→ PARTICULAR IS
   ALREADY UNIVERSAL.

"WE ARE ALL AMERICANS NOW."

TRAUMATIC ENCOUNTERS

+ MUST A WRITER ADMIT
   THE INADEQUACY OF
   LANGUAGE.

→ LANGUAGE CANNOT CAPTURE
   OR CONVEY THE
   EXPERIENCE.

→ ALWAYS POSTPONE MEANING

+ LANGUAGE CAN NEVER
   CAPTURE THE REAL.

→ STAGES A FAILURE

TRAUMATIC ENCOUNTERS

Holocaust Representation and the Hegelian Subject

Paul Eisenstein

State University of New York Press

Published by
State University of New York Press, Albany

© 2003 State University of New York

For information, address State University of New York Press
90 State Street, Suite 700, Albany, NY 12207

Production by Judith Block
Marketing by Michael Campochiaro

Library of Congress Cataloging-in-Publication Data

Eisenstein, Paul.
    Traumatic encounters : Holocaust representation and the Hegelian subject/
Paul Eisenstein.
        p. cm.
    Includes bibliographical references and index.
    ISBN 0-7914-5799-0 (alk. paper)—ISBN 0-7914-5800-8 (pbk. : alk. paper)
        1. Holocaust, Jewish (1939–1945), in literature.   2. Holocaust, Jewish
(1939–1945)—Historiography—Philosophy.   3. Hegel, Georg Wilhelm
Friedrich, 1770–1831.   4. Schindler's list (Motion picture)   5. Holocaust,
Jewish (1939–1945), in motion pictures.   6. Holocaust, Jewish (1939–1945)—
Influence.   I. Title.

PN56.H55 E48 2003
809'.93358—dc21   2002030969

10 9 8 7 6 5 4 3 2 1

For
Mac Davis

Contents

Acknowledgments

Parts of chapter 1, "Holocaust Memory and Hegel," appeared in *History and Memory* 11.2 (Winter 1999): 5–36, and an earlier version of chapter 4, "Leverkühn as Witness: The Holocaust in Thomas Mann's *Doctor Faustus*," appeared in *German Quarterly* 70.4 (Fall 1997): 325–346.

At a number of stages in this book's development, I have been the beneficiary of timely responses, discussions, suggestions, and support. I owe an initial debt of gratitude to the PLH reading group at Ohio State, particularly Ken Petri, Eleni Mavromatidou, Nathan Moore, and David Humphries, for their political commitment to theory and philosophy.

I am indebted to Hilary Neroni, for archival work that assisted the development of chapter 2, for her conversations regarding theory and film, and for her friendship and support.

I would like also to thank the librarians at Otterbein's Courtright Memorial Library, particularly Patti Rothermich and Allen Reichert, for their exceedingly generous help and assistance.

For their help in moving the manuscript toward publication, I would like to thank James Peltz, Lisa Chesnel, Laura Glenn, and Judith Block at SUNY Press.

For reading many drafts, with genuine care, insight, and enthusiasm, I would like to thank two exemplary teachers and friends, Debra Moddelmog and Marlene Longenecker.

My deepest thanks to Mac Davis, whose own commitment to philosophy, history, trauma, and ethics provided the initial fuel for this project and was a consistent source of its sustenance. This book is dedicated to him for the decisive shift in my own education that led ultimately to its writing.

Without Todd McGowan, this book would never have been written. For his companionship in the world of ideas, and for his commitment to strengthening this project from its beginning to its end, I will be forever grateful. His friendship has made all the difference.

Finally, my deepest gratitude to Emma Perry Loss, for her shared concern for the meanings made of history, and for her grace, and for several other things that cannot be put into words.

Introduction

Memory and Particularity

Nearly every thinker of the Holocaust agrees on the need to remember so as not to repeat. This consensus, of course, has not made the enterprise of memorializing history any less vexing. When we remember, when we seek to mark some aspect of the Event, we might be saving history from oblivion, but as events of recent decades indicate, there is no automatic link between our efforts and the prevention of future catastrophes. Writing in the wake of the enormous popularity of *Schindler's List* and the incredibly large number of events commemorating the fiftieth anniversary of the liberation of the camps and the end of World War II, Michael Geyer has argued that this automatic link is part of an Enlightenment fantasy involving the routine role that knowledge is assumed to play in the advancement of progressive politics. The central scenario constituting this fantasy is one that sees collective memorialization and a "coming to terms with the past" as the simple, if difficult, step in ensuring against history's repetition. According to Geyer, if there was once a basic belief in memory's automatic role in enabling the realization of Enlightenment political ideals—a belief that radical evil is best combated with enlightened knowledge—that belief is now more and more difficult to sustain. Geyer writes, "It was and is the firm belief of the politics of memory that the past will not be repeated, if only people remember. But as a politics and culture of memory grew in the 1970s and 1980s, so did a politics and culture of anti-Semitism, as well as a desperate and terrorist identity politics. These were the first indications that there was something wrong with the original argument."[1]

Geyer's inquiry has contemporary Germany and the hopes aligned with its reunification as its focus, but Germany is hardly alone in bearing out the truth of his central point—that we are in the midst of "a return of memory without the effects that once were presumed to follow in its wake."[2] This same assymetry can be discerned in nearly every country (e.g., Israel, France, etc.) that has come around to producing its own culture of memory. And in every country, the same point emerges: the crime represented by the Holocaust, a crime against whose repetition nearly everyone is rhetorically committed, is not a problem of ignorance or willful forgetting. Writing about the proliferation of Holocaust memory in America, for instance, Peter Novick sees most contemporary American memorial efforts as no doubt well-meant but so completely ritualized to the point of being practically devoid of any *political demand*. "For many years," Novick writes, "we've been talking about the culpability of by-standers and the crime of indifference. And over those years very few have thought that our standing by in the face of the preventable, if unholocaustal, deaths of millions of children annually has any connection to 'the crime of indifference.' "[3] For Novick, the very idea that attending to the Holocaust might ensure against a similar instance of atrocity has become one that virtually no one is willing to make the basis of political practice, ethical practice, or both.[4]

Despite the failure of memory as a kind of foolproof mechanism against outbreaks of racism, anti-Semitism, and/or genocide, however, few are willing to give up on its potential—which is to say, on the idea that remembering the past *can* inform a way of thinking and behaving that might lead to a better, less violent, world.[5] So, the question still remains: when remembering and repetition are invoked in the same sentence, just what *kind* of remembering is implied here? The persistence of this question as a point of theoretical inquiry is perhaps explainable enough: if it was the case that immediately after (and even during) the extermination, those who experienced it directly felt that their words could not be adequate to the horror of the Event, then is it is hardly surprising that we, today, should find a kind of automatic hesitancy attending any attempt to comprehend the enormity of the horror, any sense of feeling assured that we have discerned the proper lessons from the event, that our acts of bearing witness are adequate to the experience itself, to the "way it really was." This is why Giorgio Agamben, in his recent theoretical meditation on "the decisive lesson of the century," is forced to confess that there is little in his book "that cannot already be found in the testimonies of survivors." As Agamben sees it, the survivors already bear witness "to something it is impossible to bear witness to"—a lacuna we can only be made to listen to when we leave behind certain words altogether and begin to understand in a different sense the ones that remain.[6] Survivor testimony and literature, in other words, anticipates the arrival of philosophical and academic inquiry at a truth they both eventually espouse— that words bear no essential or affirmative relationship with things, that we lack a language adequate to traumatic experience. One need simply consider here Victor Klemperer's meditation in the spring of 1945 on the uselessness of words such as *improbable, impossible,* and *unimaginable*.[7] Or Primo Levi's descriptions of his own and his fellow prisoners' hunger and cold and fatigue, and his terrible prediction that the death camps would have given birth to a new language if they had lasted longer.[8] Or the Woman in Ida Fink's playlet, "Description of a Morning," who repeatedly takes apart her husband's naive assertion that words are "our salvation" by refusing to grant them a context or significance outside of her present, catastrophic one.[9]

Like Agamben and others, I do not mean here to suggest that the Holocaust stands as an event sui generis that interrupts like no other historical calamity the relationship between words and things. Agamben's claim that the "aporia of Auschwitz is, indeed, the very aporia of historical knowledge: a noncoincidence between facts and truth, between verification and comprehension" reads to me as an assertion that Auschwitz makes terribly *explicit* something about the gap between language, knowledge, and meaning that has been implicitly true all along. In one sense, poststructuralist theorizing is an effort to render this implicit truth explicit. Today, a felt sense of inadequacy informs our very inquiry into history. Condemned to particularity by the unsymbolizable dimension of history (the lacuna to which Agamben refers), every historical narrative becomes, in Hayden White's now familiar term, an emplotment, and every artistic representation must be regarded not as the product of an essential, transhistorical vision, but rather as the product of a limited, discursive, culturally specific, subject position. The inquiry into history has become the inquiry into memory.

If this transformation has had the effect of lending a sense of insufficiency or failure to each and every historical or artistic representation, for poststructuralism and contemporary cultural studies, this is exactly the progressive kernel that constitutes its contribution to an ethics of historical memory. In other words, it is this inadequacy, this limit, that prevents any *total* account and that necessitates the proliferation and dissemination of more and more narratives of the Holocaust—all of which are asked to demonstrate a measure of self-reflexivity, some sign that such narratives are aware of the *particularity* of their construction. It is also this account that allows for a plurality of identities to consolidate themselves, without any claiming exclusive ownership of this or that identity-bearing signifier. Rather than an enterprise with some substantial, defined end, the work of identity formation likewise becomes perpetually ongoing, caught in the Kantian loop of "infinite striving" as we come to understand the very nature of our identities in a new, pluralistic and ever-provisional, way. Jonathan Boyarin perhaps best captures the implications of this understanding when he says of his own Jewish identity, "I like to refer to myself as a 'practicing' Jew: I don't think I'll ever get it entirely right."[10]

In short, the sense of insufficiency that pervades every attempt to achieve some stable, universal point of reference has dictated an insistent problematizing of the relationship between particular narratives of history and identity and the goal of comprehensive knowledge to which such narratives aim to contribute. If for some, such incessant problematizing has seemed to create a moral vacuum, proponents of poststructuralism—specifically from the quarter of cultural studies—have countered this charge with a "positive" ethicopolitical program. Here, we might take as paradigmatic Boyarin's claim that "the best of postmodern theorizing does not stop at demystification, decentering, and deconstruction. It begins to explore how the world can be known from a multiplicity of enunciated centers. This positive moment in postmodernism is inseparable from political engagement."[11] Boyarin's sentiment highlights the gains to be made by way of thinking a plurality of *particular* loci of knowledge. Indeed, it is at some level easy to see that if our memorial efforts are informed by the fundamental poststructuralist insight regarding the inability to know or master history objectively, then we become *responsible* for the very substance of history in a radically new way, since history is constantly being fashioned and refashioned, made and remade.

For thinkers from Adorno to Derrida to Lyotard, the foregrounding of the particularity of subject position, the refusal (or endless deferral) of identity between Particular and Universal, forms the very basis for an ethics that would make another Auschwitz impossible. The refusal or endless deferral of the point of nondifference is, for such thinkers, part and parcel of an antifascist ethics. In his *Negative Dialectics*, for instance, Adorno claims that any representation of the Holocaust that does not admit its particularity, that does not measure itself by what eludes it, is "from the outset in the nature of the musical accompaniment with which the SS liked to drown out the screams of its victims."[12] The progressive possibilities of this theoretical stance for a genuine engagement with the Holocaust are not difficult to detect. For if every approach is to be measured by what eludes it, by an unrepresentable excess, then there is something in the very relation between thought and history that is forever ongoing. There is, in other words, no way to be "over and done with" an event like the Holocaust, no final "meaning" ever to be recouped from it. On the contrary, the Holocaust becomes, as Dominick LaCapra argues, the site of perpetual "working-through"—an effort that he claims depends fundamentally on an acknowledgment of the multiple and finite subject positions involved in transferential relations with it. In *Representing the Holocaust: History, Theory, Trauma*, LaCapra writes that "working-through requires the recognition that we are involved in transferential relations to the past in ways that vary according to the subject-positions we find ourselves in, rework, and invent."[13] The role of the historian-witness, LaCapra says, "is not a full identity but at most a subject-position that should be complemented, supplemented, and even contested by other subject-positions."[14]

For LaCapra, this is the first recognition at the heart of his three significant books on the Holocaust and its memorialization—that the limited and finite nature of subjectivity cannot be entirely bracketed in the act of historical inquiry, that transference has an indisputable central-ity in the writing of history, and that it authorizes the display of self-reflexivity in the effort to bear witness to a traumatic past. I am aware here that what I am calling this first recognition is followed—especially in LaCapra's later two books (*History and Memory After Auschwitz* and *Writing History, Writing Trauma*)—by a second, equally important one, having to do with subjects who take their particularity so far as to forget their *positionality* within the social order, who opt out of the dialogic process of having their views complemented, supplemented, or contested. His deployment of the notion of "subject positions," in other words, works not just to counter the pretensions of a universalizing, essentializing idea of identity but to work against the subject who *goes too far* in the direction of particularity and individualism. With respect to the latter, LaCapra has spoken of the way the Holocaust functions for some poststructuralists (most notably, Lyotard) as a kind of "negative sublime." These are subjects, we might say, who do not navigate the path from pure poststructuralism to one of its many contemporary progeny—cultural studies, post-Marxism, multiculturalism, new historicism, and Rortyean pragmatism. These subjects refuse the "positive" ethicopolitical program of poststructuralism I referred to above in my citing of Boyarin, enacting instead what we might refer to as a *total* or *incessant* deconstruction that stands in the way of any progress forward. This mode of deconstruction is glimpsed in Derrida's own refusal ever to say, "this is what deconstruction is," and in his refusal of any point of decision. In the context of historical memory, this total or incessant deconstruction ends up, for LaCapra, exemplifying an obsessive dwelling on trauma that gets stuck in repeated instances of acting out the failure to witness. This acting out then gets in the way of even a partial reconstruction or working through of the past—something that, for LaCapra, constitutes the contribution that history as a discipline can lend to the creation of what he calls a "cognitively and ethically responsible public sphere" and "a legitimate democratic polity in the present and future."[15] So, for LaCapra, an ethics of bearing witness involves not just a kind of fidelity to the excess that exceeds any attempt to know or represent the past in toto, but a commitment to uses of language that "enable processes of judgment and at least limited liability and ethically responsible agency. These processes are crucial for laying ghosts to rest, distancing oneself from haunting revenants, renewing an interest in life, and being able to engage memory in more critically tested senses."[16] LaCapra's position is thus a kind of median one.

In his commitment to these processes, to certain norms that do not automatically imply normalization, it may be tempting to align LaCapra with Habermas and his almost wholesale critique of poststructuralism (most notably, Derrida). My own sense is that such a move might mistakenly regard the "positive" political agendas of cultural studies as constituting a break from poststructuralism, when in fact, a direct link exists between today's prevailing cultural theorists and the seminal poststructuralist insights pertaining to subjectivity, discursivity, and the impossibility of fixing ultimate meanings.[17] Indeed, it is possible to claim that in recent books Derrida himself has begun to try to catch up with some of the "positive" ethicopolitical programs he helped to spawn.[18] There are additional reasons for maintaining that this direct link holds as well for the relationship between LaCapra and poststructuralism. For one thing, LaCapra's norms do not lie in a putative "idealizing presupposition" involved in the very use of language to communicate alone—that is, in the ideal of communicative reason that Habermas sees as making possible communicative action in the first place.[19] Moreover, LaCapra is far less polemical than Habermas in his view of Derrida, according a basic value to the notion of an "unrepresentable excess" that foregrounds (and may even limit) communicative action, and discerning in Derrida himself an occasional willingness to maintain a tense interaction between norms and what escapes or exceeds them. But perhaps more than this is the sense that LaCapra's contributions to theorizing Holocaust memory owe a fundamental debt to the revolutionary space-clearing gesture inaugurated by the poststructuralist critique of traditional historiography. This space-clearing gesture clears the way for affect—in particular, what LaCapra calls "empathic unsettlement"—to gain a legitimate place at the table of historical inquiry. In introducing empathy, LaCapra is careful to remain sensitive to the irreducible distance between particular and universal (between self and Other) insisted on by poststructuralism. In *History and Memory After Auschwitz*, LaCapra admits that "empathy itself, as an imaginative component not only of the historian's craft but of any responsive approach to the past or the other, raises knotty perplexities, for it is difficult to see how one may be empathetic without intrusively arrogating to oneself the victim's experience or undergoing (whether consciously or unconsciously) surrogate victimage."[20] But his central point is that an empathy that resists full identification with the Other *is* possible, and that it ought to impact historiography at the level of its form. Thus, though LaCapra is far from prescriptive when it comes to legislating the required dose of empathy for an authentic effort at bearing witness, he does see it carrying out an important function since it introduces an anxiety pertaining to *form* that works to counter narratives of history that arrive at mastery and complacency:

> Opening oneself to empathic unsettlement is, as I have intimated, a desirable affective dimension of inquiry which complements and supplements empirical research and analysis. Empathy is important in attempting to understand traumatic events and victims, and it may (I think, should) have stylistic effects in the way one discusses or addresses certain problems. It places in jeopardy fetishized and totalizing narratives that deny the trauma that called them into existence by prematurely (re)turning to the pleasure principle, harmonizing events, and often recuperating the past in terms of uplifting messages or optimistic self-serving scenarios.[21]

I shall return in detail to the significance of LaCapra's theoretical position in chapter 1, but what is most significant here is the extent to which LaCapra quintessentially exemplifies the advance—even as he warns of its "clear and present dangers"—represented by postmodernism's challenge to the stability of history, historical inquiry, and identity formation. Dispensing with the unified subject who was once the (putative) knower of a rational and transparent history, LaCapra replaces the closure and sense of community gained by unself-conscious historical representations with a notion of trauma as the repressed dimension of redemptive narratives of and definitive disciplinary approaches to the Holocaust. For LaCapra, the truth of what it means to bear witness resides in the fragmentary nature of our engagement with the Holocaust, in the fact that our memorial efforts are doomed only to produce something incomplete.

The very turn from universal to particular that LaCapra argues for in his conceptualization of Holocaust memory has been registered by Michael Marrus, who notes precisely this shift in his discussion of the historiography of the Holocaust. Invoking Isaiah Berlin's famous distinction, Marrus argues that we have indeed begun to move away from the attempt to know history in terms of master narratives (i.e., the province of the hedgehog) and to replace such narratives with the production and proliferation of a plurality of narratives (i.e., the province of the fox). As Marrus puts it,

> We have passed from a historical literature conditioned by a few grand visions to a body of writing shaped by discrete, not necessarily interconnecting perspectives. By and large, it seems to me, in the first two decades after the Holocaust writers were preoccupied with the search for a single key—something that would unlock the mystery of the massacre of European Jewry. Since then, historians have

moved more cautiously, guided by a variety of research agendas. With significant exceptions, historical writers today are uncomfortable with the frameworks they have inherited. They spend much of their time pointing to variety, paradoxes, complexities, and contradiction. Their writing is less informed by single, unitary perspectives than it was with their predecessors, and they have advanced our knowledge on many smaller fronts, in contrast to the massive, coordinated campaigns of those who went before.[22]

Marrus's point here has been echoed more recently by Inga Clendinnen, who claims, apropos historiography more generally,

> that the quest for global interpretations and grand narratives is always a mistaken one, assuming a shapeliness in human affairs and a simplicity of human motivation never encountered in muddy actuality. Nowadays no one much hankers for the panoramic view of where we all were and where we are all going once offered by Marxism or Whiggism, or the more obscure and even less testable stories and metaphors psychoanalysts offer to explain our darker private obsessions. Large theories may generate good questions, but they produce poor answers. The historian's task is to discover what happened in some actual past situation—what conflicting or confused intentions produced what outcomes—not to produce larger truths. The most enlightening historical generalisations tend to be those that hover sufficiently close to the ground to illuminate the contours and dynamics of intention and action in circumscribed circumstances.[23]

What Marrus and Clendinnen trace here, I think, is the shift from a structuralist to a poststructualist sensibility in the encounter with history, the primary feature of which is quite obviously the disavowal of a certain totalizing gesture, the refusal of any position of supreme mastery or universal vantage-point when it comes to "explaining" the Holocaust. Rather than traffic in large theories that produce poor larger truths, today's agents of memory seek to remain sufficiently close to the ground, granting a license to theory (and theorizing) only in the most local of contexts. Preferring plurality, paradox, complexity, and incompletion to monocausality, clarity, and comprehension, and finality, Marrus and Clendinnen—like LaCapra—suggest that there is perhaps a greater, ethical fidelity to history in the small, incremental steps toward understanding the Holocaust that historians and other witnesses now make on a plurality of fronts. Consider here, for instance, Raul Hilberg's insistence on asking the smallest of questions, on addressing "things which are minutiae or details," and the extent to which this insistence has been elevated into a kind of new categorical imperative vis-à-vis master-narratives.[24]

For an exemplification of this formal categorical imperative in the field of survivor memoirs, we might take as paradigmatic Binjamin Wilkomirski's recent (and now discredited) memoir, *Fragments: Memories of a Wartime Childhood*, in which Wilkomirski writes poignantly of the isolated images and events that constitute his memory of childhood and his inability to take up some vantage point from which to narrate them coherently:

> My earliest memories are a rubble field of isolated images and events. Shards of memory with hard knife-sharp edges, which still cut flesh if touched today. Mostly a chaotic jumble, with very little chrono- logical fit; shards that keep surfacing against the orderly grain of grown-up life and escaping the laws of logic.
>
> If I'm going to write about it, I have to give up on the order- ing logic of grown-ups; it would only distort what happened.[25]

These are images and events that for Wilkomirski are "just pictures, almost no thoughts," and the suggestion is clearly that if he is to remain faithful to the experiences themselves, a certain amount of self-referentiality is necessary. Wikomirski cannot pretend mastery: he cannot install these shards in some intelligible, logical, coordinated story as if he were a Subject capable of mastering them, as opposed merely to a "subject po- sition" who exists in relation to them. Thus, Wilkomirski refuses to take up the advantage of a suprahistorical position, insisting instead that he is "not a poet nor a writer"—which is to say, not someone capable of tran- scending or "intellectualizing" the fragments that constitute his memory. His memoir begins, in fact, with the self-referential claim that he does not even own a language ("no mother tongue, not a father tongue either") with which to render his experiences—a claim that immediately distances himself from any notion of mastery. Indeed, even at the close of his memoir, Wilkomirski is adamant about the impossibility of finding some sort of liberation by way of conceptualization and analogy. As he recounts his own high-school education concerning the War, he records his secret reading of books above and beyond the normal curriculum:

> I wanted to know everything. I wanted to absorb every detail and understand every connection. I hoped I would find answers for the pictures that came from my broken childhood memory some nights to stop me going to sleep or to give me terrifying nightmares. I wanted to know what other people had gone through back then. I wanted to compare it with my own earliest memories that I carried around inside me. I wanted to subject them to intelligent reason,

and arrange them in a pattern that made sense. But the longer I spent at it, the more I learned and absorbed empirically, the more elusive the answer—in the sense of what actually happened—became.[26]

Every attempt to discover some source of unity in the various Holocaust experiences he learns about, every attempt to arrange the fragments into a whole, leaves Wilkomirski feeling as if he is the embodied leftover that such a whole cannot accommodate. Seeing documentary footage of the liberation of the camps, Wilkomirski understands his own experience as the particular that defies any notion of universality, claiming that "perhaps it's true—somehow I missed my own liberation." We have here almost a perfect evocation of the sense of failure and suspicion against which any notion of a single conceptual framework or systematic ordering system appears to linger. Wilkomirski's claims are clearly consonant with a post-Holocaust ethic—a fact that accounts for the way his memoir has been *believed* in spite of its factual impossibilities. Despite the obvious poignancy of its content, it strikes me that Wilkomirski's memoir became a central Holocaust text precisely because of the attractiveness of its form. In a sense, Wiliomirski gave us exactly what we wanted: rather than aiming for a universal vantage point or some monocausal explanation, we have come to take variety, complexity, contradiction, and *unbelievability* as a sign that we are in the midst of a truthful experience of the Holocaust.

The very theoretical insight suggested by LaCapra and enacted by Wilkomirski was supposed to ensure a more genuine confrontation with the Holocaust by clearing a space for the unprecedented and the unbelievable. But it has not done so without raising its own problems in turn. Objectification may lead to fetishized narratives that deny trauma. But once dispensed with, is it possible to avoid licensing narratives that go to the other extreme? Claims concerning the (un)truthfulness of Wilkomirski's memoir are only the most recent instance where the abandonment of objective, historical methodology has given rise to problems.[27] If in theory, the turn to the particular was supposed to infuse the act of memory with a dose of trauma that could be the basis for an antifascist ethics, it has in fact created another set of problems entirely—opening the way (inadvertently or not) for particular "historicizations" (what some would call mythologizations) of the Event driven by apologetic or otherwise ideological ends. Such historicizations have produced significant debates concerning what is usually referred to as the relativization and normalization of Nazi history. From the *Historikerstreit* in Germany in the 1980s to the controversy surrounding the "eliminationist anti-Semitism" thesis of Daniel Goldhagen's *Hitler's Willing Executioners* to the more recently proclaimed "Americanization of the Holocaust,"[28] it is, I think, fair to say that this problem is perhaps more vexing than any other in Holocaust studies: To what extent does an insistence on particularity and context begin to grant a license for simplification, relativization, or unchecked transferential relations to (i.e., fixations on) specific aspects of the past?[29] When, in other words, does the insistence on particularity become a vehicle to recoup "meaning" and to guarantee the consistency of identity—or worse, to make money? When does an overabiding insistence on the "unthinkable" lead to demoralization and all that this word connotes?[30] This is a question recently raised by Omer Bartov, who notes the manner in which proponents of particularity are "paradoxically forced together and—mostly very much against their will and better judgment—found sharing their scholarly abodes with very strange bedfellows indeed."[31] For Bartov, particularizers and relativists, "though without any visible direct ties, are part of the same intellectual discourse."[32] In his introduction to *Probing the Limits of Representation: Nazism and the "Final Solution"*—the most comprehensive attempt to think through the dilemmas occasioned by this discourse—Saul Friedlander frames the decisive challenge for Holocaust studies: Once you turn history into the product of multiple, particular interpretations, how do you stop these interpretations from crossing certain political and ethical lines? Friedlander writes:

> the challenge has become more perceptible during the last two decades, as the result of ongoing shaping and reshaping of the image of the Nazi epoch. During the seventies, film and literature opened the way to some sort of "new discourse." Historiography followed and the mid-eighties witnessed heated debates about new intepretations of the "Final Solution" in history (the best known of these debates being the German "historians' controversy") and, in more general terms, about the proper historicization of National Socialism, that is, of "Auschwitz." In these various domains new narratives about Nazism came to the fore, new forms of representation appeared. In many cases they seemed to test implicit boundaries and to raise not only aesthetic and intellectual problems, but moral issues too.[33]

The crux of the complication is this: when, in the name of antifascism, we do away with a traditional belief in historical truth and representation, when we disavow the possibility of some totalizing master-narrative,[34] how are we to ensure that our accounts are not being put to simplistic or apologetic or (as alleged in the case of Wilkomirski) quite simply untruthful ends? Can the poststructuralist turn in historiography maintain an ethical sense of justice, fairness, and truth, or must a more pragmatic, more politically liberal source of meaning adjudicate the field of meaning? How, in other words, are we to ensure the place of truth and trauma in the act of bearing witness to the Holocaust?

Recovering the Universal

The chapters that follow aim to address this question. In chapter 1, I tackle this impasse head-on, as it were, by suggesting that one way out of the deadlock is to recover the very "totalizing" impulse repudiated by postmodern historiography and postmodern aesthetics. My claim is simply this: that memory work in fact depends on our willingness to occupy a "totalizing position"—not as a means for replicating totalitarian violence against particularity, but rather as the point at which we, as human subjects, fully engage the unsymbolizable trauma of the Holocaust. To recover this position for progressive memory work is to recover the name synonymous with it: Hegel. Rather than see Hegel in the way dominant liberal and poststructuralist thinkers have—as someone directly or indirectly responsible for this whole mess in the first place, as wanton totalizer who eliminates all difference—we must see Hegel's insistence on totality as in fact an insistence that we bear witness to the unsymbolizable dimension of history, the stuff of history that escapes meaning. When Hegel insists again and again in his philosophy that we must retain what is finite and begin to regard it as Absolute, he is, in my view, arguing not for the superior, self-satisfied position of Spirit, but on the contrary for that experience in which we recognize that the Universal, the Master, the order of thought itself is incomplete. Hegel's ultimate argument in the *Phenomenology* is just this—when we occupy a totalizing position, we do not achieve a static, transcendental position of substantial knowledge; we do not displace or disavow or defer an encounter with the trauma of an event like the Holocaust and its unsymbolizable, but nonetheless present, presence. On the contrary, we bear witness to its real trauma. On this view, the monocausal narrative does not *automatically* constitute an ethical breach—not if we mean by monocausal all the causes that are capable of being thought within a certain universe of meaning. In fact, as Hegel's transcendental idealism would have it, the embrace of monocausality enables one finally to confront that which cannot be reduced to cause. This is especially important today when the Holocaust—far from standing as the Event that cannot be reduced to cause—is the object-lesson for those who insist on the categorical imperatives to historicize. Here, I rely crucially on Slavoj Žižek's Lacanian reinterpretation of Hegel. For Žižek, "Hegelian 'reconciliation' is not a 'panlogicist' sublation of all reality in the Concept but a final consent to the fact that the Concept itself is 'not-all.' "[35] This thesis leads Žižek to argue for an inversion of "the standard formula of the relationship between the Universal and the Particular"— an argument that, in my view, ought fundamentally to alter our understanding of how best to bear witness to an instance of historical trauma like the Holocaust. In short, Žižek argues that the Universal and the

Particular must "change places": rather than regarding the Universal "as the genus which divides itself into particular species," we might recognize instead "a series of Universals, of universal interpretive matrices, which are all answers to the 'absolute particularity' of the traumatic Real."[36] We can, I think, see this plurality of interpretive matrices both in the attempt to historicize and account for Hitler's evil, and in the attempt to understand what motivated those who involved themselves in Jewish rescue: indeed, one way to account for such pluralities of interpretive matrices is to see them as testifying to their very condition of possibility—that is, to the fact that something particular and traumatic has already (and irrevocably) receded from our purview.

This inversion that Žižek advocates has the advantage of distinguishing the proper ontological domain of trauma, since trauma is not only that which eludes all attempts to symbolize it but is also that which gives birth to cognition, to freedom, and to symbolic orders of meaning. Like the Kantian moral law or the paternal Law in psychoanalysis, the trauma involved in Spirit's Universality has for this reason something "creationist" about it, since, logically speaking, it is only insofar as something appears that eludes our understanding that we begin to think that words and things and actions have meanings—as opposed to being mere material or mechanical entities. Only when our particularity has been negated, only when we are *no longer* in the domain of particularity, are we able even to cognize that which we have lost (and long to recover). Freud's "Negation" essay articulates this basic phenomenological point in its paradoxical contention that a certain symbol of negation endows thinking with a measure of freedom from the consequences of repression. The traumatic negation carried out, say, by the paternal Law might shatter the ego's claims to understanding, but at the same time, the ego begins to lay claim to cognition itself. In short, negation may entail a loss of that which is primordially repressed, but at a deeper level, it also entails its *gain*, since that which is repressed by way of negation only becomes intellectually available for consciousness by way of negation. This is what Freud means when he says that "negation is a way of taking cognizance of what is repressed . . . it is already a lifting of the repression, though not, of course, an acceptance of what is repressed."[37] Taking seriously the creationist dimension of trauma, we might outline a way of thinking that fundamentally takes away the ground, say, of certain neo-Nazi groups who likewise assert their legitimacy as one of a series of particular groups who ought to be tolerated. From the psychoanalytically informed Hegelian standpoint that this book advocates, particular groups ought to demonstrate their universality, which is to say, their direct tie to the unsymbolizable trauma—the non-sense at the core of the Master-signifiers with which they identify—that even permits their taking cognizance of the plenitude they believe they've lost, that catalyzes and ultimately limits the meanings they generate. (This, of course, would be difficult for a neo-Nazi group, since that which is responsible for the meanings they generate is always *historicizable* and *symbolizable*, and this fact is at the core of their construal of identity-bearing signifiers—of both their own and of others.) Ultimately, psychoanalysis helps us to see how Hegelian dialectics diagnoses a host of problems associated with memorial efforts that always remain within history and within the symbolic order: if Hegel's Master-Signifier functions as a kind of traumatic, nonsensical quilting point that allows a universe of meaning to consolidate itself, then we might read the path toward the encounter with it not as the triumphant realization of the "end of history," but rather as an encounter with its beginning as well—which is to say, an encounter that shares an affinity with those moments where the meanings associated with a given historical epoch break down. Moreover, we might read those whom we pass on this path as exemplifying some of the categorical symptom-formations uncovered by psychoanalysis—for example, obsession, hysteria, paranoia, and so on.

In chapter 2, I consider one such exemplification by taking up what might rightly be called the false Hegelian position of the memorial effort that would seem to "know all" when it comes to representing the Holocaust—Steven Spielberg's *Schindler's List*. The wider context for my discussion here is the interpretive problem the act of Jewish rescue has posed for liberal and left-leaning political philosophy and the desire within that philosophy to secure a mobilizing maxim or normative core as the "lesson" of such heroic conduct. In this chapter, the dynamics of Hegelian negation in the service of a final reconciliation appear, then, on two related levels. First, there is the case of Spielberg himself and the extent to which he has been credited, with *Schindler's List*, for having no longer displaced the trauma of history (and of his own Jewish identity). Spielberg would here appear to follow the stereotypically Hegelian path of "progress" as an artist—in which some radical element of difference is finally sublated within his artistic canon. Second, there is the case of the desire of the rescuers themselves, and the extent to which that desire, too, must seemingly be sublated in order for it to have some political or moral efficacy today. What I aim to do in this chapter, however, is to turn Hegel himself against this construal of him in order to problematize the reconciliations aimed at on both of these levels. In short, I hope to demonstrate that far from cinematic triumph, *Schindler's List* in fact reveals the fantasy of mastery beneath the "false universal"—the universal qua site of meaning as it is imagined from the standpoint of the symbolic. Moreover, I want to suggest that the very point of focus of Spielberg's film—the heroic act of Jewish rescue—has coordinates within the obsessional economy within

liberalism more generally. This obsession is driven largely by the confrontation with fascism forced on liberalism at the very moment of its
triumph with the demise of Soviet Communism. An obsession with rescue thus becomes a way for liberalism to recoup its self-image: the mobilizing maxim it derives from the heroes who involved themselves with
saving Jews becomes a way to protect the viability of liberal moral norms
by showing them as operative even then. Spielberg's film thus typifies a
trend within liberalism, imagining a universal maxim as something external but not ultimately incompatible with the symbolic order. This maxim,
exemplified by the conduct of Jewish rescuers, can then be affirmed by a
plurality of identities within a democratic society. This explains, I believe,
why rescuers are central to contemporary debates within political philosophy about how to live today as moral citizens. The notion of an
imagined universal that both respects difference at the same time that it
provides a basis for a fair, tolerant, and just society is what links Spielberg
with contemporary liberal discourse. My own contention is that the ontological dimension of this basis—it is, after all, a symbolic credo ("Whoever saves one life, saves the world entire") that exists entirely at the level
of consciousness—betrays the genuinely ethical dimension of the heroic
Act, and in this way evinces all of the liberal worries about direct inter-
ventions into history that may have unforseen consequences.

In chapter 3, I take up an aesthetic approach antithetical to
Spielberg's. If Spielberg has traversed the path of the Hegelian dialectic
both in its narrative and in its form in order to arrive at a position of final
reconciliation, D. M. Thomas's *The White Hotel* works self-consciously at
both levels to postpone such a reconciliation. The implicit critique
Thomas's novel raises for Spielberg's film concerns precisely a bringing to
the fore of those acts of negation that enable Spielberg to stage his reconciliation. My claim here is that the multiple narrators and narrative
forms of a novel like *The White Hotel* can function to "hystericize" the
obessional discourse underlying Spielberg's liberal message. In its proliferation and multiplication of stories and viewpoints, *The White Hotel* can
thus be read as a poststructuralist rejoinder to the liberal attempt to arrest
the signifying chain by way of a mobilizing political maxim or moral
norm. That Thomas's central character suffers from hysterical symptoms
speaks precisely to the symptoms of the novel's form as well, since in
genuine hysterical fashion, Thomas seems to want to make our desire
come alive apropos the perpetrators and victims of history. This marks,
in my view, the ethical advance represented by the postmodern qua
hysteric's approach to memorialization: contra Spielberg, one must be
made to linger with an object of history whose opacity cannot so easily
be made translucent. Thomas's novel forces us to ask what is history,
without every providing a single, definitive answer. But if *The White Hotel*

at least enables trauma to enter the equation by pointing toward the impossibility of a single, univocal approach, it does beg the question of how to ensure that trauma remains in the equation. This is especially problematic in terms of Thomas's commitment to a Jungian theory of the soul and Thomas's rendering of a deeply affirmative afterlife for those who died at the hands of the Nazis.

In chapter 4, I show how simply entertaining the question is not enough—that the genuine witness to the horror of history is one who does not simply remain within the confines of self-mediation, of thinking. Any discussion of mediation begs reference to Lacan's understanding of the symbolic and his later claims regarding the extent to which analysis is aimed not so much at maintaining one's position within the symbolic, but rather at taking the whole of one's symbolic identity towards an experience in which one *bears witness* to the real. A modern exemplar of this kind of witness resides in a place we perhaps would not think first of looking—in Thomas Mann's early postwar novel *Doctor Faustus*, and in the artist that is that novel's principle subject—Adrian Leverkühn. Though Leverkühn dies before the genocide even begins, his art, and specifically the "absolute" form of his final masterpiece, anticipates and addresses the most sensitive and long-standing moral and philosophical tension concerning artistic representation and its relation to horror. Leverkühn's art bears witness to the real of historical suffering—not by holding back within symbolization, by gesturing toward a limit, or by acknowledging the limitation of individual perspective, but rather by exercising thought so absolutely that symbolization itself is pushed to the brink of horror. To read the novel in this manner is not only to provide a corrective to long-standing opinions in Thomas Mann scholarship regarding the moral and aesthetic nature and function of Mann's fictitious composer, and thus of the novel itself, but also to provide an example of how we might profitably address the question of how to bear witness to—to represent—the Holocaust.

If Leverkühn's art testifies to the ethical exigencies of encountering the real, it does so only at the level of the content of Mann's novel. That is to say, the *form* of *Doctor Faustus* does not go as far as the composer who is the novel's main subject. Put another way, we might say that Mann remains a bourgeois novelist. To complete the through-line of the book, then, I turn to a novel which exemplifies Nietzsche's insight that "one is an artist at the cost of regarding that which all non-artists call 'form' as content, as 'the matter itself.' "[38] I refer here to David Grossman's *See Under: Love*—a novel whose very *form* exemplifies what it means to occupy a totalizing position in the act of bearing witness. The achievement of Grossman's novel lies in the extent to which it dramatizes the frustrations and impossibilities that attend to particular narrativizations that attempt either to redeem the Holocaust or to infinitely defer a final encounter with it. The first three sections of the novel are examples of such narrative efforts: in the first, Grossman shows us a nine-year-old boy trying to build the "Nazi Beast" in his basement for the purpose of finally *knowing* history completely; in the second, he shows us that same boy (now grown) trying to commune with a poet (Bruno Schulz) killed by the Nazis so as perhaps to gain a kind of deliverance from history in the form of a lost manuscript entitled *The Messiah;* in the third, he shows us this grown man again trying and failing to recapture a story told by his grandfather about the life of a child in the Holocaust. If all three of these sections testify in one way or another to a kind of paranoia in the face of history—that is, that something meaningful does exist out there that either needs to be recovered or alternatively prohibited from being grasped—the final section of Grossman's novel executes a formal gesture designed to undo such paranoid fantasies and thereby bring about a direct encounter with the traumatic real. All of this is to say that in "The Complete Encyclopedia of Baby Kazik's Life," Grossman collapses the paranoid quest enacted by his protagonist (Momik Neuman) in the novel's first three sections by permitting his protagonist to *exercise his paranoia in an even more unreserved way.* In so doing, Momik—in the final section of the novel—writes in the form of an encyclopedia the story of a child of the Warsaw Ghetto, and thus exemplifies the extent to which a totalizing gesture—far from securing some position of comfortable rest—can bring about a memorial effort that meets at its most genuine level the horror of the Event.

1

Holocaust Memory and Hegel

The finite has always to be maintained and made into an absolute.

—Hegel

Hegel and His Critics

To invoke the name Hegel in the context of the Holocaust—and what it means to remember it—will surely be for some to strike a discordant note. As cardinal spokesman for German Idealism and its version of an absolute subjectivity, Hegel is usually more frequently aligned with clearing a conceptual space amenable to the commission of an event like the Holocaust than with ensuring against any future recurrence of it. Given this affiliation, to make the case for a return to Hegel in the service of an ethics of historical memory—a case this book aims to make—is to invite from a variety of quarters a series of immediate objections. Few may be as explicit as Karl Popper—for whom Hegel is the decisive link in the emergence of modern totalitarianism[1]—but the lion's share of contemporary critical-theoretical positions (especially those informed by poststructuralism) still depend fundamentally on a rejection of Hegel on political and ethical grounds. What virtually all of these rejections have in common is an overabiding suspicion of the putatively "universal" or "absolute" dimension of Spirit that Hegel advocates so unequivocally. Indeed for many, Hegel's systematic dialectic of History—in which every immediacy, every experience, every particular is already and automatically swallowed up by the Whole—points up the violent flip side of an Enlightenment master-narrative concerning the universality of Reason at its worst. In its deployment of such a notion of universality, Hegel's master-narrative of Spirit would seem to entrap and subsume so many different *material* or *historically specific* markers of identity (bodily, ethnic, gender, socioeconomic status, etc.)—markers which for Hegel gain their apparently singular bearing solely

19

by means of what is universal and absolute (i.e., speculative logic and the activity of thinking). The critique to be waged here against Hegel's idealism would seem to be self-evident: in its drive for sameness, Hegel's Spirit lets nothing go free. Even Kojève (though for him, this is not a reproach) notes this feature of Hegel's thought, pointing out that "one cannot bring up any discourse in opposition to [Hegel's] own discourse, which would not be reproduced in a paragraph of the System as a constituent element (*Moment*) of the whole."[2] In Hegel's system, nothing is permitted to resist the grip of the sovereign concept of reason and its meaning-making abilities. In this regard, one need only recall Hegel's paean to the sacrificial logic of the "cunning of reason" in his introduction to the *Philosophy of History*, in which Hegel claims quite explicitly that "the particular is for the most part of too trifling value as compared with the general." There, Hegel unreservedly asserts that when it comes to *phenomenal being*, "part is of no value, part is positive and real."[3]

It is perhaps safe to say that the Hegel who champions the cunning of reason in *The Philosophy of History*, the Hegel who accompanies this championing with a more or less cavalier avowal of just what reason's cunning entails for that which has been deemed valueless ("individuals are sacrificed and abandoned"), is the Western metaphysician par excellence *against* whom so much contemporary discourse concerning ethics defines itself. Indeed, from the liberalism of Rawls and Rorty to the poststructuralism of Deleuze and Derrida, this is precisely the Hegel we are told we must avoid. Within Holocaust and Jewish cultural studies especially, this devaluation of the particular sounds an especially keen series of alarming ethical questions. Does not Hegel's idealism simply take to its very extreme a longing for the univocal and the universal initiated by the Greeks and made the foundation of anti-Judaism (via the discourse of Paul) in Christian Europe?[4] Does not Judaism, in Hegel's teleological understanding of religion, represent merely an "adolescent" stage in the progressive life of Spirit coming-to-itself—a stage soon eclipsed by and incorporated into a universally and absolutely true Christianity?[5] Was not the anti-Semitism and dictatorial power that fueled the Holocaust itself a product, at least in part, of the sort of universalist or absolutist thinking whose clearest philosophical underpinning rests with Hegel? And must we not, in our attempt to bear witness to what happened, avoid reproducing a certain Hegelian gesture whereby even this ultimate of catastrophes is "overcome" or redeemed—that is to say, made to serve the advance of a meaningful, universal Idea?[6]

In his essays on Judaism, Emmanuel Levinas perhaps sounds this theme most forcefully, indicting Hegel's notion of Spirit for presiding over a philosophic operation by which (and this phrase cannot help but give us pause) Jews are made to vanish. In Levinas's reading of Hegel,

The particularity of a people is identical to its finitude. It is Hegelian logic that presides over this announcement of disappearance. The particularity of a thing has significance in fact only in relation to a whole; and from that point on, in the name of Hegelian logic, the necessary disappearance of a people is announced, for everything that is finished must finish.[7]

From the standpoint of Hegelian logic, Levinas notes, any claim by Jews to some independence from history, some existence apart from the universal (read: "Christian") History that Hegel advocates, is simply illusory. The Jewish claim to be an "eternal people," for example, cannot survive what Levinas sees as a less than just litmus-test for legitimation—

> The exaltation of the judgement of history, as the ultimate jurisdiction of every being, and the affirmation that history is the measure of all things. The judgement passed by a conscience on events that succeed, that have an efficacity, an objective visibility, would, you know, according to the exaltation of history, be merely a subjective illusion that vanishes like smoke in the face of the judgement of history. For this conception, there is no eternal people liable to live free in the face of history. Every people is part of history, bears within it its determined essence, and contributes in its way to the universal work that incorporates and surpasses it—into which, consequently, it is finally absorbed and disappears. What would be eternal is the universal history itself which inherits the heritage of dead peoples. (200)

That such "dead peoples" whose own judgments are made to vanish like smoke (again, phrases that warrant pause) might insist on a kind of vitality is, according to Levinas, from the standpoint of Hegelian logic chalked up to a mere "subjective belief [whose] purely subjective significance is denounced at the very moment at which the real curve of events is drawn" (200). Under the pressure of Hegel's "synoptic gaze," history is turned into teleology, its "progress" thereby granted an almost sacred warrant. Levinas's concern rests with the ways this warrant gets sustained. That is to say, the prestige Hegel accords history depends fundamentally on the fact that no one locate him- or herself in opposition to its meaning and forward direction. For this prestige to be thus maintained, Judaism (or any other particular ethnic or cultural tradition for that matter) faces two choices—integration into Christianity or a judgment of insignificance:

> Philosophy, as it is summed up and crowned by Hegel, would precisely end up by integrating the individual and collective wills to the

extent that they are real—that is to say, effective—into a reasonably
structured totality, in which these living totalities are represented by
their works, but in which these works derive their true—that is to
say visible—significance not from the subjective intentions of their
authors but from the totality, the only one to have a real meaning
[*sens*] and to be able to confer it. The intentions of the authors and,
consequently, everything that—to return to Judaism—the Jews think
themselves, the whole of our *Aggadah* and *Halakhah*, would be just
an old wives' tale, a theme for a sociology or psychoanalysis of
Judaism. Judaism would not be true in what it wished, but in the
place where the universal history would have left it. (200)

As Levinas suggests here, grand narratives of history are ultimately inimical to the particular exercise and manifestation of unique beliefs and
practices. In short, the very desires of Judaism—the will and wishes of
Jews themselves—are seriously threatened by universalizing or totalizing
narratives of whatever stripe (e.g., Hegelian, sociological, psychoanalytic)
that claim to possess the *real* meaning of these desires. Levinas may not
go as far as *Anti-Oedipus* in hailing the schizophrenic dimension of this
desire, but his basic argument is similar: these grand narratives, functioning as reasonably structured totalities, might claim to operate in an osten-
sibly neutral fashion, but in their claim to comprehensiveness, their interests
are far from merely objective or neutral. This is the case because their
versions of history do not allow for alternate narratives, laws, and desires
to have a kind of autonomous significance in the face of the grand
narrative's definitive social determinations in the act of its coming-to-
fruition—that is, the story of Hegel's self-realizing Absolute, Marx's pro-
letarian class, or Freud's Oedipal narrative. According to Levinas then,
the Jew today is not one who merely believes in Moses and the prophets;
on the contrary, to be a Jew is to insist on and be granted a kind of *prior*
philosophical ground that permits and enables that belief. To quote Levinas
again,

> To wish to be a Jew today is therefore, before believing in Moses
> and the prophets, to have the right to think that the significance of
> a work is truer in terms of the will that wished it into being than
> the totality in which it is inserted; and, even more brutally, that will
> in one's personal and subjective life is not a dream whose death will
> allow us to draw an inventory of the work and the truth, but that
> the living willing of will is indispensable to the truth and under-
> standing of the work. (200)

In Levinas's key qualifier ("even more brutally"), it is clear that the terrain of philosophy is one with ramifications of violence for real, live Jews—the prevention of which would seem to be predicated on a clear rejection of Hegel.

Levinas's essays on Judaism render even more urgent his political concern voiced initially in *Totality and Infinity* having to do with the sacrifice of interiority and desire on the altar of history so as to comprehend being. In his elaboration of this political concern, Levinas is—as my cursory reference to *Anti-Oedipus* begins to make clear—part of the wider dismissal of Hegel and Hegelian dialectics in poststructuralist French thought.[8] Decisive in the history of philosophy, it is this comprehension of being that deprives the past and the present of its radical alterity, of that which (to take the title of another of Levinas's books) is "otherwise than being." This sacrifice of interiority betrays the categorical ethical imperative that underwrites Levinas's defense of transcendence and metaphysics. To sacrifice interiority is already to sacrifice the plane on which the subject is most radically called into question: it is to synthesize the irreducible orders of totality and infinity, by taking both to belong to the same sociosymbolic, minimally consistent, life-world. The pitfalls of this synthesis ultimately apply to Hegel, who by "including the real" in a universal narrative of history—that surplus exterior to totality and nonencompassable within it—has determined the real in its "historical objectivity" without regard for what Levinas refers to as "interior intentions." These intentions institute an order of time that cannot be completely synchronized with historical time, and this, for Levinas, is their particular virtue (and the virtue of particularity more generally). Interior intentions determine the real from a "*secrecy* that interrupts the continuity of historical time"—a secrecy that makes possible the pluralism of society.[9]

The problem with treating Judaism as merely historical, then, is that it overlooks the extent to which Jewish (or any other religious) subjects occupy a position before an infinite other—a part of whom remains incapable of being integrated into a meaningful totality. Though we are, as particular subjects, not "exterior to history," Levinas claims nonetheless that we do "find in the Other a point that is absolute with regard to history—not by amalgamating with the Other, but in speaking with him. History is worked over by the ruptures of history, in which a judgment is born on it. When a man truly approaches the Other he is uprooted from history."[10] For Levinas, *this*—and not a quantity of knowledge to be had at the putative "end of history"—is what is Absolute: an experience of the Other in a *conversation* that does not commit historiography's "totalizing" crime of reducing the Other to the same. This is how Levinas thinks his ethics would ward off future genocides: in the recognition that human discourse or conversation is *already* the result of the subject's receipt of a prior summons to it by that which is absolutely Other, Levinas situates intersubjective relations on the ground of nonknowledge, on the face to face encounter that cannot be historicized.[11] Constituting an irremediable breach of totality, this summons is for Levinas the inaugural event of ethics, since it dispossesses me of a world hitherto mine and gets me paradoxically to offer the world to the Other. This version of the advent of subjectivity informs Levinas's dictum that "Transcendence is not a vision of the Other but a primordial donation."[12] What triggers this advent is a primordial Signifier carrying out its expressive function, its breathless performance of an act of "signification without context" that maintains the alterity of the Signifier despite its own subsequent thematization. In discourse, we experience something absolutely foreign, something Infinite that is not integrated for having been spoken. According to Levinas, language may institute a relation between a human being and the Infinite—between the metaphysician and the metaphysical—but both parties "*absolve* themselves from the relation, remain absolute within the relation."[13] This is what is absolute about language for Levinas—the extent to which we are, in conversation, indebted to a nonhistorical instance of the Other's saying that exceeds what is merely said. When Levinas says that to be Jew today is to be granted a ground prior to belief in Moses and the prophets, this is what he means: that Judaism *begins* with a nonhistorical encounter with the Other/God in and after which both parties maintain an *absolute* particularity.

I make this slight digression toward Levinas's own ethics not for the purpose of dismissing his alternate account of what is Absolute, but rather to telegraph briefly how much Levinas's critique of ontology and his insistence on a diachrony that survives synchronization in fact relies on Hegelian insights. Indeed, as I shall show shortly, Hegel, too, sees the ultimate alterity of the Other—the absolute particularity of sense particulars—as likewise "absolved" from the relation that our symbolization of it institutes. Language may appropriate the Other or object, but for Hegel, too, this appropriation is not entirely successful. The absoluteness of the subject instituting the relation lies for Hegel, however, in the direction of *universality* and *infinitude* as well, since the symbolic order of meaningful language is precisely that which has already eclipsed the finite, particular raw matter that words are. Against the Levinasian insistence on an exalted infinitude of the Other, the Hegelian point to make here is that this very designation is only intelligible if conceived as the result of a finite subject's self-negation. This is what Hegel means when he says that finite beings raised into the infinite are in no sense acted on by an alien force: "the

finite is not sublated by the infinite as by a power existing outside it; on
the contrary, its infinity consists in sublating its own self."[14] For Hegel,
then, language is, as it is for Levinas, that which institutes a common
world, while at the same time preserving something absolutely uncom-
mon, but this commonality—contra Levinas—means that we have already
reached a domain of universality. In addition, like Levinas, Hegel sees our
encounter with the Other's alterity as incommensurable with the order of
ordinary historical experience, as involving an encounter with trauma in
which we (in Levinas's words) are uprooted from history. But this encounter
may be more terrifying than the pure experience or pure knowledge of
the transcendent which Levinas deems a "traumatism of astonishment."[15]
My own reading of the Hegelian subject below will aim to establish that
Hegel does not eliminate metaphysics in the act of realizing it terrestrially, that the totalization of history does not bring to a halt all relationship
with alterity and infinity. Whereas Levinas (and the group of French
postwar thinkers of whom he is a part) believes that a totalization of
history must be avoided in order to bring about a more genuine relationship with alterity, my own reading uncovers the extent to which Hegel
reveals the achievement of very same relationship as the *product of* a totalizing gesture—and achieved only by way of such a totalizing gesture.
For Hegel, such a gesture can and ought be repeated. The Hegelian
endorsement of totalization, on this view, does not announce just the
"end" of history—as if Hegel was the first and only individual in human
history ever to have fathomed it. On the contrary, the "end" that Hegel
claims to have grasped ends up executing a kind of replay of history's
beginning[16]—and all of history's epistemic "crises" in which bodies of
knowledge and universes of meaning face traumatic material that cannot
be accounted for.

    Even devotees of Hegel who concern themselves directly with eth-
ics and the Holocaust and the formations of cultural identity, even those
who clearly see themselves as working in the tradition of Hegel, likewise
cannot escape the idea that there is something about the Hegelian claim
to a universalist or comprehensive speculative position that associates his
metaphysics with atrocity.[17] The case of Adorno is here no doubt paradigmatic, since despite his clear praise of Hegel,[18] there is for Adorno nonetheless something in the philosophy of the latter that, in the last instance,
is complicit with the mentality of fascism and anti-Semitism. In Adorno's
work, this idea receives any number of articulations—from the explicit
linking of totality and anti-Semitism in *Dialectic of Enlightenment*; to the
claim in *Minima Moralia* that "the whole is the false," which rewrites
Hegel's famous equation in the *Phenomenology* that "the whole is the true";
to the decidedly counter-Hegelian assertion in *Negative Dialectics* that

"No universal history leads from savagery to humanitarianism, but there is one leading from the slingshot to the megaton bomb. It ends in the total menace which organized mankind poses to organized men, in the epitome of discontinuity. It is the horror that verifies Hegel and stands him on his head."[19] To grasp the whole of history is, for Adorno, a worthy task for theoretical understanding, but that whole would have to be defined not as the positivistic realization of a redemptive reconcilement between some universal Idea and all phenomenal occurrences but rather as "permanent catastrophe" or "historic suffering." As Adorno sees it, "There is hardly another way to interpret history philosophically without enchanting it into an idea" (320). To counter Hegel's "enchanting" of history under the spell of a self-realizing idea or identity, Adorno thus puts forth the notion of a "negative dialectics": against the Hegelian claim to have achieved some final identity between universal and particular, Adorno grounds a kind of ethical disposition on "the consistent sense of nonidentity," on a "negative dialectics" that is always faithful to the "remainder" that eludes our ways of knowing. Adorno defines dialectic as precisely the recognition that all most assuredly cannot be reduced to Spirit, that philosophy cannot presume to bring all phenomena into the orbit of meaningful, conceptual knowledge. Hegel, for Adorno, "cut short" dialectics in his positing of some final position of reconciliation (an "all-subjugating identity principle"), and this is likened specifically to the attitude of the Nazis in Adorno's remarkable claim that "if thought is not measured by the extremity that eludes the concept, it is from the outset in the nature of the musical accompaniment with which the SS liked to drown out the screams of its victims" (365).

If Levinas's and Adorno's critiques are at all representative, as I think they are, of the disfavor under which Hegelian thought labors today, the fundamental source of this disfavor lies clearly, as we can see, with the implicit violence toward difference believed to lie at the core of Hegel's idealism and the "transcendental subject" who takes it up. The now-standard critique of this subject, from the quarters of both liberalism and deconstruction, has as its target precisely this subject's radical exercise of power in order to make idea and actuality correspond—that is, a cognitive gesture said to erase the divide between spirit and matter, between soul and body, and thereby realize a (fictive) unity or final identity between the two. In one sense, this identity-relation has always been problematic for the insult and injury it poses to one of the two terms. If in Hegel's day, advocacy of such an identity constituted an ethical breach against the very qualities of Spirit, since it was to beg the charge of having executed a "pantheistic" degradation of Spirit to claim that Spirit *is* the infinite multiplicity of individual things, today of course, the ethical breach lies in the other direction. To be sure, few critiques of Hegel take issue with the pantheistic diminishment he imparts to Spirit by asserting its identity with each and every particular thing, but many, however, recoil from the unfreedom to which Hegel condemns each and every particular thing by locking them in an identity-relation with Spirit. If one of the commonly understood lessons of the Holocaust concerns precisely the resolute need for a tolerance for, and indeed fostering of, multiplicity and the free expression of different identities, the identity-relation Hegel asserts between the multiplicity of things and Spirit would seem to fail to anticipate or be adequate to this lesson. One need only, as Karl Popper does, read Spirit as State or Race or Nation, and Hegel appears to be quite obviously an enemy of democracy and the "open society."

One of the difficulties here has to do with Hegel's insistence that particular, finite entities only gain minimal integrity by way of their link to Spirit, to what can give them meaning. In this basic idealist gesture of dialectical negation, Hegel denies an autonomy to the very *existence* of particular things with respect to the generation of their meaning—an autonomy that he nonetheless grants to Spirit. Because the autonomy given to Spirit then appears to have something transcendent about it, Hegel here runs squarely up against the historicist or anti-imperialist methodological imperative that today enjoys virtual hegemony when it comes to conceptualizing an ethics of bearing witness to history and an understanding of the formation of cultural identities. Hegel runs afoul of such an imperative is this way: in his insistence on an ultimate identity between particular entities and universal Spirit, Hegel's phenomenology "historicizes" the particular—insisting, indeed, that every particular phenomenon is the product of *mediation* by Spirit—but exempts Spirit itself from the same operation. In this way, Hegel refuses to see Spirit *itself* as something particular, as something that is *not* universal or transcendent but rather historical, finite, conditioned, "ethnocentric."

Hegel, Psychoanaylsis, and Their Kantian Antecedents

Here, we might recognize a connection (evoked already by Levinas, if only negatively) between Hegel's thought and psychoanalysis—a connection the vitality of which I believe is critical in helping us to develop a responsible ethics of Holocaust memory. Indeed, I think the claim can be made that psychoanalysis clarifies the ethical stakes of Hegelian epistemology and the need to think and act a way out of history. This bears directly on the urgent question—taken up most notably by Dominick LaCapra—in Holocaust studies concerning a working through of the

past. I shall develop in more detail the way a psychoanalytically charged
Hegel can help us to address this question, but suffice it to point out here
the fundamental similarity between the exemption, as it were, that Hegel
gives to Spirit qua unhistoricizable (i.e., not conditioned by some external, mediating force) and the exemption given by psychoanalysis to the
creation and existence of the unconscious as the repository of traumatic
material that we can never fully or completely "remember." Noteworthy
in this context is the fact that in the case both of Spirit and the unconscious, we are in the presence of a universal frame or horizon whose
universality is insisted on—that is, whose particular manifestations can be
historicized/analyzed—but which is itself claimed to have a nonhistorical
status. Indeed, according to Hegel, the very order of history ensues only
with Spirit's own self-division—an act of primordial negation in which, as
Hegel would put it, Spirit "thinks itself" and thus navigates the path from
being (*Sein*) to existence (*Da-sein*). And psychoanalysis, too, suggests that
the very condition of historicity depends likewise on an act of primordial
repression, a "shock without affect," in which the unconscious becomes
"for itself" at the same time that it becomes for the ego and thus available
for the contents of "normal" repression. Here we can see why so much
of the historicist suspicion evinced toward Hegel is likewise evinced toward psychoanalysis: the Oedipal narrative, the Law of the Father, and
the notion of unconscious desire would appear to function in much the
same way as Hegel's Suprasensible Idea—as a kind of absolute and un-
touchable anchoring point or Law from which to make meaning out of
phenomena.[20] For critics of both German Idealism and psychoanalysis,
this universal anchoring point seems nothing but a weapon of epistemic
(and sometimes actual) discipline and punishment, since in the tradition
of logocentrism, it appears to harness the freedom and spontaneity of the
particular under the heavy yoke of the universal.[21] According to this view,
both Hegel and psychoanalysis are guilty of positing that something
definitely *does* exist that *is* the ultimate, universal ground of meaning (e.g.,
Reason, the Paternal Law)—something that cannot be regarded as one
more particular phenomenon to be grouped among a host of other particular phenomena.

For those who would memorialize the Holocaust, the questions to
pose at this point are these: What precisely is to be understood by the
apparently self-evident contradiction of a universal "something" that is
yet nonhistorical? How close are we here to participating in the fascist
fantasy of a Universal Reich—or of a "pure" Aryan Identity purged of its
perceived (historical) contaminants? Can this constitute a working through
of the past? The answer to these questions necessitates a bit of a detour
back to the figure who first opened up the path down which Hegel and

psychoanalysis travel. I am referring here to Kant and the space he clears for freedom in the *Critique of Pure Reason* and the *Critique of Practical Reason*. In the *Critique of Pure Reason*, of course, Kant had ruled out Reason's speculative knowledge of its ultimate, transcendent basis, claiming that there is no way to validate or document the truth of pure Reason's assertions by referring to something that is *already* the product of Reason's cognition. Seeming to promise us nothing less than an expansion of our knowledge beyond all bounds of experience, "pure" reason for Kant ends up containing "nothing but regulative principles." This is what constitutes the decisive "negative benefit" of critique: rather than discovering truth, it prevents errors.[22] By being referred back to the a priori conditions for its cognition, Reason finds itself checked by a discipline that cures it of its extravagance and self-conceit, and that diminishes the tendency toward aggressive attempts to secure its assertions and claims.[23] The entirety of Kant's efforts rests on the phenomenological fact that Reason's claim to have authoritative knowledge of transcendental ideas by way of historical experience always leaves unanswered a prior question concerning the conditions (e.g., space and time) that make experience and knowledge possible. Logically speaking, these conditions cannot themselves be historical without simply eliciting the same question pertaining to the conditions of *their* possibility. It is this logical necessity that ends up disciplining Reason in its tendency toward dogmatism. Refusing the conflation of transcendental idealism and transcendental realism, Kant protects the original import of the word *idea* by maintaining that an idea is a notion that surpasses the possibility of intelligible experience. Kant's ultimate result in the first *Critique* is thus essentially one that informs the prevailing attitude toward metaphysics and epistemology that sees no way to bring about a genuine encounter with something transcendent (and in the case of pragmatism, no reason even to try): as knowing subjects, we are confined to the theatre of history and finitude; we cannot know the transcendent realm, since ours is only a world of appearances; even our very selfhood is but the way we appear to ourselves.

As it turns out, however, this is not Kant's last word on matters historical. Indeed, as the second *Critique* makes abundantly clear, there is one transcendent speculative idea that we can know a priori and this is freedom. Mindful of his claims regarding direct cognition of Reason's ultimate ground in the first *Critique*, Kant says that we know this a priori without having any insight into it. That is to say, freedom does not extend cognition to the supersensible realm; on the contrary, it manifests itself practically in our capacity to act in conformity with a Law without concern for our interest and inclination—in short, to act morally. As Kant sees it, freedom is not beyond causality: it is the inexplicable locus of causality that is self-caused—in Kant's words, "the power to begin a state *on one's own*."[24] Only this transcendental idea allows us to take literally the notion of working *through* the past: to act freely, which is to say ethically, we do not take our cues from nature or from intelligible history or from objects or ideas we imagine as the bearers of plenary meaning. Indeed, for Kant, the traumatic object/idea outside the world of appearances has nothing natural or intelligible or meaningful about it: it is not even an object of knowledge. But it can have a determinative effect on the world of appearances. Here, then, is the ethical dimension to our encounter with transcendent, which is to say traumatic, material: it allows us to think and act in such a way that arrests the violent and vicious circle of history. Only the transcendental idea of freedom allows us to think a history that is radically incomplete, a history that is not synonymous with nature—in short, a history already structurally conditioned by trauma. If we as historical agents are not mechanical entities, if every cause is not to be regarded as beholden to natural laws, if it makes any sense at all to speak of human responsibility, then we must, following Kant, exempt something from history. Each of us, insofar as we are free, are not *only* historical agents caught in the nets of ordinary space and time. On the contrary, we are the bearers of a causality that is not subject to another cause. Kant implies that this is an aspect of the subject radically cut off from ordinary consciousness—the real (or noumenal) part of ourselves capable of beginning "its effects in the world of sense *on its own* without the action's beginning *in the subject* itself."[25] In his working out of the nature of a genuine moral act, Kant can be credited, by extension, with having theorized a way to *free* the act of memorialization—a way of conceiving a memorial act that avoids its being put to ideological or otherwise affirmative uses. Kant thus addresses the dilemma that I referred to in my introduction involving the effects of postmodernism on Holocaust memory. This problem is not that far from Kant's: how to conceive ethics apart from pathological motives. Kant's response is to show that the most ethical instance of bearing witness is the freest.[26] And the freest instance is the one that does not neatly resign itself to a historicizing gesture. On the contrary, the freest act would be the one that takes up Reason's own traumatic, nonhistorical ground.

Though Kant may have wavered at times on the feasibility of a free act carried out terrestrially by human agents, Hegel and psychoanalysis do not. Both insist that we try to take up for the purpose of encountering a universal, metaphysical, nonhistorical anchoring point of subjectivity. What we achieve by doing so is not the pure object of the fascist fantasy, but rather the traumatic hole in history—a hole occupied not by a missing source of plenitude but by material incapable of being historicized.

The Lacanian name for this material is the traumatic kernel of the real—that *irreducible presence* voiced by someone or something that both sets in motion and forever eludes all of our attempts to comprehend or symbolize it. According to Lacan, the aim of analysis—of attempting to get the unconscious to speak—is to isolate for the purpose of recognizing that there is something of substance internal to every identity that cannot be made to mean, and that we are forever cut off from this substance even as it is lodged within us. The position of the subject, then, involves attempting to bear witness by a kind of proxy—in the stead of that which might bear witness directly on its own if it only had a language to do so. As Lacan puts it in *Seminar XI*, the aim of analytic interpretation "when it is a question of the unconscious of the subject" is to "bring out" those irreducible signifiers to which we as subjects are subjected."[27] Lacan is most deeply Hegelian on precisely this score, since the aim of analysis is to bring about the recognition that one *is* this thing of substance, even as one cannot master it. Both Spirit and the unconscious betoken the existence of this substantial, traumatic kernel, because their cause *refuses ordinary historicization*, because their cause is *internal to* that which comes into existence by way of it. One implication of this insight is simply that there is no way to speak meaningfully or empirically about a chain of causes that creates Spirit or the Unconscious other than to posit the definitional, if not tautological, necessity of their own self-formation. Hegel never tires of claiming that Spirit *is* its own finitizing of itself, its own becoming an object for itself, and that the Understanding only distorts things when it believes it can separate Spirit from its ground, for the purposes of representing the latter for consciousness.[28] And Freud, replacing an early hypothesis concerning seduction with a metapsychological one, likewise provides a picture of the formation of the unconscious rooted in the notion of death drive and in a quantity of excessive excitation that remains unpresentable.

In both cases, then, the universality of Spirit and the Unconscious entails a substantial content that cannot present itself in sensible form that enables Spirit and the Unconscious to appear *to themselves*. Thus, Spirit and the unconscious qua universal frames of reference both exist as the lifeblood of what we can know but can never be fully or meaningfully known themselves. That the presence signified by this traumatic kernel of the real is not in itself meaningful does not mean that we can make it can mean anything we want it to, nor does it mean that we cannot *encounter* it. Indeed, that we *can* encounter it is precisely what links Hegelian phenomenology and psychoanalysis—the idea that an absolute or universal position places one not in a comfortable position whereby all is reduced to univocal meaning, but rather in a position to *bear witness to trauma,* to that unsymbolizable nugget of nonmeaning to which we are subjected. What must become clear here is the extent to which psychoanalysis elucidates the trajectory toward trauma in Hegelian phenomonology. When Hegel—inheriting from Kant the notion of an act that breaks from the ordinary temporal sequence of intelligible causes—claims that we have *already* performed such an act and must in the name of ethics do so again, he is in fact urging us toward a traumatic encounter. If memorializing the Holocaust is to work in the service of ensuring that it is never again repeated, if we are to take up Adorno's categorical imperative to "arrange thought and action so that Auschwitz never repeats itself," then we will have to find a way to bear witness to its trauma in its ultimate form and place. My claim here is simply that the *path* of the Hegelian dialectic— substance, negation, negation of the negation—corresponds to moments within a psychoanalytic mode of inquiry aimed at producing an encounter with trauma. Indeed, an understanding of this path is crucial to the locating of those points at which a given theoretical or artistic response to the Holocaust gets "stuck" on it. As I hope to show below, the diagnostic categories of psychoanalysis (e.g., obsession, hysteria, paranoia) might best be regarded as moments at which a given theoretical or aesthetic response to the Holocaust fails to go all the way through the Hegelian dialectic and thus works to redeem or disavow the existence of trauma. Understood in this way, then, the return of Spirit to itself that Hegel likens to its recognition of its own absolute or universal nature is akin to an encounter with the unconscious—an ultimate encounter with Reason's freedom, with the place of traumatic knowledge that cannot itself be known. This is what various aesthetic representations of the Holocaust confront and cope with by way of symptoms ripe for psychoanalytic investigation.

When Hegel, however, is understood to deliver up the wholeness and closure that only the cozy confines of an abstract Idea can deliver, this is where the problems begin. For rather than bringing about the recognition that we are irreducibly split off *from within* from that which would make us whole, Hegel—in this reading—only ties up what is contingent and irrational into the neat bow of rationality and necessity.[29] Ignoring a kind of antifascist ethical imperative—to recognize that any universal interest is only and always a particular one—Hegel prepares the ground, inadvertently or not, for an exercise of power predicated on the pursuit of an absolute identity between Spirit and what stands over against it. For Levinas, this is tantamount to announcing the disappearance of a people, and for Adorno, this amounts to the ideological sanction of violence par excellence. For these reasons, Hegel's insistence on the universal or absolute nature of Spirit is, more often than not, seen to be inseparable from the workings of totalitarianism and from the fundamental fantasy of fascism. It is this fantasy that virtually every single theoretical articulation or artistic rendering having to do with the Holocaust and an ethics of bearing witness to it seeks to contest—that subjects and societies *are* organic, singular and yet universal totalities which *are* implicitly and absolutely whole, that the Holocaust is somehow compatible with the foreordained telos of Reason's development toward perfection. With the Holocaust and fascism precisely as a reference point, ways for how to combat this fantasy have usually come from one of two quarters—liberalism or deconstruction. I shall discuss in more detail below—apropos *Schindler's List* and *The White Hotel*—the manner in which assumptions emanating from these quarters underwrite aesthetic approaches to Holocaust, but my turn now is to these assumptions themselves, and their ways of coping with the fundamental fantasy of fascism. Here, my aim is to understand the liberal-democratic and deconstructionist positions vis-à-vis memorialization by way of the questions they would pose to Hegel and his notion of an Absolute or Universal Spirit. What I hope to enact here is a kind of dialectical progression toward the encounter with trauma in its most genuine form—an encounter that necessitates our *going through* the liberal and deconstructionist positions for the purpose of arriving at a moment best suited to the undoing of the fascist fantasy of mastery. This final moment, of course, is the *absolute* or *Hegelian* one. My claim regarding this final moment is simply this: that Hegel allows us to structure a relation to the fact that all of our forms of knowing and exercising power are rooted in the fact that we are creatures of trauma, subject to that which we cannot master *in the very act of mastery*. Rather than aiming to repair the trauma or to postpone infinitely the encounter with it, Hegel brings us to the recognition that we are in fact encountering it all the time.

Liberalism as an Antidote to Fascism

The liberal-democratic critique of Hegel and the fascist fantasy of legitimacy might be boiled down to the following questions: How can Hegel's dialectic of Spirit avoid enacting a self-sanctioned, tyrannical monism antithetical to certain values that must be *constructed* via persuasion and not force—for example, moral recognition, justice, consensus, and solidarity? Can Spirit itself ever be subject to the norms of reasonable debate? Can Spirit safeguard the basic liberties seen to be essential to a well-ordered society? If totalitarianism is predicated on the belief that human subjects, human society, or both *are* implicitly and absolutely whole, the liberal response is usually to insist that wholeness is not something given in any organic or exclusive or foundationalist way. Indeed, the liberal-democratic suspicion of a nonhuman idea of the whole usually centers on the sense that when conceived of as *immanent* in society, its realization can only be achieved by means of violent force. In his *Conscience and Memory: Meditations in a Museum of the Holocaust*, for example, Harold Kaplan suggests an inevitable ethical trespass constituted by the attempt to realize in actuality some organic *idea* of wholeness. According to Kaplan, "Those lumbering abstractions of the German philosophic tradition—Fichtean, Hegelian, Marxist, then Fascist—sought immanence and became deadly, perhaps because immanence could be found only in violent form. History mounted a stage and demanded sacrifice."[30] Here, the liberal democratic heritage would seem to claim that subjects and societies are *not* whole, but that liberal values—for example, rule of law, universal rights of property and contract, the methods of the social sciences, democratic reform, community-based norms for reasonable communication and behavior, and so on—can *fill in* what is missing. If the fascist fantasy disavows the existence of antagonism from its very conception of society—as Juliet Flower MacCannell has succinctly put it, fascism copes with its own fantasy by short-circuiting it[31]—the liberal response admits the existence of social antagonism but seeks to rid us of its source, believing that reasonable people's fantasizing can reveal a ground of agreement prior to conflict and capable of warding off its outbreak.

This notion is perhaps most clear in the well-known Rawlsian wager that the creation of a just society comprised of free and equal citizens, a society conceived as a fair system of cooperation over time between generations, depends fundamentally on the securing of some point of view from which to determine the transparent rationality of its just structure. The securing of this point of view is achieved by way of what Rawls notoriously refers to as "the original position."[32] This point of view is, for Rawls, to be regarded as the essence of a "thought experiment" (i.e., a fantasy): the original position is a "device of representation"—part expository tool and part intuitive notion—that functions to convey a kind of reasoning likely to reach agreement about the necessary governing principles for a just and fair society. Freely confessing that the "parties" of the original position are not actual persons in society (and insisting that no general assembly has occupied this position immanently and en masse at some particular instant of history), Rawls claims that it is our responsibility to imagine these "artificial" persons to be as pure as possible. The strategic value of these fantasmatic idealizations for Rawlsian liberalism cannot be underestimated: the more we can eliminate self-interest and other pathological factors from the ideal figures with whom we are imaginatively to identify, the more likely we will be—when we role-play from the original position—to make fair and reasonable decisions about the basic structure of society. As Rawls puts it, "Remember, it is up to us, you and me, who are setting up justice as fairness, to describe the parties (as artificial persons in our device of representation) as best suits our aims in developing a political conception of justice."[33] This elimination of self-interested or pathological factors informs the critical Rawlsian notion that the parties that model the kind of reasoning that is the signature of the original position are situated behind a "veil of ignorance." Behind the veil of ignorance—the warrant for which Rawls has said is implicit in Kantian ethics—the parties of the original position reason not from the standpoint of the particular facts that characterize their own social position or historical epoch, but rather from a position of detachment. As a result, they are able to take a "clear and uncluttered view of what justice requires when society is conceived as a scheme of cooperation between free and equal citizens from one generation to the next."[34] Their envisaging of a just and fair society is thus such that they do not know if the principles they adopt will be to their particular advantage or not: they are obliged, as Rawls puts it, to evaluate principles solely on the basis of general considerations. In this way, the veil of ignorance nullifies the accidents of natural endowment and the contingencies of social circumstances that are often exploited in directions that do not take fairness as the *sine qua non* of justice. Rawls has referred to the veil of ignorance as a way to remove differences in bargaining advantages, of "correcting" the arbitrariness of the world, and this effort depends on the exclusion of knowledge: in my emulation of the kind of rational reasoning modeled behind the veil in the original position, I am thus emulating parties who are supremely ignorant of the social positions, race, sex, able-bodiedness or comprehensive doctrines they represent. I am even immune to what Rawls refers to as "special psychologies" (e.g., envy, aversion to risk, desire for mastery, etc.). In this way, Rawls secures a subject whose reasoning about the basic structure of society takes place in the purest, most disinterested way. No subject in the original position, in other words, would risk willing a world in which he or she might be disadvantaged. Pure, disinterested reasoning means only one thing: the exercise of our moral nature. And the exercise of our moral nature can only lead to one result: a consensual recognition that justice qua fairness ought to determine social and political policy.

In one sense, Rawls's debt to German idealism is clear, since he is performing the characteristic idealist gesture of situating the subject prior to so-called objective knowledge, of repudiating the notion of a one-to-one correspondence between Nature and a given religiopolitical order. In short, it is possible to see Rawls as merely following through on the "Copernican" gesture Kant calls for in the first *Critique* and that Hegel radicalizes in his positing of an Absolute Spirit who is the basis of all historical reality: rather than see our cognition as determined by an objective or Natural religiopolitical order, we should instead see the way the latter is in fact the product of a gesture that gets *it* to conform to our cognition. When we perceive a world whose hierarchical relations are said to be the immanent realization of a divine chain of being, we are not, in other words, perceiving this world *as it really is*, but rather only *as it appears to us*. When liberalism sets out after the questions that every political order seeks an answer to—what justifies political power? what unites a *polis*?—it thus discovers not a mind-independent, suprahistorical object (e.g., a religious doctrine, national myth, or economic theory), but a process or a method carried out by autonomous, reasoning subjects. The commitment to this process or method is what ensures that even if one dislikes the policies that are the outcomes of this process, one affirms them nonetheless. Because the process protects the inviolable freedom of the subject, it is ultimately more important than any end it produces. In his putting the subject first, Rawls wants clearly to contest both the monarchical or aristocratic idea of a "natural" ordering of society and the "naturalness" of the utilitarian apology for how goods and liberties are distributed in a given society. But in another sense, what gets discovered beneath the aristocratic or utilitarian idea of the natural is a liberal version that lays claim to the same title. Why does a Rawlsian subject, role-playing the original position behind a veil of ignorance, discover principles of justice therein? Because the capacity to discern justice and to remain faithful to it is a *natural* attribute. This is an attribute that "no race or recognized group of human beings" is without: only "scattered individuals are without this capacity, or its realization to the minimum degree, and the failure to realize it is the consequence of unjust and impoverished social circumstances, or fortuitous contingencies."[35] The exercise of this natural attribute enables a critique-free consensus to emerge regarding the natural principles on which to structure a well-ordered society. As Roberto Alejandro has noted, the monopoly Rawls grants to justice over the deepest recesses of our identity—as "the virtue that best expresses our nature"—places the principles of that justice beyond revision and reevaluation.[36] These principles include first a commitment to the notion of citizens as free and equal persons, since all persons possess moral powers and the power of reason; second, a commitment to basic liberties, equal opportunity, and the idea that insofar as social and economic inequality must exist, such inequality should benefit the least advantaged members of society; and third, a commitment to measuring one's comparative position in society by way of units Rawls designates as "primary goods"— not units of wealth, utility, or desire. Primary goods are things persons need as free and equal citizens trying to develop their moral powers and to pursue their determinate conceptions of the good.

What is crucial here to Rawls's thought-experiment, and the thought-experiment of liberalism more generally, is that it allows for the free expression of a *plurality* of individual identities and communities. Like the Kantian critique of pure reason, Rawls' thought-experiment functions as a kind of tribunal that puts law in the place of war. In this regard, Rawls never tires of insisting that his brand of liberalism aims not at truth (i.e., Reason's direct cognition of objects) but at reasonableness, and that he makes no claim to comprehensiveness because he "takes to heart" conflict and wants only a charter for the well-ordered society that will be accept- ← able to all parties. What Rawls calls the "fact of reasonable pluralism" means that citizens can never agree on an authoritative doctrine that applies to all subjects and covers all values. But what they *can* agree on is a political conception of justice. Thus, while Rawls does argue for a certain procedure that enables us to "enter the original position" at any time for guidance, he also subjects the description of the original position to revision in the hopes of one day achieving a kind of final identity between the dictates of the original position and our own judgments bereft of the veil of ignorance. Even here, however, Rawls points out that this identity is provisional.[37] One point that becomes clear here is that if the fascist fantasy is predicated on a univocity of identity and community that is somehow pregiven—and that forces the creation of the anti-Semitic caricature of the Jew in order to cement this univocity—the liberal response is to insist on the polyvocity by means of which individuals and societies organize themselves. As David Johnston in his summary of Rawls's political liberalism puts it, "Rawls assumes that different people pursue different projects and hold different values, and that these diverse projects and values—or comprehensive conceptions of the good—are equally reasonable. That is, for him, the defining assumption of political liberalism. ← The principles of justice are intended to guide adjudication of people's *conflicting* claims, so that each person's capacity to pursue her own conception of the good will be protected, as long as that conception is consistent with justice."[38]

Liberal-democratic values, then, operate quite clearly as a kind of reference point about which there can be "overlapping consensus"—even and precisely among those who hold different views. Even liberals who might quarrel with the ahistorical position Rawls assigns to those conducting the thought-experiment—Richard Rorty and others, for instance, have remarked on the extent to which those behind Rawls's veil of ignorance "look remarkably like twentieth-century American liberals"—do not quarrel with the vital importance of Rawls's assumptions for the integrity of democratic society, that being the value of consensus among and between members of a community, and not simply fidelity to some objective, transcendent, nonhuman idea (e.g., the self-realization of Spirit). That Rawls's liberalism does not aim for synchronicity with some "nonhuman idea"—this is here perhaps an implicit reference to an absolutist version of the figure of Hegel—is inseparable from its claim to an ethical mandate. Preferring politics to philosophy, its scope is decidedly more narrow: we might say that its morality is inseparable from its modesty. This move toward modesty informs what has been called Rawls's shift to the political from *A Theory of Justice* (1971) to the more recent *Political Liberalism* (1992). In the latter, Rawls aims to be even more forthright about the fact that his liberalism is "not comprehensive liberalism," that it seeks neither to replace comprehensive doctrines (religious or nonreligious) nor to provide their "true" foundation, and that its articulation of principles and values which all can endorse must be taken as having to do only with politics and not metaphysics. Much of this has to do with the now well-known communitarian critique of Rawls and the extent to which *A Theory of Justice* is said to rely on a comprehensive Kantian philosophical theory of what has been called an "unencumbered and antecendently individuated subject."[39] According to the communitarians, Rawls does in fact rely on a comprehensive metaphysical doctrine about the subject—one that risks fixating on the reasoning subject's pure process of self-reflection and thus ignoring altogether the way a subject's attachment to various ends, values, conceptions of the good, and communities might in fact be a constitutive part of the "pure" subject on whom Rawls depends. In his reply to these charges, Rawls is quick to distance himself from any reliance on metaphysics: the veil of ignorance, he says

> has no specific metaphysical implications concerning the nature of the self; it does not imply that the self is ontologically prior to the facts about persons that the parties are excluded from knowing. We can, as it were, enter this position at any time simply by reasoning for principles of justice in accordance with the enumerated restrictions on information. When, in this way, we simulate being in the original position, our reasoning no more commits us to a particular metaphysical doctrine about the nature of the self than our acting a part in a play, say of Macbeth or Lady Macbeth, commits us to thinking that we are really a king or a queen engaged in a desperate struggle for political power. Much the same holds for role playing generally.[40]

This disavowal of precisely the metaphysical moment in which one thinks— and acts on the basis of—that which is without foundation betrays the prevailing disavowal of metaphysics within liberalism more generally, in which no Idea is ever seriously to be realized or taken up on the ground. This disavowal, in ways I hope to make clear shortly, constitutes a departure from Kantian ethics (and the Hegelian subject who takes it up) for reasons that are difficult to sustain. Though realized practically, we should recall that those ethics remain tied to a metaphysical idea of freedom— a traumatic encounter or instance of bearing witness that cannot be reduced to mere role-playing, as if there were no *real* stakes to our ethical attempts to meet the historicity of history. Rawls genuinely wants reasoning subjects to generate principles aimed at consolidating a just and fair society, but he is unwilling to seize the mantle of metaphysics, believing that it compromises the autonomy of liberal citizens and sets up a scenario in which (pragmatically) agreement will never be reached. It strikes me, in fact, that just the opposite is the case: as Kant shows (and Hegel takes up), subjectivity implies already that the physical world has been transcended. The autonomy of the subject is necessarily metaphysical, involving an encounter with trauma that is part and parcel of our ethical freedom and solidarity. Indeed, if we think honestly, it may be the one thing on which we can all agree: we are all creatures of trauma, and the (metaphysical) reexperiencing of this trauma in the act of bearing witness can function as a universal tie that binds. Today, however, liberalism continues to think metaphysics as transcendental realism, a view that mandates the repudiation of metaphysics (and trauma) in toto. In his fundamental statement of liberal pragmatism, Rorty thus claims that the best way we now have to make sense of our lives involves solidarity and not objectivity. As Rorty puts it, "We must look not for skyhooks but for toeholds."[41]

Most liberal-democratic narratives in response to the Holocaust are grounded in precisely this Rawlsian "thought experiment," the liberal pragmatist ethos it gives rise to, and finally what both are able to produce—something *actual* that might restore balance and stability to social  relations. This actuality usually takes several related forms—be it a recognition that individual citizens ought to be the ones who reasonably decide how best to structure the social order of which they are a part, a categorical imperative to practice tolerance, a recognition of human rights, a commitment to undoing instrumental reason's domination of communicative reason,[42] and so forth. According to this view, the lesson of the Holocaust lies in the direction of a renewed pledge to some meaningful positivity capable of guaranteeing the consistency of the social order. This

borders clearly on the contested question of just what the Nazis wished
to destroy. For those who conceive the human subject as a moral agent,
as a bearer of rights, as an individual capable of elevating into Law a
fundamental respect for the essential freedom of others, the answer is
clear: Nazism is the violation of the moral order itself, of the rights of
other human agents, of the social contract and its democratic values (e.g.,
freedom, consensual agreement, human rights, etc.). In short, Nazism
consists of a frontal assault on the very origins and tenets of liberalism.
Richard Wolin perhaps gives this view its ultimate expression when he
writes, "The fascist program, whose ideological origins date from the
counter-revolutionary doctrines of the early nineteenth-century (Bonald,
de Maistre, etc.), was above all bent on forcibly extirpating the liberal-
democratic heritage of the French Revolution."[43] One crucial insight to
note here is the liberal-democratic critique of the manner in which fascism conceptualizes conflict. According to the liberal-democratic critique,
this is one of fascism's decisive and deleterious features: under the sign of
fascism, the very phenomenology of conflict is transformed from that
which exists between autonomous, moral agents capable of articulating
their grievances and of relying on persuasion to settle claims, and is felt
instead to exist between the moral agent and an impersonal, imperative
fate that both beckons and threatens him (e.g., modernity)—a fate met
inexorably by the elimination of other moral agents. This, ultimately, is
what leads fascism down the path to violence and evil: it does not treat
conflict politically as an intersubjective problem of solidarity, capable of
being adjudicated reasonably; instead, it hyperbolically conceives social
conflicts as crises with "eternal" implications.[44] To make this point explicitly in terms of National Socialism, we need only refer to the controversy
surrounding Heidegger's Nazism and the extent to which liberals routinely assert a degree of continuity between that Nazism and Heidegger's
commitment to the "presencing" of Being. Heidegger is one of liberalism's
object-lessons for this reason: in his fidelity to (impersonal) Being that
reveals itself in ways that eclipse all conventional philosophical or scientific
modes of verifiability, in his privileging of this Being over (personal)
existents, the capacity for sound political judgment is seriously jeopar-
dized.[45] According to the liberal critique, this focus on the impersonal
foments an almost inevitably criminal failure to recognize the essential
freedom of a multiplicity of others. Thus Kaplan's claim that "the Nazi
attack was against all forms of pluralism—racial, ethnic, religious, political, and cultural. Democracy, internationalism, egalitarianism, freedom—
these formed the precise antithesis." Nazism, for Kaplan, is but the extreme
instance of "the power concept [which] eliminates negotiation, consensus,
dialogue, agreement."[46]

One paradox of the liberal-democratic position as it pertains to bearing witness involves its account of *how* democracy loses ground to fascism, and in this respect, a crucial echo emerges between liberal democracy and its opposite. I refer here to the manner in which the failure of liberal-democracy to consolidate itself must necessarily be chalked up to *external* causes—for instance, to those who refuse the veil of ignorance proffered by Rawls's thought experiment. These are individuals and groups who continue to aim for truth and not reasonableness, who look for some transcultural reality as opposed simply to the best way of *coping with* one's particular (necessarily ethnocentric) reality, who continue to conceive of political relations in metaphysical terms that necessitate the exercise of power and coercion.[47] Rawls is one who definitely has Nazism in mind here:

> The wars of this century with their extreme violence and increasing destructiveness, culminating in the manic evil of the Holocaust, raise in an acute way the question whether political relations must be governed by power and coercion alone. If a reasonably just society that subordinates power to its aims is not possible and people are largely amoral, if not incurably cynical and self-centered, one might ask with Kant whether it is worthwhile for human beings to live on the earth? We must start with the assumption that a reasonably just political society is possible, and for it to be possible, human beings must have a moral nature, not of course a perfect such nature, yet one that can understand, act on, and be sufficiently moved by a reasonable political conception of right and justice to support a society guided by its ideals and principles.[48]

Several questions for Rawls here emerge: Why *do* people betray their nature by continuing to look for some transcultural Truth as opposed to subscribing to more reasonable, if merely political, coping mechanisms? Might not the nature of fantasy be such that the very hegemony of such reasonable coping mechanisms in fact *exacerbates* the desire for Truth? Can we in fact say that the lesson of the Holocaust lies in the failure of certain people to fantasize in a shared and reasonable way? Is there not always something about fantasy itself that is "unreasonable"—a coping mechanism aimed more at "fantasizing" oneself into existence than at achieving this or that scenario promised by the fantasy? Is not the fantasy object—that is, one's *self*—then an entity whose meaning is entirely groundless and contingent? Interestingly enough, Rawls touches on precisely this aspect of the fantasy when he claims that without the fantasy, *there may as well be nothing*. Liberalism's affinity with obsession emerges here in the sense that the compulsion driving the thought-experiment (i.e., our going behind the veil of ignorance) functions to ward off some deeper source of doubt pertaining to the very structural conditions of society to which that doubt bears witness. What Rawls seems to fear most of all is the dissolution of identity that looms in this specter of doubt. So, rather than allowing this fact to highlight the groundlessness (and freedom) of political liberalism's fantasy, he busies himself with the construction of a meaningful fantasy scenario that might guarantee fairness and justice in the world. The lesson of the Holocaust hereby becomes "have the right fantasy"—a lesson that stops well short of thinking through the workings of fantasy itself, especially its relation to trauma.

Toward the Origins of Liberal Fantasy

Far from *equating* liberalism and National Socialism, my claim here is simply that a deeper insight than the liberal one may hold the key to the prevention of future catastrophes. Or at least, that we might learn from liberalism's past failures to act decisively by breaking from the compulsive (and compulsory) fantasy. This insight lies with conceptualizing the lesson of the Holocaust not so much in terms of the rightness or wrongness of this or that fantasy but with the origins of fantasy itself and the fact that one's *fantasy object* or *fantasy scenario* always has something nonsensical or unconscious about it. Having ruled out a priori a notion of the subject as *split off* from one's desire (and thus one's fantasy) and therefore constitutionally incapable in some sense of exercising some natural propensity for justice, liberalism assumes that fantasy is somehow the result of a *conscious* choice, that we must subject our fantasies to more conscious or circumspect deliberation. In misunderstanding the terms of its own fantasy, what the liberal-democratic position disavows is the traumatic instability/inconsistency that is *internal* to democratic social relations—that is to say, the extent to which the thought-experiment on which it outlines a just and fair society is itself *already* a pathological, violent, purely performative act of foreclosure. The assumption that a reasonably just political society is possible is itself unreasonable, and this is the best reason for clinging to it! It is, in other words, fundamentally an act without ground, an act that grounds itself. This is, however, precisely what the liberalisms of Rawls and Rorty try to get around, arguing instead that what counts as reasonable is *freestanding*, which means that rather than being linked to some a priori comprehensive doctrine—Rorty refers to such doctrines as ladders that we should now throw away since they have become encumbrances—it relies on public culture for justification and legitimation. Already here, however, is a step back from the rhetorical question Rawls borrows from Kant above—a question that hints that the *real* legitimacy of liberal views and values belongs at an entirely different ontological level than public agreement. In other words, public agreement already hints at a disingenuous use of the word "freestanding" to characterize the way liberal values are legitimized. Because liberalism fails to seize the precisely metaphysical source of its legitimacy, its remedies do not really address the causes that animate historical instances of violence and murder: these remedies never really aim to bring liberal institutions and citizens toward an encounter with trauma. In this way, liberalism circumscribes its own freedom by resting its case on a scenario with some bearing in the real capable of managing social relations in a fair and equal and reasonable way. The "truth" of this scenario is solidified by a plurality of subjects' identification with it. But precisely here, in the belief that truth is somehow a property of the real or of nature, the liberal-democratic fantasy misunderstands the terms of fantasy in a way that prevents its mounting the best possible opposition to fascism. This is because fascist ideology and aggression, too, is underwritten by a fantasy scenario that transforms the real in order to master it. If fascism sought to preserve the truth of the real by interpreting its absence as theft (i.e., why is the German nation unable to experience its essential identity *for real?*—because the Jews have hijacked a significant portion of it), liberal democracy takes the real itself to reside in a symbolic scenario in which social relations are anchored in a belief in basic liberties, justice as fairness, and human rights conferred by *nature* and agreed on by the citizens of public culture.

As I have intimated above, the problem with liberalism is that it does not take Kantian ethics and the Hegelian subject seriously enough: when Kant theorizes a moral act as the *freest* gesture of the noumenal subject, when Hegel urges on a universalizing gesture that prepares the ground for this subject's ethical sacrificial act, neither imagine mastery or stability or fairness to be the necessary (or even desired) result. That is to say, neither outline scenarios in which we are to preserve the truth of the real and to disavow its traumatic dimension. For liberalism and fascism the case is otherwise. In their case, the absence of real solidarity can be accounted for coherently by pointing to an *external cause* capable of explaining the current inability of a society to gain full possession of itself. In the case of fascism, this cause is the anti-Semitic, paranoid construction of the Jew; in the case of liberalism, this cause is always the fascist/terrorist who will not agree to fantasize in a liberal-democratic way. The point to register here, of course, is that the cause of a subject's or society's incompletion/inconsistency is no more singular than it is entirely symbolizable. What liberalism forecloses thus always exists at the same ontological level of that which is thereby constructed—the just, well-ordered society. The trauma the liberal-democrat discerns in the Holocaust is thus always a symbolic entity—the Nazi machine that forsook all rational means of adjudicating disputes and killed scores of innocent human beings. But does this picture sufficiently address the structural trauma for which a given society might seek redress by way of fascism?

The remedy implicit in liberalism's diagnosis of the problem seems to me to be overlook the predicament for which the anti-Semitic construction of the Jew sought redress. As the comprehensive signifier that unifies all those sites where the symbolic is experienced, on the ground so to speak, as failing to correspond to the real itself, the ideological figure of the Jew takes up the function of a transcendental, noumenal "realistic" object—an intelligible source of all causality. To conceive this object realistically or anthropomorphically is already to misrepresent German idealism's claims regarding transcendence and the noumenal object. To see just how, we might consider how the ideological figure of the Jew carries out—and perverts—the role of what Lacan terms the *point de capiton* (i.e., the quilting point). In the *Psychoses* seminar, Lacan argues that the quilting point is simply an invented signifier, a "remedy for a world made up of manifold terrors," a means for replacing "innumerable fears by the fear of a unique being."[49] Lacan has in mind here the traditional belief in God, but his insight is equally applicable to anti-Semitism and to what we might call, no doubt parodically, the traditional belief in the Jew. In the latter, the figure of the Jew functions as a kind of master-signifier, a kind of transcendent Other the idea of whom "quilts" together a number of contingent phenomena in order to find behind those contingent phenomena some ultimate (and perennially inhabited) locus of causality. Though aligned with psychosis, Lacan eschews the antimetaphysical circumvention that would dispense with quilting points altogether. Properly conceived, quilting points exist for Lacan as primordial signifiers irreducible to the order of meaning and necessary for the latter's consolidation. Quilting points enable us to navigate the path from nature to culture, to begin to gain our bearings in a social world. The quilting point's metaphysical dimension is a logical and welcome necessity: only when a signifier emerges that does not belong to the physical circuits of demand and satisfaction, do I gain some separation from those circuits; only as I am moved to wonder if things really are as they appear to be, do things emerge as discrete entities. This is the quilting point's indispensable function. But as Lacan never tires of pointing out, there is always a kind of "stupidity" that pertains to it—something about it that is traumatically nonsensical. In this way, Lacan remains faithful to Kant's dictum that the concept of the noumenon is not the concept of an object: it is, as Kant puts it, a "mere title" for a concept. One finds and clings to a quilting point in order to build a rampart against the trauma of the real, and at its deepest level, the quilting point cannot get free of this ineluctable proximity. To take up a quilting point absolutely is to experience this proximity: it is to bear witness to (or bring about again) a fundamental gesture of foreclosure that enables a sociosymbolic order to consolidate itself. The problem with the ideological figure of the Jew is that it gives to the quilting point a context, a history, *from the beginning*. The ideological figure of the Jew qua quilting point thus does not so much foreclose the real. Instead, it allows for a fantasy in which the ultimate loci of causality are treated empirically as matters of realism, are conceived of as entirely the province of sociopolitical struggle and violence. The deployment of the quilting point in this direction, as Slavoj Žižek has noted, constitutes the fundamental gesture of an anti-Semitic ideology, transforming by means of a purely formal conversion a number of inconsistent, disparate, unsymbolizable elements—that is, "manifold terrors"— into so many manifestations of the same ground. In this gesture, the signifier Jew is rid of its constitutive, "transcendent" stupidity, and is instead called on to serve as the meaningful name that enables a regime to account, in a coherent historical narrative, for all those instances wherein identity is experienced as something incomplete and marked by lack. In his concise description of the process of accounting, Žižek insists that

> The designation *"Jew" does not add any new content*: the entire content is already present in the external conditions (crisis, moral degeneration . . .); the name "Jew" is only the supplementary feature which accomplishes a kind of transubstantiation, changing all these elements into so many manifestations of the same *ground*, the "Jewish plot."[50]

That a formal conversion, a final reconciliation of all contradiction, only concretizes a lack internal to the notion of a national identity—this is what accounts for the paranoia that comes increasingly to drive the fantasy: the anti-Semitic construction of the Jew was at one and the same time the construction of a figure who was to be eliminated but who could never finally die. This is why anti-Semitism became more severe where there were the fewest Jews, why the more Jews that were annihilated— the more they disappeared—the more they were said to be executing their secret, international conspiracy.

We might see in the liberal democratic response to the Holocaust an identical gesture in terms of embodying or symbolizing the cause of societal antagonism and imbalance. Let us return here to a text that argues for liberal democracy as the legacy of the Holocaust—Harold Kaplan's *Conscience and Memory*. Like those of most liberal democrats, Kaplan's intentions are no doubt in the right place, but his argument that conscience is fascism's primary target—"the fuhrer principle was obviously a device to erase conscience. . . . Brute power recognizes its primary enemy"[51]—seems already to rely on a meaning of "conscience" that is somehow prior to the symbolic network of meanings in which it is inscribed. This belief in a presymbolic entity that is nonetheless socializing constitutes the liability of the liberal democratic argument and the redemptive scenario outlined therein. Would it not have been—and indeed was it not—fruitless to present the Nazi regime with the claim that their program of annihilation contradicted the imperatives of conscience? In short, what the liberal democratic argument appears to disavow is where precisely the acquisition of the real places one: once you point toward an external signified believed to have the capacity to rid the world of its imbalance, to master its foundations, to restore an essential value to each and every individual human life, you have already mistaken what, as I shall argue later, the Hegelian commitment to universality in the absolute sense entails—the unsymbolizable real that is the universal's condition of possibility.

Kaplan's claim here is precisely to the contrary. As he sees it, "one has to say that the Holocaust is a lesson in positive democracy."[52] It is the Holocaust here that is invoked as an exemplary instance of the trampling of human rights—rights that would be the foundation of a valid world order. The Jew here becomes, if retroactively, the bearer of these rights:

> It would have been grotesque at the time for the Jews to see themselves as the chief ideological enemies of Nazism. But now, after the Holocaust, we must give more credit to Nazi belief, even if Jews were selected to spearhead democratic values in order to deface them. [. . .] Even if the Jews were pathetically innocent of leading opposition to Hitler, should we not now accept that imputed representation of liberal humanist and democratic values?[53]

In this clear liberal critique of Nazism, Kaplan's claim in short is that the fascist quilting point lacks external support. Arguing the terms of anti-Semitism in their positivity—as Kaplan clearly does in his suggestion that Jews were not at all in fact guilty of organizing some overthrow of German society—one can clearly refute any number of the particular features of the anti-Semitic construction of the Jew. But in this very critique, the liberal view once again mitigates the *necessary* contingency or groundlessness of the quilting point itself. This is the crux of the liberal democratic position: the quilting point that guarantees meaning in a society is not to be seen as a purely arbitrary, tautological, empty signifier, installed by us and thus without the capacity to heal the world. On the contrary, liberalism asserts a replacement for this signifier—this time, one that *does* have external support (e.g., in the reality of the French Revolution, or in the reality of "communal consensus" arrived at without force and constantly willing to be revised). We can see here that in one sense, the Nazi and the liberal operate within the same universe. Thus, Hitler's claim that conscience is the business of the Jew is, if only by means of a retroactive formal gesture, to be taken seriously.[54] Kaplan cannot admit the total contingency of Hitler's *point de capiton* because he would have to admit the total contingency of his own and all others. By conferring, if retroactively, some meaningful mandate on the anti-Semitic construction of the Jew, Kaplan is able to hold on to the possibility of a quilting point, a normative core—call it democracy, egalitarianism, pluralism, whatever—that has an integrity capable of cementing the social contract. To be sure, the Jew is certainly not the quilting point for most liberal democrats. As we have seen, the more common go by the name of justice as fairness (Rawls) or solidarity (Rorty). But by conferring a meaningful substance to his quilting point, Kaplan nonetheless exemplifies the liberal democratic position. If there is a gap between ideal and real, between the social contract and the actual society, it is not one that cannot be filled—even only if imaginatively or on a community-by-community basis. So it is, Kaplan writes, that "the doctrine of human rights appears as if to fill a void in democratic values."[55] In this view, there does exist a referent which all of us agree to recognize by a certain name, which has a value that is irrefutable, and which guarantees the meaning and consistency of rational communication and sociopolitical interactions. The social order itself appears here as the shared experience of this referent

It is by no means the case that this liberal democratic position has nothing to teach us. Kaplan has rightly identified the void at the core of democratic values; his mistake, however, consists in giving a measure of positivity to cause for this void, and then in seeking to replace those actors with exemplars of universal human rights. This suggests the point at which liberal democracy and totalitarianism converge: both refuse a society split from itself, marked by an "excess" that sticks to it but yet it cannot incorporate. As Renata Salecl puts it in *The Spoils of Freedom:*

> The discourse of universal human rights thus presents a fantasy scenario in which society and the individual are perceived as whole, as non-split. In this fantasy, society is understood as something that

can be rationally organized, as a community that can become non-conflictual if only it respects 'human rights.' [56]

The proper rejoinder to the fantasy is simply that this void is internal to democracy and democratic values themselves: the will of the people is not something that can be realized in actuality, for it is, in fact, all the time beset by contingencies that impede efforts to determine it definitively. And more important, the will of the people is split from itself: the people, we might say, do not really want what they want. Far from something to bemoan, democracy's insecure position—it is without a definitive Master to guarantee its self-possession and smooth functioning—is a sign of its progressive potential. The break from the obsessional economy under-writing liberalism lies here, in the notion that *doubt* and *precariousness* are the central ingredients of democracy, and that one *can* act from a position of insecurity. In other words, we need not, in the manner of obsession, substitute security-guaranteeing acts or maxims in place of the possibility of an Act without any basis in the real. "The essence of democracy," Salecl says, "is that it can never be made to the measure of concrete human beings: the basis of democracy is the subject as pure empty place. [. . .] As soon as we try to fill it out with concrete, 'human,' con-tent, we risk falling into totalitarianism."[57] In their *Hegemony and Socialist Strategy*, Ernesto Laclau and Chantal Mouffe make a similar point, insist-ing on the notion of "antagonism" as constitutive of a "radical democ-racy": "This moment of tension, of openness, which gives the social its essentially incomplete and precarious character, is what every project for radical democracy should set out to institutionalize."[58] What a radical democracy entails is thus a recognition antithetical to the carrying out of Holocausts: there is something in the very structure of society and in the identities we assume within language that, exempted from the ordinary, intelligible, temporal chain of causality, cannot be managed or evaded.

Deconstruction as a Memorial Practice

Laclau and Mouffe's challenge to the hegemony of class as the master-signifier of leftist politics already signals a movement from liberalism to deconstruction. The questions Laclau and Mouffe ask of vulgar Marxists are the same questions that deconstruction poses more generally to Hegel. Indeed, it is difficult to call for a totalizing gesture in the service of encountering trauma without coming up against the long shadow still cast by Derridean deconstruction, and specifically, its insistence that even the encounter with some traumatic kernel of the real is part of capturing the play of difference within a metaphysics of presence. Since deconstruction (and the cultural studies it has spawned) is wary of the manner in which Hegelian master-signifiers carry out this capturing, its questions for Hegel are these: Why isn't Spirit itself *also* a phenomenon, and thus also subject to mediation by some other Spirit, and so on, and so on? Is not Spirit also a temporal/discursive formation, and thus never fully present or total? Do not the negations performed by Spirit represent only the most ultimate of appropriative acts? It should be apparent simply from these questions the extent to which the deconstructionist critique of the fascist fantasy entails a negation also of the liberal position as well. In short, the deconstructionist reply to the fascist fantasy is not to say that we can erect or agree on a meaningful Law capable of guaranteeing the consistency of intersubjective relations; it is to say, on the contrary, that we must never fill in the missing gap. We might be able to conceive the "original position," but we can never take the principles discovered therein to have a genuine metaphysical basis. (Rawls's own commitment to role-playing is compatible with this deconstructionist insight, even if he does not draw the same conclusions from it.) In other words, what liberalism is able to produce as the Signifier which would occupy the missing piece in the puzzle—justice as fairness, solidarity, and so on—deconstruction insists is forever doomed to elude us. In the language of psychoanalysis, obsession aims at satisfaction, while hysteria aims to perpetuate dissatisfaction. What deconstruction recognizes in the liberal position is that the anchoring of society and subjectivity in a recognition of Law, justice, solidarity, and a plurality of identities *is itself* a universal, which risks misunderstanding its own terms of being. Just when we believe we have found that which arrests the incessant slippage of meaning—a secure foundation, a ground, a Signifier that does refer absolutely to something (e.g., public culture)—we must at the same time always realize that what we think we have secured is caught within a differential economy. In the language of psychoanalysis, we might say that deconstruction recognizes that something forever remains unconscious, despite our efforts to consciously arrive at an acceptable fantasy that would render transparent the unconscious.

The critique aimed by deconstruction at liberal-democratic premises concerning the organization of meaning rests fundamentally on its critique of the quilting point, of the master-signifier or normative core which provides an anchoring point that arrests the incessant slippage of meanings and allows us to symbolize. But since deconstruction's critique is aimed at the very notion of a quilting point—a synchronic moment within language, a symbolic Law that operates as a kind of rampart against the traumatic real—its critique of Hegel and the Hegelian premises of psychoanalysis has primarily the same contours. What I would like to

suggest here is that although deconstruction is obviously no longer practiced in any orthodox way, its theses still inform the vast majority
of approaches to culture, history, and memory—specifically in the form
of a kind of wariness with respect to an end-of-the-line in the matter of
bearing witness, a skepticism concerning the deadlock that characterizes
one's encounter with trauma in which there is nothing that remains to be
symbolized, mediated, disseminated, and so on. Derrida's objection to
this deadlock dates as far back to his earliest critiques of psychoanalysis
(specifically Lacan's rereading of Freud), and his notion that psychoanalysis is all-too Hegelian in its embrace both of the Hegelian method and
system. Although Derrida admits that both psychoanalysis and deconstruction have somewhat of an affinity in terms of attempting to situate
that which escapes or resists the order of language—"the concept of
castration," Derrida has said, "is indissociable from that of dissemination"—he nonetheless insists that dissemination has a sort of leg up on
the *jouissance* conferred on the place of the Law, since dissemination "designates that which can no more be integrated into the symbolic than it
can form the symbolic's *simple* exterior under the heading of its failure or
its (imaginary or real) impossibility."[59] For Derrida here, dissemination is
that which exceeds even the conceptual category of the traumatic real—
that is, the irreducible point of nondifference—and his suggestion is simply that to bring such a point to rest within such a category is only to
force its articulations to participate in a "closure that shelters the question
of writing." For Derrida, the traumatic real may resist analysis "but as
sense it is analyzable; *it is homogeneous to the order of the analyzable. It comes
under psychoanalytic reason. Psychoanalytic reason as hermeneutic reason.*"[60] In
order to problematize this reduction of the real to sense—a gesture he
openly aligns with a kind of dogmatic Idealism—Derrida insists again and
again on the infinite divisibility of that which eludes symbolization—as if
paradoxically to keep the prospect of something outside the symbolic
alive by infinitely deferring the encounter with it. As Derrida puts it in
his *Resistances of Psychoanalysis,*

> The question of divisibility is one of the most powerful instruments
> of formalization for what is called deconstruction. If, in an absurd
> hypothesis, there were one and only one deconstruction, a sole *thesis*
> of "Deconstruction," it would pose divisibility: differance as divis-
> ibility. Paradoxically, this amounts to raising the analytical stakes
> for a thinking that is very careful to take account of what always
> rejects analysis (the originary complication, the nonsimple, the ori-
> gin under erasure, the trace, or the affirmation of the gift as trace).
> The paradox is merely apparent: it is because there is no indivisible

element or simple origin that analysis is interminable. Divisibility, dissociability, and thus the impossibility of arresting an analysis, like the necessity of thinking the possibility of this indefiniteness, would be perhaps, if one insisted on such a thing, the truth without truth of deconstruction.[61]

An ethics of deconstruction and an ethics of the Absolute are here clearly seen to be antithetical, since Derrida's explicit claim is simply that in the issue of the relation between thought and matter, *there is always something to say*. In virtually every one of Derrida's works, this point emerges: there is never simply a "truth" of deconstruction; whatever truth it can be said to put forth is always a kind of contradiction in terms, a game of hide-and-seek that never ends—that is, a "truth without truth." For Derrida, this is how deconstruction raises the ethical stakes of thinking itself: it insists on the impossibility of bringing the game to an end, and, indeed, on the prohibition of any such end.

One consequence of this praxis for historical memory, of course, is to maintain a minimum of distance between our own subject positions within language and the positions of the witnesses and victims. Rather than attempting to bear witness to the real of history—an experience that might require the experience of the sociosymbolic order's temporary suspension, the loss of our moorings in a network of circulating signs—bearing witness entails instead listening to the stories, honoring the dead by keeping the memory of the victims alive, repeating the phrases "Never forget" and "Do not let it happen again," and realizing that our obligations to the dead are interminable. The aim of such remembering is to communicate the point that the truth of history eludes us at every turn, since we can never render it unproblematically, since any given historical phenomena is always already an instance of textuality. Obviously informed by deconstruction, these claims underwrite the fundamental historicist assumptions of cultural inquiry today, and they work to maintain the illusion that we are not now living in the time of the Holocaust. Derrida no doubt understands the extent to which historicism and the signifying chain guards one against the suspension of the temporal plane and a frontal encounter with trauma. When we experience this suspension, Derrida claims,

we are exposed, absolutely without protection, without problem, and without prosthesis, without possible substitution, singularly exposed in our absolute and absolutely naked uniqueness, that is to say, disarmed, delivered to the other, incapable even of sheltering ourselves behind what could still protect the interiority of a secret.

There, in sum, in this place of the aporia, *there is no longer any problem.*[62]

But despite this eloquent articulation of the place we occupy in the moment of aporia, this place is ruled off limits since it brings about a situation for the subject wherein which there is "no next moment"—that is, the moment of symbolic death in which "time stands still," in which the very temporal plane of experiential possibility has been closed off. Because closure of any kind—even the closure involved in the cessation of life—smacks of triumphant accession to the siren call of a metaphysics of presence, this experience is prohibited, thus making the deconstructionist ethical credo: act in such a way so that aporia always remains a *possibility* for you, so that your death is always an event still to come. One never, for Derrida, experiences aporia or death *as such*. This is ultimately the hysterical dimension of Derridean deconstruction: it denies the possibility of the very thing that constitutes it as a philosophy. I say this because Derridean deconstruction *is* nothing if not a philosophy of aporia.

I have rehearsed these well-known deconstructive theses in order to highlight the extent to which they inform the prevailing theoretical approach to the Holocaust and the bearing of witness to it. While these theses provide a necessary critique of the liberal-democratic position that has clearly managed to anchor the meaning of the Holocaust in some substantial notion of tolerance, respect, rights, and constitutional democracy, my claim here is that this critique—because it makes *no ontological distinction* between the signifiers that consolidate liberal society and the traumatic real—goes awry when it sets its sights on the traumatic real. Put another way, Derrida seems to see the consolidating signifiers of liberalism and the traumatic real alike as latecomers on the scene, aiming to compensate for the *différance* that marks any attempt to secure an origin or site of ultimate causality. Thus, deconstruction objects to the liberal exercise of power in the form of a reasonable charter that secures universal or communal agreement because it arrests the metonymic play of the dialectic, and it subjects the traumatic real to the same critique. The precise relation of trauma to the discursive/temporal chain is critical to this ethical dispute. Insisting on the infinite divisibility of the trauma of the real, deconstruction effectively claims that we cannot genuinely be said to have experienced a primordial or founding trauma. Thus for Derrida, there is something about the encounter with trauma that is always *futural*, always yet-to-come. Here, Derrida remains with the Kant who wavers about the actual execution of a free, moral act—the Kant who posits the immortality of the soul and the existence of God so that death does not really involve a coinciding with the eternal, but simply the continuation of human finitude into an afterlife. The effect in Derrida is similar: to claim that the encounter with trauma ought always to be regarded as something futural is in effect to infinitely sustain the symbolic order and our subject positions within it by forever postponing the experience of the death of that order—that is, our own symbolic deaths. To put this another way, under the guise of demonstrating again and again the inability of the symbolic order to gain full possession of itself, deconstruction in fact keeps alive the fantasy that it might. The alternate path, of course, is to view the experience of trauma as having *already* happened, as a structural necessity capable of (and worth) being reexperienced again. Derrida's insistence on the infinite divisibility of the real refuses these possibilities and stands, in my view, as a result as the "vanishing mediator" between the Holocaust and contemporary theories of how best to bear witness to it.

Where the presence of this vanishing mediator is most apparent is in the work of Dominick LaCapra, and specifically his clarion call for a kind of *interminable* working through of the Holocaust and its trauma. LaCapra locates his work under a "rethinking of psychoanalysis" not to be identified with any definable position or foundation. His view of psychoanalysis, he says, "is relatively nontechnical and does not strictly conform to the principles of any given school. Rather it selectively appropriates aspects of the work of Freud and of those responding to him in ways I judge to be fruitful for reconfiguring historical understanding as a process that requires a critical exchange with the past bearing on the present and future."[63] Aware that even his own advocacy of working through must not presume itself to be immune from working through (i.e., deconstruction), LaCapra sounds a clear Derridean motif when he claims that "one cannot give a full account, adequate definition of working-through. Indeed, any inclusive and exhaustive definition would distort the concept."[64] According to LaCapra, "working-through" the Holocaust depends on an acknowledgment of the multiple "subject positions" involved in transferential relations with it. In his *Representing the Holocaust: History, Theory, Trauma*, LaCapra contends that "working-through requires the recognition that we are involved in transferential relations to the past in ways that vary according to the subject-positions we find ourselves in, rework, and invent."[65] History is, in this sense, fundamentally social, even as it acknowledges that something eludes any and every particular vantage point within the symbolic. As LaCapra sees it, the role of the historian "is not a full identity but at most a subject-position that should be complemented, supplemented, and even contested by other subject-positions."[66]

On one level, LaCapra's claims are clearly intended to introduce the force of negativity into any simple, propositional statement concerning history—any unself-conscious witnessing position—and in this sense, his claims are clearly a part of a postmodern challenge to the stability of history and historical inquiry. Like many poststructuralists (informed by Hegel's method if not his system), LaCapra has rightly dispensed with the unified subject who was once the strictly objective knower of a rational and transparent history: "Nowhere more than in discussions of the Holocaust," LaCapra writes, "do positivism and standard techniques of narrowly empirical-analytic inquiry seem wanting. How the historian should use language with reference to the subject-positions that he or she occupies and is attempting to forge is a pressing issue with no prefabricated or pat solutions; the issue cannot be obviated through a reversion to type."[67] This kind of recognition enables LaCapra to see, among other things, trauma as the repressed dimension of redemptive historical narratives, as well as to note various blind spots in contemporary accounts of the Holocaust and those thinkers now irrevocably associated with it (e.g., Paul de Man, Martin Heidegger, etc.).

Up to this point, we might see LaCapra's thesis as consonant with the earlier affiliation of dissemenation and castration: something traumatic eludes the order of language and reason and returns to destabilize our positions within that order. But while LaCapra insists on the acknowledgment of this destabilization, he is wary of what might be called the Hegelian tendency within psychoanalysis to consider one's particular subject position as in any way universal or absolute. For LaCapra, this move always involves an ethical trespass, since it risks conflating structural and historical trauma:

> Although one may contend that structural trauma is in some problematic sense its precondition, historical trauma is related to specific events, such as the Shoah or the dropping of the atom bomb on Japanese cities. It is deceptive to reduce, or transfer the qualities of, one dimension of trauma to the other, to generalize structural trauma so that it absorbs historical trauma, thereby rendering all references to the latter merely illustrative, homogeneous, allusive, and perhaps equivocal, or, on the contrary, to "explain" all post-traumatic, extreme, uncanny phenomena and responses as exclusively caused by particular events or contexts. Indeed, the problem of specificity in analysis and criticism may be formulated in terms of the need to explore the problematic relations between structural and historical trauma without reducing one to the other.[68]

For LaCapra, the affective encounter with structural trauma—like the Hegelian suprasensible Idea—too often threatens the specificity of historical trauma, obfuscating its potential lessons. An affective encounter with structural trauma has a place within his ethics of witnessing, but only when one is "attentive" to its possible abuses. Invoking the well-known barbershop scene in Claude Lanzmann's *Shoah* in which Lanzmann "forces" Abraham Bomba to relive the trauma of his role as a barber in Treblinka, LaCapra's fear is that such an absolutizing gesture risks a kind of "acting out" which fixates on trauma and motivates destructive repetitions:

> With respect to traumatic events, and certainly with respect to the extremely traumatic limit-event, one must, I think, undergo at least muted trauma and allow that trauma (or unsettlement) to affect one's approach to problems. In treating these events, a kitsch, harmonizing, or fetishistic narrative that denies trauma is particularly objectionable. But one should not remain at the level of acting-out or absolutize the latter in the form of an attempt actually to relive or appropriate other traumas.[69]

As LaCapra sees it, there is no doubt something "inappropriate about modes of representation which in their very style or manner of address tend to overly objectify, smooth over, or obliterate the nature and impact of the events they treat." But by the same token, it is just as worrisome when one "go[es] to the extreme of dissociating affect or empathy from intellectual, cognitive, and stylistic or rhetorical concerns."[70] For LaCapra, one counteracts the existence of trauma by attempting to "work-through problems, mourn the victims of the past, and reengage life in the interest of bringing about a qualitatively better state of affairs."[71] The key to this attempt is careful mediation so that the study of history fulfills what LaCapra sees as its public, sociopolitical purpose: "to generate anxiety in tolerable, nonparanoid doses so that one is in a better position to avoid or counteract deadly repetitions."[72] Tolerable doses of anxiety permit actual, if partial, reconstructions of the past, reconstructions that enable politically necessary judgments of liability and responsibility. This focus on the actual, present world is the explicit crux of LaCapra's more recent *Writing History, Writing Trauma*, in which LaCapra laments the way the inquiries into trauma and the use of psychoanalytic concepts sometimes "become a pretext for avoiding economic, social, and political issues." Mindful of a need to renew the link between theory and practice, LaCapra cautions that the appeal to psychoanalytic concepts "adds a necessary dimension to economic, social, and political analyses but does not constitute a substitute for them."[73] In other words, claims about the (nonhistorical) dimension of structural trauma must not completely run roughshod over historical trauma itself; the encounter with trauma must not completely overwhelm the demands of accurate reconstruction and critical analysis.

LaCapra is no doubt correct to insist that there is something factually or contextually different about the situation, say, of an individual death camp survivor and a contemporary reader of a Holocaust memoir. As creatures who exist in space and time, the identities of these two hypothetical individuals cannot be conflated. Indeed, even the death camp survivor's claim, in the act of testifying or everyday living, that he or she *is* "back there," is for LaCapra a problematic one worthy of questioning (though certainly not blame). But again, the questions that confront Derridean-inspired historicism rear their head here: Are we only spatial and temporal individuals? Does ethics belong solely within the coordinates of space and time? And is the encounter with what does not belong to space and time *in fact* of a piece with "deadly repetitions"? LaCapra's claim that structural trauma is "in some problematic sense" historical trauma's precondition hints only generally at the ethical stakes of the matter. As we have seen, structural trauma—from Kant onward—is that which allows a social order to constitute itself: logically speaking, some rupture must have occurred for a human world of lack to have eclipsed a natural world of plenitude, for us to be the free, desiring subjects that we are. This rupture is a kind of terrible gift we carry around with us all the time. If trauma conditions the existence of the finite world, it also constitutes the nature and being of the finite subjects or that world. There is thus no way for us to live an intelligible moment that is not indebted to structural trauma. Our death (or incompleteness) is thus no mere possibility. As Hegel puts it, there is no way for a finite being to be without ceasing to be: "The being as such of finite things is to have the germ of decease as their being-within-self: the hour of their birth is the hour of their death."[74] So, generally speaking, structural trauma, insofar as it is responsible for the finite world in which human beings act according to desires (and not as automatons), is a precondition for the execution of historical trauma. But its status as precondition goes deeper than this, since it is also the *disavowal* of structural trauma that has often motivated the agents responsible for the execution of the historical traumas to which we now feel ourselves summoned to bear witness. Indeed, have not the myriad historical "crimes against humanity" been driven by a fantasy of *redressing* structural trauma—a fantasy of treating structural trauma as *historical* and thus capable of reversal? And as Eric Santner has suggested, does not the avoidance of "future adventures in fascist politics" depend on a deconstruction of the fantasy of such a reversal (and the lethal narcissisms to which it caters)?[75]

crushing by universal

Avowing Structural Trauma

To designate the preconditional link between structural and historical trauma merely as "in some sense problematic" thus may leave a few decisive ethical questions unaddressed: How can contemporary subjects be made to see the futility of aiming to redress a trauma that is in fact structural? How can we philosophically, artistically, or both take apart the way the *disavowal* of structural trauma has in fact functioned to condition/ motivate historical trauma? And must not the first imperative of an ethics of historical memory focus on the method that constitutes this disavowal— the (fascist) historicization of structural trauma? These questions lead me to see a basic ethical value in *the reexperiencing of structural trauma* that happens when we encounter in the material evidence or testimony of historical traumas that which eludes our discursive, meaning-making abilities. This is not to say that all historical trauma *is* structural trauma, but that the bearing witness to historical trauma, while *beginning* with historically specific instances, ought to *lead to* a recognition of the struc- tural trauma antecedent to it. Thus I find suggestive Cathy Caruth's claims regarding the ethical centrality of a more structural *awakening* in the act of bearing witness—an "itinerary" that moves us from thinking of trauma strictly as an exception (i.e., in its historical specificity) to thinking of it as "the very origin of consciousness and all of life itself."[76] The terminus of this itinerary involves simply the recognition that the act of knowing is inseparable from the question (and difficulty) of what it means to know. It is by no means clear to me that this itinerary automatically constitutes the complete reduction or absorption of historical trauma, since the particular historical trauma that catalyzes the journey is, in some ways, just as present at the end as it is at the beginning. Nor is it clear to me that this itinerary is always inimical to accurate reconstructions of the past. A film like *Shoah* is apposite here: certainly Lanzmann repeatedly stages ("acts out") the failure to witness, but does this come at the expense of what his film reconstructs—the everyday machinery of the extermination, the phenomenology of the bystanders, and so forth?

I am no doubt aware of the by-now frequent criticism my endorse- ment of this itinerary is bound to elicit—the suspicion that Caruth and others have simply enlisted particular historical traumas to support their larger, pet philosophical theory. This is the charge leveled, in one way or another, at all of the structuralizers who move from the Holocaust to an antecedent trauma it is said to render explicit. Ruth Leys, for instance, has recently indicted Caruth for having forsaken the genealogy of the concept of psychic trauma in an attempt to "use the notion of trauma as a *critical concept* in order to support her performative theory of language."[77] Leys is among the more vocal critics of those who arrive at a structural trauma antecedent to the historical one, ridiculing the notion of an "intergenerational transmission of trauma" and linking the structuralizers to our contemporary culture of victimhood.[78] Evincing a clear hostility to theory, these criticisms rest almost entirely on the circumvention of the ways history itself has been thought *philosophically*—for instance, the fundamental notion that something nonhistorical conditions the very emergence and existence of history. It is without question true that this philosophy opens up the possibility of trauma's manipulation, but it also makes possible an ethics rooted in the complex witnessing of the traumatic encounter.[79] In addition, because the dismissals of Leys and others rely on a fairly broad sweep of the historical brush, they risk overlooking some decisive differences in the methods and outcomes vis-à-vis the way some of these theorists have executed the move from historical to structural trauma. As I have suggested, the trespass does not consist in *ending up* at a recognition of structural trauma, but rather in how one gets there. James Berger may have a point when he notes the extent to which influential theorists such as Foucault, Lyotard, Baudrilliard, and Jameson all take as their starting point the idea that something cataclysmic and irrevocable has happened—without ever focusing in a sustained manner on particular disasters. According to Berger, "The theories of the postmodern initiated by these thinkers diagnose a postapocalyptic condition. At the same time, insofar as these theories tend to focus on developments in epistemology or economics and lose sight of more concrete social and political disasters, they are themselves symptomatic of the traumas they fail to mention."[80] No mention, or needlessly elliptical circumlocutions, are indeed problematic. If Berger's point is that there should be some explicit reference to the extermination of Eastern European Jewry in these works, then I am in complete agreement. But beyond that, I wonder what are to be the standards for measuring a "sustained" focus on particular disasters? And in insisting on such a standard, do we not risk downplaying the extent to which a book like Lyotard's *Differend*—in its explicit mentions of Auschwitz—has had the effect of getting people to think about the particular disaster of the Holocaust in a precise manner? Moreover, it may be unfair to lump critics who *do* spend time explicitly with texts that have specific historical referents—I am thinking here of Shoshana Felman's discussions of Lanzmann's *Shoah*—with theorists who perhaps begin and remain at the level of structure, or who take the step from history to structure too quickly.

In any case, my own sense is that in our everyday experiences of memory, this move toward structural trauma—what I have called its reexperience—happens all the time, and that its commonness is not reason enough to dismiss it: in the effort to memorialize the victims of the gas chamber, of Hiroshima, of imperialism and colonialism, of economic degradation (or of some other instance of historical trauma, e.g., the World Trade Center bombings), we end up arriving at the same, horrible limit-point pertaining to what we can know. This is the lacuna Agamben finds at the heart of all testimony, what he calls (after Primo Levi's remarks in *The Drowned and the Saved*) "Levi's paradox"—that only the dead are the "complete witnesses" capable of furnishing testimony with some general meaning. The temptation this lacuna invites is to believe that prior to the specific historical trauma we are dealing with, we enjoyed a kind of innocence in which this paradox did not pertain to us. (This is a temptation sometimes given into by those who claim an exceptionality for the Holocaust.[81]) But if, as we are attending to the specific historical dimensions of a particular trauma, we are led to an experience that results in the recognition that structural trauma is anterior to historical trauma, another recognition dawns in us: we did not need this latest instance of historical trauma to render up the lesson that our knowledge of things or grip on the world is not really what it seems. This "universal" experience, as I have said, does not automatically constitute a trespass against the specificity of historical events—unless we are dogmatically opposed to anything universal. Those memory texts that end up "using" specific historical events in order to lead potential witnesses toward the avowal of structural trauma seem to me not so much to make the *historical* trauma happen again (which would, in fact, constitute a deadly repetition), but to make *the structural trauma happen again. As a kind of reminder,* the latter happening remains at the level of ethical remembrance and not deadly repetition. My own sense is that this effort can (to put it in Kantian terms) get us to realize the paradox of our freedom, making us see the extent to which fascism (and its historicization of the structural) constitutes a betrayal of that freedom. On this score, LaCapra evinces a more liberal worry that a Law of sorts (even if provisional) must be erected to check this freedom: he worries that the reexperience of structural trauma might be accompanied by a feeling of elation or *Rausch* and sees as a remedy for this some commitment to the critically tested methods of historiography. But what this view overlooks is the Idealist thesis that sees the Law (something that limits and motivates my conduct) as something that *founds* freedom, rather than limiting it. Here then, I am essentially endorsing an ethics of historical memory centered on the reexperiencing of structural trauma—as a way of realizing the terms of our freedom, of realizing that all is not historical. This structural trauma should come *on the heels of* an attentiveness to historical trauma: only when we move from the historical to the structural do we cease implicitly treating the Holocaust as a dead relic of the past; only then can we perhaps begin to make memorialization have significant effects on the way we think and act in the world.

My own sense is that the very outcome LaCapra advocates—"muted trauma" or "unsettlement"—might in fact be result of the reexperience of structural trauma he wants to discourage. Like Derrida, he refuses to endorse any experience in which the temporal order itself might be suspended, any experience that places in jeopardy the very notion of subject positions involved in transferential relations with history or the Holocaust. In LaCapra's argument, everything up to *but not including* subject position is to be risked in the engagement with history. Only by exempting from ultimate danger the symbolic identity of the subject can LaCapra counter what he sees as one of the less appealing products of poststructuralist theorizing—that "quasi-theoretical situation in which problems lose all specificity by being everywhere and nowhere—a situation that easily lends itself to apologetic uses." Wary of the "troping away from specificity" that is part of a memorial effort rooted in the repetition of trauma, LaCapra insists again and again on the historicist imperative that we implicate our subject positions in the very object of his or her inquiry. The basic source of concern here is that the break from history—the dissolution of identity—is part and parcel of deadly repetitions. But to repeat the point raised at the close of the preceding paragraph, if we never break from history, how does the working through promised by historiography itself not end up turning into a kind of acting out? In other words, LaCapra may overlook the possibility of memorial efforts that would only strengthen his political project. Indeed, how *have* various changes in the historiography of the Holocaust actually taken place? Can these changes be entirely accounted for at the level of symbolic, dialogic exchanges between and among historians?

Though LaCapra clearly refuses any formalized or systematized notion of working through—"One cannot give a full, adequate definition of working through. Indeed, any inclusive and exhaustive definition would distort the concept"—what must be insisted on here is that every single one of his utterances depends for its meaning on a strictly formalized totality of meaning. We might say here that LaCapra is deeply, if unwittingly, Hegelian. If liberalism pledges fealty to a false universal, deconstruction pledges fealty to a false particularism. This is one of the central paradoxes of any mode of historical inquiry in which any proposition is understood as diachronic, as taking its meaning from other propositions (and not from some pragmatic belief in reference to actual objects). As Joan Copjec points out,

Once one breaks up the signifying chain, the statement, into a series of minimal units, of diacritical terms or signifiers that take their meaning only from their reference to another signifier, which in turn refers to another, and so on and on, and once this endless deferral is no longer considered to be grounded in some external reality (language being conceived as autonomous, as self-sustaining), we are obliged to wonder how it is possible to produce any statement at all."[82]

What in short is the condition of possibility of the signifying chain itself? What sets it in motion? And how can we establish *new* signifying chains? Again, we return to the experience of structural trauma in the act of bearing witness to the past and the need to rethink or reexperience the universality that underwrites particular subject positions. What becomes clear here is that there is *no getting around* the ethical priority of structural trauma in the prevention of future historical traumas: we can grasp the transcendental object *as such* because we *already have* grasped it. When we begin with historical traumas and arrive at the implicit structural trauma they render explicit, we simply bear witness to the fundamentally counterfascist ontological fact of our division. What this amounts to is the recognition that one must adopt *more than* merely a historical attitude toward history, since one's cognitive abilities are all the time testifying to their failure. Every attempt to bear witness to historical trauma is in fact at the same time a bearing of witness to structural trauma, just as every statement of diachrony is at the same time an instance of synchrony. In other words, there is no historical trauma without structural trauma: we must have synchrony to arrive at diachrony—the critical necessity of the Hegelian Absolute, the Hegelian system.

Hegel's Ethics of Memory

The whole of Hegel's place at the cornerstone of historical memory rests on the fundamental thesis of Hegelian phenomenology—that the particular *is already universal*. At first glance, the radicality of this proposition appears to lie entirely in a conservative direction. That is to say, Hegel's proposition appears on the face of it to grant an equally legitimate position to any individual formulator of the proposition itself, thus opening up a universe of radical relativity, aggression, or both in which every particular interest is given license to believe its interest to in fact be universal. The political valence of Hegel's idealism has seemed always to center on the subjective exercise of power it authorizes. It is Hegel who

theorized (and encouraged) this exercise of power more thoroughly than
anyone, insisting that every material reality experienced by this subject is
always and only the product of his or her mediation; as Hegel puts it in
the preface to the *Phenomenology*, "Everything turns on grasping and expressing the True, not only as *Substance*, but equally as *Subject*."[83] In this
stroke, Hegel's idealism challenges the very status of objectivity, claiming
that objectivity itself is the product of subjective mediation, that what
counts as an object can only be determined by a subject. In this respect,
objectivity is in a sense an illusion: it does not exist "out there" but is
rather the result of a distinction between subject and object made by the
very subject in question.

For Hegel, this very distinction is a structural feature of consciousness or selfhood itself. According to Hegel, there is a fundamental "disparity which exists in consciousness between the 'I' and the substance
which is its object" (21). Moreover, this disparity—what Hegel refers to as
the "negative in general"—is absolutely critical for the survival of subject
and object. Here, we return to an insight of Hegel's registered above
apropos the necessity of structural trauma: since finite things are determined by an act of negation, since they owe their consistency to a certain
"disparity," there is no way for such finite things to exist without the
simultaneous recognition that they must necessarily one day cease to
exist. This is what Hegel means when he says that the hour of the subject's
birth is the hour of that subject's death as well, and it is why Hegel says
that the disparity, conventionally thought to be a "*defect* of both," is in fact
"their soul, or that which moves through them" (21). The key point of
Hegel's phenomenology is to recognize that the disparity between the "I"
and its objects is at the same time the disparity of all substance with itself,
and it is this latter disparity that even clears the way for the subject to
emerge and for substance to be known or to exist for us at all. This is but
another way of saying that our knowledge of the world and ourselves can
never be an immediate one because something substantial must be given
up if there is even to be anything at all to be gotten back: the consistency
of reality itself, then, depends on the sacrifice of substance and the process that sacrifice commences whereby reality itself depends on the subject's
ability "to appropriate and subdue it to himself." As Hegel puts it in the
lesser *Logic*,

> The "I" is as it were the crucible and the fire which consumes the
> loose plurality of sense and reduces it to unity . . . This view has at
> least the merit of giving a correct expression to the nature of con-
> sciousness. The tendency of all man's endeavors is to understand the
> world, to appropriate it and subdue it to himself: and to this end the

positive reality of the world must be as it were crushed and pounded, in other words, idealized.[84]

As the imagery here makes clear (so much so that one is tempted to cringe), Hegel does not simply recognize the process whereby the object world (i.e., positive reality) is created. On the contrary, he urges this process on, insisting that the subject exercise his mediation of material reality without reserve. What Hegel is after, of course, is the identity of identity and nonidentity, the seemingly oxymoronic "concrete universal"—that is to say, the universal thought that is nonetheless universal despite its existence within a particular consciousness. To this end, Hegel insists that the subject "crush and pound" his or her way toward a totalizing vantage point vis-à-vis material reality, a position Hegel baptizes Absolute Knowledge or Spirit.

In the case of Holocaust memory, this would appear to be a recipe for disaster; one can imagine all sorts of apologists invoking this thesis of Hegel's to justify the truthfulness of their particular interpretation or memorialization of history. What if, however, at a deeper level, Hegel has something far different in mind than providing the theoretical foundation for a certain "reconciliation" with history? What if, on the contrary, Hegel's insistence on the universality of every particular interest is designed not to secure the legitimacy of all particular interests (and thus of a radically conservative philosophy of relativity), but instead to point up the insufficiency/inadequacy of any and every particular interest? What if Hegel's aim is finally to grasp the source of this insufficiency at its most genuine level—as pertaining not to the realm of particularity but to the order of the Universal itself? If this is the case, then Hegel is far from granting license—without regard to truth—to any and every particular approach toward history; he is far from writing a blank check to fascism that would enable the latter in fact to regard their particular interest as Universal and thus carry out whatever barbarity might be necessary to realize a palpable universality. On the contrary, when Hegel instructs us that our particular is *already* universal, he forces us toward an encounter with a more primordial form of difference, the terms of which involve not two particular interests but rather the order of something and the order of nothing—that which can be thought and that which cannot. Thus the difference between Hegel and the liberal and deconstructionist positions might already be discerned, since the latter two (albeit in different ways) tacitly maintain the existence of a self-sufficient or adequate universal. Hegel's claim that the particular is already universal, however, shifts radically the direction of our inquiry: the difficulty of testifying to history lies not in finding a way from the particular (i.e., a starting point) to the universal but rather from the universal to the particular. As Hegel sees it, the universal is always the point from which we start. Both the liberal hope for an adequate universal and the deconstructionist repudiation (even prohibition) of it are, from the beginning, at loggerheads with this fact.

Hegel's insistence on the absolutely universal ground for everything that exists for human subjectivity, then, might be seen to serve antifascist ends by reversing the way we conceptualize our memorial efforts. For Hegel, it is not the Universal or Total account (i.e., master narrative) that is outside of our reach and must remain so; rather, it is the Particular. It is not, in other words, the universal that lies in some suprahistorical domain, but rather the particular—that inert, material presence that stymies the order of intelligibility and meaning from within. We might refer back briefly here to Binjamin Wilkomirski's memoir, *Fragments: Memories of a Wartime Childhood*, which in his words consists of a series of pictures severed from virtually all thinking. Wilkomirski's ambition, in this respect, is nothing short of trying to give the literary text the ontological status of a rebus. His aim is to use words in order to draw certain images "exactly the way my child's memory has held on to it,"[85] and these particular memories, indeed, would seem to defy perspective—that is, defy the capacity of thought altogether. Wilkomirski's memoir, for example, recounts without embellishment several horrific sensory images—of two boys with little twigs jammed into their penises (this as punishment for having not been able to make it to the camp's latrine ditch); of two infants who eat the very skin off their own fingers before dying of hunger; of the smashed skulls of two children whose brain matter mix with snow and mud to form a terrifying puddle that Wilkomirski must leap over to avoid detection by a camp warden. The Hegelian point to register here, however, is that each of these images stand not as particulars that defy the systematic pretensions Hegel gives to the order of thinking; according to Hegel, these images would be more properly regarded as *already universal:* they have already been seized by thought in order even to be rendered in words. Hegel's thinking here has the Kantian separation of sensibility and understanding into two separate faculties as its target. For Hegel, thought cannot be regarded as the opposite of sense, since the very perception and recollection of sensory images is simply a specialization of thinking. What is elusive to such a testimony, then, is not the universal but some traumatic kernel of the real—what we might call the particular or undifferentiated substance itself—that cannot be made sensible. Read in this way, the vignettes that make up Wilkomirski's memoir stand not as a series of particular, but rather wholly *universal*, fragments: they are "concrete universals" in the sense that Hegel intends. This interpretive twist is decisive: rather than representing a series of negative presentations of the

Whole—a series of indicators that the Whole of his childhood (or even of the Holocaust) lies outside the purview of representation—Wilkomirski's images can be said to present the Whole of his childhood itself. To read them as particular fragments is to maintain the existence of Wilkomirski's childhood apart from his recollections of it—as if other essential happenings that he is simply unable to access lie just on the other side of his representations. To read them as universal fragments, however, is to bring about the recognition that there is nothing beyond the anecdotes Wilkomirski has remembered—only the trauma that every universal gesture bears witness to. Indeed, for Hegel, since this trauma is *all the time with us*, the Universal is its vehicle and must be taken up resolutely if we are to bear witness to it—if we are to risk a confrontation with otherness in its unsymbolizable form. Hegel's relevance to the our remembrance of the Holocaust might be said to lie precisely here, in the notion that every time we utter a meaningful word, we are at the same time saying that trauma is *all the time with us*. All we need do is to work toward an avowal of it. Thus, for Hegel structural trauma is a logical condition of history—and not yet historical trauma. The latter would seem to emerge when historical subjects themselves historicize this logical condition, when they aim to speak in a way that is not subtended by structural trauma.

Hegel makes this point by insisting on a fundamental truth concerning our status as speaking beings: that every time we open our mouths to designate this or that particular entity, every time we think the particular, every time we reduce it to sense, we are all the time speaking and thinking from the position of the Whole.[86] This is, in Hegel's lesser *Logic*, the basic insight of phenomenology: "thought is the universal in all acts of conception and recollection."[87] It is, as Hegel says, "the agency of thought [that] gives universality to particular contents."[88] This is clearly the most crucial of Hegel's claims concerning universality: thought, or the universal, is thus not that which harms or threatens to engulf the particular—as it is for Adorno and others—but is, rather, the absolute ontological ground for everything said to exist. The very designation of something particular is merely an instance of universality. The instant an "I" is spoken (is perceived, is heard), its real existence, according to Hegel, dies away. Once again, the link between Hegel and psychoanalysis emerges in the insistence of both on a subject split from itself, a subject whose speaking of a thing already suggests the annihilation/absence of the thing. In his simple proposition involving the relationship between speech and objects, Hegel indicates the extent to which the symbolic order—the order of meaning—is predicated on the death of the thing, which is but another way of saying that our very entrance into a world of meaning is coterminous with the split in the subject. As Hegel puts in the *Phenomenology*, the particular place from which the "I" speaks is thus never where we think it is, because the instant the "I" speaks itself, it has in fact vanished or become unconscious:

> The "I" that utters itself is *heard* or *perceived;* it is an infection in which it has immediately passed into unity with those for whom it has a real existence, and is a universal self-consciousness. That it is *perceived* or *heard* means that its *real existence dies away;* this its otherness has been taken back into itself; and its real existence is just this: that as a self-conscious Now, as a real existence, it is *not* a real existence, and through this vanishing it *is* a real existence. This vanishing is thus itself at once its abiding; it is its own knowing of itself, and its knowing itself as a self that has passed over into another self that has been perceived and is universal. (309)

What Hegel anticipates here is the basic Lacanian maxim that the position of the enunciation is always Universal, no matter how Particular the position of the statement is. We usually think it is just the other way around; we think that our statements are universal and the position from which we enunciate them is particular. But Hegel reverses this. Hegel's link to psychoanalysis is perhaps most marked here, since Hegel's point is that we never say what we "want" to say or what we "mean" to say because there is always a split between the *meaning* and the *sense* (the physical properties) that our words have. The universal is thus not to be repudiated as that which acts violently toward particulars; the particular emerges only in so far as it has always already been touched by what is universal, in so far as it has reached the level of thought.

Hegel makes this clear at the close of the Sense-Certainty section of the *Phenomenology*. There, he says that the sensuous particular cannot be reached by language, because language—which is for Hegel always inseparable from thinking—enjoys no unmediated relation with the raw material encountered by our senses. Even the Kantian recourse to unmediated intuition does not manage to escape dependence on that which is universal. What such a claim amounts to is simply that even the image, the perception of which we might be tempted to claim somehow short-circuits the symbolic order (the order of language and thinking), is always still the product of an idealizing or appropriative gesture. As Robert Pippin argues, "We must admit that there is no way in which the intuited particular, or formally characterized domain of intuited particulars, can play a cognitively significant role except as already minimally conceptualized particulars. Always involved in such judgments is my having taken *this* to be this-such, even in a quite minimal or highly abstract way."[89] When we speak or think about some particular sense-experience, then, we do so only because paradoxically we are no longer experiencing it an unmediated way. There is always—even if only minimally—a dimension of universality to our meaningful utterances. This is why Hegel can say that language has "the divine nature of directly reversing the meaning of what is said, of making it into something else, and thus not letting what is meant *get into words* at all" (66). This is the case because consciousness belongs to language, which is inherently universal: whenever something is thought or spoken about, then, we are already in the domain of universality. The attempt to actually "say" or "think" or render imagistically a particular entity would result in either that entity's crumbling away or in the speaker's inability to complete his description. Again, Hegel's point is this: that any reference to a particular—even the particular that eludes our finite mind—is still the product of the Whole. This is the thrust of Hegel's critique of empiricism, which holds that sensory objects (i.e., concrete particulars) "ha[ve] absolute truth for consciousness" (65). Empiricists would seem to be good pluralists: they counter the egoistic tendencies of Idealism by recognizing the unique inviolability of every particular. As Hegel points out, they "speak of the existence of *external* objects, which can be more precisely defined as *actual*, absolutely *singular, wholly personal, individual* things, each of them unlike anything else; this existence, they say, has absolute certainty and truth" (66). But to say that these external objects have "absolute truth for consciousness," for Hegel is to make an assertion in which one does not "know what one is saying, to be unaware that one is saying the opposite of what one wants to say" (65).[90] Any meaningful designation of a particular only indicates what is universal about it: "When I say: 'a single thing,' I am really saying what it is from a wholly universal point of view, for everything is a single thing."[91] Thus, the sense of the unsaid that pervades so many memorializations of the Holocaust might in fact be regarded in a different light—not as the inability of the particular to pass itself off as the universal, but rather as the inability of the universal (i.e., the order of thought, the order of language) to render intelligible the particular, the raw matter of historical events.

The entirety of Hegelian phenomenology rests exactly on this point: for the particular to be grasped, thought must have already gone beyond it. Every meaningful statement is made from a totalizing position. As Hegel puts it, "The Here that is *meant* would be the point; but it *is* not: on the contrary, when it is pointed out as something that *is*, the pointing-out shows itself to be not an immediate knowing [of the point], but a movement from the Here that is *meant* through many Heres into the

universal Here" (64). Were this not the case, any utterance designating a
particular could never complete its task; its very capacity to designate is
thus linked precisely to its universality, because were an utterance really
to correspond to an "immediate knowing"—that is, really to be truly
singular—it would simply be another particular that exists—like those
entities it is to designate—only at the level of sense and not at the level
of meaning. The exercise by which sound emerges from our mouths
would thus not be a "pointing out," but rather a purely mechanical gesture, and one without meaning because the meaning of our words is
inseparable from the whole, or universality, of the discourse in which they
are put. We might again refer to Lacan, who in claiming that "the symbolic order from the first takes on its universal character . . . It isn't constituted bit by bit. As soon as the symbol arrives, there is a universe of
symbols," is only rearticulating this basic Hegelian point.[92]

The totalizing practice that might follow this recognition, then,
would do nothing to confirm the superior position of the Absolute Spirit.
It would, on the contrary, make explicit what has been implicit all along:
the precariousness of the universal, and the ridiculous desperateness that
underwrites its securing of particulars. In other words, when the Universal subsumes individual particulars, the Universal is telling us by this very
process something about its ontological status as well—that sense always
eludes it, that it is in the first/last instance without an intelligible ground.
Exaggerated acts of totalizing make this message unmistakable: the Universal itself is not all, is external to itself. Even the Universal is lacking,
and looking for that which might make it complete. Try as it might to
symbolize the cause responsible for its lack, its project is doomed to fail
because that cause cannot be symbolized. This is why, though we speak
all the time from the position of the absolute, it is significant whether or
not we take it up absolutely: to take up totalizing in this way is to counter
the use made of totalizing by fascism—its conceiving of totality as *exterior*
to a given sociohistorical milieu.[93] The point to be made here is simply
that every position taken up absolutely is a radical one, since it opens one
up to alterity in its unsymbolizable dimension. One must note here, then,
the fundamentally conservative nature of the fascistic employment of the
universal: far from carrying out some radical embrace of universality, we
must see this employment stuck at a certain point short of such an embrace—at the point where otherness is already invested with meaningful
qualities. We spoke of this earlier in the context of the historicization of
the quilting point: rather than risk a genuine uprooting from history,
history is the barrier fascism erects against trauma—that is, our having
been determined by an object/Other whose determinations do not belong
to intelligible history. In its historicization of these determinations, fas-

cism *concedes* its having been determined by an Other, but this concession is part and parcel of a paranoid view of the Other that aims to *eliminate altogether* the very condition of society and subjectivity. So, fascism *does* respect the alterity of the Other, but this is not synonymous with treating the Other respectfully.

My Hegelian argument here, then, is that there is no such thing as an absolute position taken up in the service of conservative ends. Or, to put this in a more paradoxical way, a fascism without reserve *at the level of the Idea* is no longer fascism, and would be incapable of leading to actions meant to consolidate or round out the Idea. This is the case because to take up an absolute position is to expose the manner in which even the universal Law that structures the order of language lacks stability and substance; to occupy the position of the Absolute without taking it up, however, is either to reassert the existence of a universal, half-intuited, half-constructed natural Law (liberalism) or to postpone the experience of the groundlessness of any and every Law (deconstruction). In both cases, the Law is spared a traumatic encounter with the real. In her *Hegel Contra Sociology*, Gilian Rose is thus right to note the disservice done to Hegel by those who would separate his method from his "system." Absolute knowledge, Rose argues, means only this recognition: that what are "apparently 'universal' laws turn out to be the fixing of particularity."[94] What eludes the Law, then, what stands in the way of a harmonius, whole, transparent socius is recognized finally for what it is: not an actual object to be acquired, incorporated, or eliminated, but a condition of the whole of the symbolic order itself. Though he has been routinely misread on just this point, Hegel is the one who makes this clear. "The equilibrium of the whole," Hegel writes, "is not the unity which remains with itself, nor the contentment that comes from having returned into itself, but rests on the alienation of opposites. The whole, therefore, like each single moment, is a self-alienated actuality" (295). Neither peaceful unity nor contented homecoming, but rather epistemology meeting its ontological limit. As Hegel puts it on the penultimate page of the *Phenomenology*, "The self-knowing Spirit knows not only itself but also the negative of itself, or its limit" (492). This is the Absolute Spirit's point of reconciliation: not an experience of harmony, but rather the realization that the lack of satisfaction that is our *condition humaine* is due not to external factors, but to the constitution of the subject itself.

This sort of reconciliation might go a long way toward undoing the paranoid construction of the Jew as that "external" figure who is fingered as the embodied cause of an individual's or society's inability to constitute itself as a closed totality. Anti-Semitism, then, would have nothing to do with Jews, per se.[95] When in the lesser *Logic* Hegel claims that "the consummation of the infinite End, therefore, consists merely in removing the illusion which makes it seem yet unaccomplished,"[96] he articulates a truth that drives a stake through the heart of fascist anti-Semitism: all of your projections onto the figure of the Jew as that which must be eliminated for your identity/society to become an organic, harmonious whole in fact only mask a negativity internal to identity itself. What Hegel calls the consummation of the end—the position of Absolute Spirit—is thus not a static, transcendental position of substantial knowledge. It entails not a pure comprehension of the object. Nor does it portend the resolution of all contradiction in some final, speculative synthesis. On the contrary, it represents that position wherein one finally comes clean about the impossibility of total knowledge, wherein one experiences the abyss between all that we are able to signify and the real itself. Only by showing the manner in which a universal system arbitrarily organizes the meaning of particular symbols is it possible to dramatize the defects of that system, and to place it at risk against that which bars its consistency: the real of History.

Absolute Knowledge is the subject's knowledge of the impossibility of its self-coincidence: like the psychoanalytic "cure," it names the moment of the subject's recognition that one's identity gains consistency only in its opposition to itself. Absolute knowledge does not thus subsume all particularity, it recognizes particularity as its very lifeblood—not some element alien to its consciousness and to be overcome. The result is a ceased quest for some unchangeable Being—that is, the real—as an actual existence, as something capable of cementing the social contract against contingency. In short, one gives up the notion that the pursuit and recovery of the vanished "real" can become a socializing entity. In the *Phenomenology*, Hegel again makes this clear, claiming that the consistency of any social or individual reality can only recognize itself as having the life taken out of it, as always already in a state of decay. As Hegel puts it,

> Consciousness, therefore, can only find as a present reality the *grave* of its life. But because this grave is itself an *actual existence* and it is contrary to the nature of what actually exists to afford a lasting possession, the presence of that grave, too, is merely the struggle of an enterprise doomed to failure. But having learned from experience that *the grave* of its *actual* unchangeable Being has *no actuality*, that the *vanished individuality*, because it has vanished is not the true individuality, consciousness will abandon its quest for the unchangeable individuality as an *actual* existence, or will stop trying to hold on to what has vanished. Only then is it capable of finding individuality in its genuine or universal form. (132)

HOLOCAUST MEMORY AND HEGEL 71

Hegel's point is that the real has no actuality within symbolization, and that attempts to symbolize it cannot hope to produce the Signifier capable of comprehending the whole of a particular historical event. The "absolute knowledge" that all such enterprises are doomed to fail might in fact lead us to a new form through which to represent/memorialize the Holocaust: that form that no longer conceals the whimsy and the weakness of its ordering principle. This ordering principle is taken up absolutely by the human (which is to say, *Hegelian*) subject so that he or she might encounter that place of the real where one finds one's individuality in its genuine form. This discovery, Hegel would appear to say, cannot be achieved by asserting a historically derived signifier such as human rights or positive democracy capable of bringing the corpse back to life. Nor can it be achieved as a more postmodern or deconstructionist sensibility would assure us—by acknowledging the limitation of any and every individual perspective, for this position leaves the Law guaranteeing symbolic relations untouched. Memory remains within the realm of the symbol—in the conversation involving different, discursively produced viewpoints—without exposing the universality of that realm as a necessary and groundless fiction. An alternate, more "totalizing" form, on the other hand, might lay bare the necessity of the fiction by revealing the purely performative nature of any universal Law. It deploys, in plain sight, an ordering principle in all of its arbitrariness in order to make the following point: that the very social reality in which we live is no less the product of such an arbitrary deployment, that our very identities as social creatures are no less dependent on a force whose ways and means make no sense. Its use of such a principle in this way radically differs from the absoluteness of the fascists: no Nazi would tell you that the vision of a Third Reich is merely a nonsensical, purely performative Master-Signifier that does nothing to confer essence on his symbolic identity and the identity of his countrymen. Overidentifying with this Signifier is thus perhaps the attitude that most undermines the point where fascism takes hold: it exposes the ridiculousness or stupidity of the principle that enables us to make any sense of the world. It reveals the Law as something we institute, but whose ultimate ground cannot be found within the domain of reason. Brought out in this way, we see the "universal" Law for what it is: a contingent institution that marks the defect of the whole, an entity of "sublime stupidity."[97] One cannot just name the stupidity of the master-signifier, one must *show* it: this is why the *Phenomenology* is such a long book. If our memorial efforts are truly to combat the paranoid fantasies of fascism, this is precisely the (Hegelian) realization they must seek to bring about.

2

Obsession and the Meaning of Jewish Rescue

Oskar Schindler as Spirit

Contextualizing the Focus on Rescue

As we have seen in the preceding chapter, the significance of Hegelian idealism for historical memory rests on three related claims. First, that when we are involved in grasping and expressing historical truth, everything turns on regarding such truth *equally* as substance and subject. Second, that the subject and the historical truth that he or she would express both already have something *spiritual* or *metahistorical* about them, since their very grasp by thinking and language means that what is most real about them has necessarily vanished. And third, that this *real* dimension can be reaccessed or encountered in and through the wholesale exercise of the subject's spiritual, metahistorical powers. This is what Hegel means when he speaks of our finding our individuality in its "genuine or universal form": insofar as we speak of historical truths, neither those truths nor we ourselves are the specific, particular, material entities they claim to be. What gets discovered in a subject's wholesale exercise of his or her spiritual powers is not so much the meaningful narrative or comprehensive signifier that would allow us to say that History belongs, once and for all, to the province of the known. For Hegel, just the opposite is the case. The Hegelian subject who realizes that the historical truths with which he or she is engaged are, in fact, all of them metahistorical, does not find a cozy, locatable spatiotemporal abode. On the contrary, that subject stands on the threshold of an encounter with history proper—that is to say, history in its particularity, in its traumatic dimension. The deepest

73

paradox of history emerges here in the recognition that the acts and events of history proper were, when they happened, *not yet* historical. The specific material that occasions this recognition is no doubt varied; we know well enough that the Holocaust is not the lone instance of historical trauma that makes us feel that the things we can say and know about history fail to capture what is most genuine about the past. But despite the plurality of instances that might occasion it, the experience of trauma remains the same. The solidarity that this Hegelian insight might engender would seem to mandate a shift in our thinking. Today, many say that we are confined to history and should, on ethical grounds, remain there. Hegel's rejoinder, however, is that we are confined to metahistory and should not fall prey to believing that history is ours for the knowing. To remind subjects of this fact, Hegel outlines an ethics rooted in the encounter with history proper—the traumatic encounter with the stuff of history (testimonies, images, acts) that cannot be grasped or expressed or made sense of. This is why Hegel's ethics is an ethics of reminding and remembrance. Here, it is Hegel who refuses to render compatible the actuality of this trauma with the domain of discursive (i.e., metahistorical) or political history. For this reason, Hegel's advocacy of Spirit is not ultimately a gesture that consigns us to traffic in ghosts. Nor is it a straightforward appeal to a real-life, historical event that might secure an overarching normative principle. Put another way, the trauma toward which Hegel charts a path is neither a *spiritualized* trauma (as deconstruction would have it) nor a *politically pragmatic* one (as liberalism would have it).

My consideration of D. M. Thomas's *The White Hotel* in the next chapter is an examination of a "memory text" that embraces or exemplifies a deconstructionist spiritualization of the Holocaust's trauma. In this chapter, my focus is on the way the Holocaust is looked to within liberal and left-leaning political philosophy in order to secure our identification with a mobilizing maxim or doctrine believed capable of warding off future catastrophes. The quintessential text made to bear such a maxim or doctrine is Steven Spielberg's *Schindler's List* (1993). Indeed, by reading both the discourse surrounding Spielberg's film and some of its key textual features, I hope to reveal the extent to which *Schindler's List*—and the conduct of those who engaged in Jewish rescue—is a problematic object-lesson for liberal political philosophy. That the film was only finally made and distributed in the aftermath of the Cold War (more than a decade after the publication of Schindler's story in Thomas Keneally's *Schindler's Ark* [1982]) seems to me to be germane to its deeper, obsessional workings: bereft of a long-standing and legitimizing raison d'être (i.e., Communist totalitarianism and the Soviet Union), it is as if liberalism finds itself experiencing a kind of return of the repressed. On the one hand, in the wake of its decisive victory, liberalism stands poised to declare that the era of ideological struggle is over.[1] But alongside rhetorical claims regarding the end of history and partisan political strife appears a clear need to revisit the specific interaction between liberalism and fascism that the Cold War functioned to mask. This fact might in part explain the astonishing and in some ways disconcerting coincidence between the collapse of Communism, the explosion of Holocaust memory, and the emergence of the largely depoliticized field of Holocaust Studies. Empirically speaking, of course, it is possible to offer a cogent (and sanguine) enough explanation for this coincidence: once free of the pressing political concerns of the Cold War, citizens and scholars of various countries implicated in World War II began to be free to memorialize the pre–Cold War histories of such countries, to gain access to documents and archives previously unavailable, to accumulate and disseminate as much testimony as possible. What this account appears to minimize, however, is the degree of *anxiety* underwriting this coincidence and the extent to which the explosion of memory has sometimes had the feel of a kind of compulsory civic performance—as if some deeper and more threatening source of doubt or confusion pertaining to the global efficacy of liberalism cannot any longer be avoided. This doubt would have as its object the extermination of Eastern European Jewry in the face of little and virtually negligible help from Western liberal-democratic nation-states. In the preface to her book on rescuers, Eva Fogelman claims that "people in the 1990s are hungry for role models. They are ready to hear the rescuers' stories and to learn from them."[2] And Hillel Levine, in his book focused on Chiune Sugihara—the "Japanese Schindler" directly responsible for the rescue of some 10,000 Jews in Kovno—makes the equally suggestive point that the "rescuer has so much to teach us" because his or her heroic act "overcomes the confusion that we all share about the moral ambiguities of intervention and the politics of the post–Cold War world."[3] But the hunger and ambiguity to which Fogelman and Levine refer might have as much to do with the *pre*–Cold War world and the various ways liberal nation-states and institutions found ways *not* to intervene.[4] In its attempt to resurrect a pacifying and balancing liberal ethicopolitical mobilizing maxim, by showing it to be operative during the Event itself, we might see *Schindler's List* as a kind of cipher for the obsessional structure at the heart of the veritable explosion of memorial representations at the very moment of liberalism's triumph. It is as if, faced with its older, more feckless version of itself, an obsession with the Holocaust and with rescue and survival and virtue signals a kind of belated expenditure of energy at the level of representation that might (back then) have been directed in the service of action. Is this not what Freud means when he says that the function of an obsessive or compulsive thought is "to represent an act regressively"?[5] Rather than confront its own complicity, ineffectualness, or both in past and present instances of historical aggression, *Schindler's List* exemplifies and catalyzes what will become a much larger project of memorialization that returns to the *spirit* in and by means of which Jewish rescue was undertaken in order to try to discover a legitimizing and mobilizing core. The spirit of Schindler—or better, Schindler *as* Spirit— is thus congealed in a maxim with which all of us are to identify; as the talmudic inscription in the ring that he is given to wear indicates, Schindler himself is made to bear this maxim on his very person: Whoever saves one life, saves the world entire. In this way, liberalism's very conceptualization of social relations—its eschewal of transcendence and trauma— remains essentially unscathed by the extermination. In short, the Holocaust signals neither a central deficiency within liberalism, nor some indication of its complicity, nor some sign of its impossible need for certainty. If we focus our gaze on the right sorts of behavior, we will see at micrological levels behaviors capable of being elevated by liberalism into ethicopolitical doctrines (e.g., instances of solidarity, respect for human rights, tolerance, pluralism, etc.). If these heroic behaviors were part of the struggle against fascist evil from the beginning, then the doctrines they embody can lay claim to the same distinction. Because one salient debate within liberal political philosophy has centered precisely on the so-called Righteous Gentiles and what it was that motivated their virtuous acts of rescue, it is to the contours of that debate that I shall now turn.

The Search for Motive

I have intimated briefly above that the contemporary preoccupation with instances of rescue and survival and virtue—extending cinematically from the enormous popularity of *Schindler's List* (1993) to the almost-as-popular *Life Is Beautiful* (1998) and characteristic of both a host of contemporary memoirs as well as resurgent social science research on altruism—has coordinates within liberal political theory, liberalism's self-image and the compulsion to erase doubts about the efficacy of norms to mobilize human behavior. The products of this compulsion (e.g., films, books, museums, etc.) in many cases *acknowledge* instances in which liberal nation-states failed to act to avert the catastrophe before it happened, but these instances are not accorded a general or lasting significance. Instead, they typically end up being absorbed by larger redemptive historical narratives, and by specular images of heroic conduct or dispensations of legal justice. These narratives and images aim basically at getting us to feel *satisfied* with liberal political ideas and institutions. The implicit teleology that structures one's chronological journey through the United States Holocaust Museum—and its very placement on the mall in Washington, D.C.—aims essentially, I think, at working to produce this satisfaction. For reasons related to this, there are some who no doubt see the very choice to represent rescue and survival as reactionary. Claude Lanzmann's "fundamental criticism" of *Schindler's List*—what he lamentably terms a "fashion for 'the just' "—speaks directly to this point. For Lanzmann, the very formal decision to contend with the Holocaust through the story of a German runs afoul of a fundamental prohibition: "Even if he did save Jews," Lanzmann contends, "it's a completely different approach to history, it turns the world upside down."[6] Lanzmann's sense that the memorial products of such an approach have almost always functioned in an ideologically affirmative way certainly has much to recommend it, since the focus on rescue and survival has lent itself to linear, chronological storytelling that almost inevitably directs attention away from the parties most implicated in the crime (perpetrators and bystanders) and from the very phenomenology and machinery of mass murder.[7] Thus Lanzmann's decisive question, "Now, if there were so many just people saving the Jews, how come so many Jews perished? Here again, things have got out of all proportion."[8]

Though we must, of course, be mindful of this need for proportion and of the way the culture industry works to reconcile contradictions that undo its own mastery, my own sense is that a categorical prohibition on representations of rescue risks minimizing the practical ethical significance of our conceptualization of rescue—what Hegel will refer to at the close of the *Phenomenology* as the act for which Spirit's self-knowledge readies one for: knowing how to sacrifice oneself. Without ignoring the need to keep things in proportion, then, I think there is something to be gained from asking the question posed most trenchantly by Norman Geras: "How far may we take the example of rescuers as the image, or anticipation, of an alternative possible ethical landscape?"[9] Rather than wholesale dismissal on formal grounds alone, we might rather ask specifically what happens or what is revealed in the representation of rescue? How do such representations betray their obsessional economy, and how might they be read against the grain in order to break from that economy? Can we conceptualize rescue in a way that makes it compatible with an ethics of bearing witness rooted in the encounter with trauma?[10]

To begin to address these questions is to start with the implicit point on which there is consensus across the political spectrum: for the conduct of rescuers to have any general ethicopolitical relevance, the mere act of rescue alone does not leave us with enough to go on. Let us

return simply to the historical person of Oskar Schindler: in virtually
every conversation concerning him, it is now almost a commonplace to
note a point of fascination with him deeper than simply the extraordinary
success of his method. More important than how many Jews Schindler
was able to save, the deeper and more significant source of attraction—
and this is true, I think, of our relationship to so many rescuers—pertains
to the inscrutability or opacity of his motives. The reference point for
liberalism's obsessional economy has roots in precisely this deeper and
potentially more dangerous source of attraction, for if Schindler's motives
remain opaque, we are likely to be dissatisfied with any mobilizing maxim
they are said to exemplify. Put another way, if the maxim "Whoever saves
one life, saves the world entire" is to arrest the signifying chain destabi-
lized by the Holocaust (and immediately restabilized by Cold War net-
works of political meaning), the motives that moved someone like Schindler
to act must be shown either to be self-evident or else explained and made
meaningful. In short, if we are to transmit some normative core about
tolerance or about selfless conduct or about the fundamental value of
existence ("life is beautiful"), it simply is not good enough to have the
outcome of the rescuer's behavior: one wants a clear picture of something
that brings to a halt the metonymy of desire and that can be elevated to
the status of mobilizing civic contract—the *reason* a given rescuer acted as
he or she did.[11] Although Schindler himself tried after the war to give a
self-evident moral rationale for his actions—"If you saw a dog going to
be crushed under a car," he is said to have claimed, "wouldn't you help
him?"[12]—his membership in the Nazi party (and even the arguably infe-
licitous analogy within his stated rationale) makes it fair to say that the
desire or *spirit* informing Schindler's actions is much less self-evident to
us. The prologue to Keneally's novel places this issue front and center,
introducing us to Schindler's "strange virtue"—his "quotidian acts of kind-
ness" juxtaposed both with his influence as businessman and Nazi and his
other moral failings (e.g., womanizing and drinking).[13]

Here, however, is where the problem arises: Can some garden-
variety lesson about moral conduct emerge from the example of those
who saved Jewish lives, if we are at loggerheads as to what *moved them* to
act heroically? What if the reasons that moved them to act heroically are
not, themselves, purely moral? What if these reasons are stained with
some pathological or unfathomable interest?[14] We expect portraits of the
perpetrators to reveal to us certain pathological, irrational motives. Ron
Rosenbaum's recent *Explaining Hitler,* for instance, documents various
theories that account for Hitler's conduct by pointing to the psychological factors, physical pathological factors, or both at the root of Hitler's
subjectivity, his "thought-world." The list of such factors is a long one—

from the "Genital Wound school of Hitler interpretation" to claims regarding Hitler's syphilitic encounter with a Jewish prostitute to theories centering on Hitler's sexual relationship with his niece, Geli Raubal, and his subsequent involvement in her murder.[15] But when it comes to those whose conduct might become the basis of an "alternative ethical landscape," the presence of the pathological or unfathomable is troubling.

It would seem here that in presenting us with an act that resists easy insertion into the order of intelligible knowledge, the desire or spirit of Schindler—and the desire/spirit of other rescuers as well—stands as a quantity of energy exterior to the sociosymbolic order that threatens to destabilize the capacity of moral norms to legitimize that order. The claim for such exteriority already begets the crucial question as to its spatial coordinates. Indeed, it is possible to say of Schindler and so many rescuers that their very status as a minority means that they were somehow able to transcend the given historical situation in which they found themselves. When so many chose to look the other way, they chose not to. But if, following Hegel, the social order itself is already a transcendent entity, implying our distance from the *real* of the social relations, the notion of rescuers as having transcended transcendence would seem to etherealize their conduct only further, placing those who acted heroically further and further from what they actually did—intervene directly and materially in history.

Here, I think we can see how, in the context of the meaning to be gleaned from rescue, it is tempting to fall prey to a certain caricature of Hegelian Spirit. By this I mean that it is tempting to regard the exteriority of the subjects who acted to save Jews—which appears only after the fact, after the owl of Minerva's flight—as *compatible* before the fact with the sociosymbolic, historical order. This is what allows a duty-bearing maxim from the Talmud ("Whoever saves one life, saves the world entire") or from Leviticus ("Do not stand on your neighbor's blood") to render explicable the desire that motivates a just and ethical act. This maxim's compatibility with the sociosymbolic order—its ability to find expression in words—would square with the stereotypical view of Hegel that sees him as wanton totalizer who allows nothing to elude the clutch of Spirit or discourse. In keeping with his earlier remarks about language, however, Hegel claims that an act by Spirit is never present at that point where we imagine it to be—in a specific duty *declared* to be the truth of Spirit's ethical act. For Hegel, an ethical act places before us something that it also " 'displaces again, or rather has straightway 'displaced' or dissembled.'"[16] This is because the *particular actuality* of the act has no validation outside the subject who executes it: once we try to symbolize its motive in the form of a stated duty, we have already missed the very thing that enabled it be a *real* ethical act. This is why Hegel argues against trying to reduce or reconcile a lasting ethical act to the intentions said to motivate it. Analyses aimed at uncovering what the executor *meant* by his or her deed only diminish the radicality of the act; such analyses, Hegel claims, should "be left to the laziness of mere conjecture" and to "idle thinking."[17]

Such an assertion amounts to the claim that any attempt to interpret an ethical act cannot ultimately get free of the pathological stain that stymies that attempt. This is why Hegel insists that the conscience that acts and the universal consciousness that acknowledges this action as (moral) duty is "a relation of complete disparity, as a result of which the consciousness which is explicitly aware of the action finds itself in a state of complete *uncertainty* about the Spirit which does the action and is certain of itself."[18] So, according to Hegel, for a genuinely ethical act to have occurred, something *incompatible* with the sociosymbolic, historical order has had to have intervened. The surest sign of this incompatibility is the interpretive difficulty posed by the heroic act itself, and the sense that whatever proffered explanation given by rescuers themselves bears deep within it something *unsaid*—something that cannot be said. The Spirit who is the source of this incompatibility does not move from the given social reality to the transcendent, but rather in the opposite direction. The consequences here are significant: if Spirit moves *from* the transcendent position of language and thinking *toward* the real of social reality, then its motives can never fully be symbolized from the position it has forsaken in acting—let alone become the normative basis of a political theory.

My point here is that rather than claim that we can never find the necessary or sufficient condition for the ethical act of rescue, *the very absence of such a condition* is the sign of its ethical credibility. In the debate concerning what motivated Jewish rescue, however—and the normative core or political theory secured thereby—the symbolization of motive has proceeded apace. This debate has basically centered around two poles: at one end, Richard Rorty's claims concerning the "parochial" (i.e., particular, ethnocentric) motivations of those who involved themselves in Jewish rescue; on the other, Norman Geras's insistence on a "universalist moral outlook" and "shared sense of humanity" that motivated those who acted heroically. According to Rorty, the time has come to give up the definition of human solidarity that involves "something within each of us—our essential humanity—which resonates to the presence of this same thing in other human beings."[19] As Rorty sees it, the very behavior of rescuers testifies to the fact that human beings do not act morally on the basis of a common human nature. Put another way, rescuers act not in reference

to some belief that is beyond history and historically specific social institutions, but rather according to feelings of solidarity that are wholly a
product of some historically contingent situation and system of meanings—for example, Danes saved Danish Jews because the latter were "fellow" Danes. In some cases, these systems of meaning mobilized action; in
other cases, they functioned as a barrier to it.[20]

The same, alas, is true of the perpetrators, who for Rorty simply
cannot be called "inhuman." To designate the perpetrators in this way is
to proceed as if they "all lacked some component which is essential to a
full-fledged human being." For Rorty, there is no such transhistorical
component: "What counts as being a decent human being," he contends,
"is relative to historical circumstance, a matter of transient consensus
about what attitudes are normal and what practices are just or unjust"
(189). Rorty is, to his credit, aware of the dangerous slope down which
he risks sliding: bereft of a reference to something universal, we may
indeed "feel that there is something morally dubious about a greater
concern for a fellow *New Yorker* than for someone facing an equally hopeless
and barren life in the slums of Manila or Dakar" (191). But for him, two
factors work against the steepness of the slope. First, there is too much
morally and politically practical persuasive power in parochial identifications for them to be given up. As he sees it, a rescuer (or contemporary
liberal) might claim to have helped someone in need because he or she
was a "fellow human being," but we are more likely to discern or produce
a more efficacious mobilizing core of solidarity when that core is
parochialized. As Rorty puts it, "our sense of solidarity is strongest when
those with whom solidarity is expressed are thought of as 'one of us,'
where 'us' means something smaller and more local than the human race.
That is why 'because she is a human being' is a weak, unconvincing
explanation of a generous action" (191). Second, these parochial identifications are part of a conceptualization of moral progress centered on
rendering ever more inclusive just who counts as "one of us." That is to
say, the Rortyean project *includes* the effort that would make as many of
those belonging to the "they" a part of the group designated by the term
"we." Moral progress here means being able to see more and more traditional differences as insignificant, as no reason to prevent an Other
from being included in the range of "us."

In this way, Rorty converts the historically contingent condition of
liberal society into a positive sociopolitical proposition. Greater solidarity
is Rorty's object, but the very idea of solidarity cannot entirely escape its
rhetoricity. This is why Rorty prefers novels and ethnographies to philosophy. Indeed, the virtue of a liberal society is that it looks for mobilizing exemplars of ethical conduct not in treatises that expound on the

will of God or the nature of man, but in poets and revolutionaries of the past who *speak* in a certain way. Undaunted by the idea that conscience and morality do not escape the clutch of contingency, Rorty insists instead that to *recognize* this fact is "to adopt a self-identity which suits one for citizenship in such an ideally liberal state" (61). "A belief," he says, "can still regulate action, can still be thought worth dying for, among people who are quite aware that this belief is caused by nothing deeper than contingent historical circumstances" (189). One can, in other words, form common purposes and agreement as to which descriptions of reality—that is, which truths—should be believed even in the absence of some supracultural point of reference.

While Rorty does invoke rescuers who cite motivations deeply rooted in particular, cultural frames of reference, Geras claims on the contrary that such citations are actually rare. His quarrel with Rorty, however, is not simply an empirical one. At issue for Geras is the way antiuniversalist, postmodern philosophical attitudes risk minimizing the revolutionary heroism and courage of the rescuers. Defending a version of human nature different from that of Rorty's, Geras wants to take up and widen just what is meant by the word *substantial*. As Geras sees it, to call human nature substantial is not *necessarily* to say that there is an inner, apriori link between the individual and some immanent theological or metahistorical purpose:

> You can define 'human nature' in so narrow a way that there will not be one. You may then want a word for what there nonetheless is in that domain. A longer response is that the judgement as to what does and does not count as substantial or useful can, however, also be put under scrutiny. By what criterion or in what context, bearing on the understanding of the ways of human beings, is a notion of their nature according to which they are susceptible to pain and humiliation, have the capacity for language and (in a large sense) poetry, have a sexual instinct, a sense of identity, integral beliefs—and then some other things too, like needs for nourishment and sleep, a capacity for laughter and for play, powers of reasoning and invention that are, by comparison with other terrestrial species, truly formidable, and more shared features yet—not substantial enough?[21]

The answer to Geras's rhetorical question is precisely that these common features *do* in fact constitute substantiality, that a cumulative accounting of shared features *can* eventually reach an endpoint.

This notion that the process of accumulation implicitly acknowledges a whole—that Zeno's arrow does eventually hit its target—informs another set of questions Geras poses apropos the matter of progress: Where, precisely, does Rorty *stop* in his imagined expansion of the "us"-group? Can a commitment to greater and greater solidarity do without some pretension to universality? Here, Geras indicts the pragmatic advocacy of parochial identifications on pragmatic grounds. The movement from the particular outward, he suggests, will either work or it will not:

> One can move from fellow Americans, for instance, to Mexicans, Brazilians, and then others, or from fellow Catholics to all Christians, and then to Muslims and Jews. But either this process stops short somewhere, so as to leave a 'one of them' that can be contrasted with the 'one of us' and then Africans, say, or atheists, are excluded from the sense of moral community, and they can go hungry or be massacred for all one cares. This is a strange kind of 'human' solidarity. Or, on the other hand, the process need not stop short, and one's sense of moral community can be extended to all human beings. In this case the identification with humanity as such is not impossible after all. Why should it be? Why, for someone who allows that a sense of 'we' might cover all fellow Americans, and then be expanded? Americans are some 250 million people. With only Mexicans and Brazilians added on, 'we' comes to embrace approximately 500 million people. If this scale of identification is feasible, then so is humanity in general. It is not credible that the relevant limit to human compassion lies somewhere beyond several hundred million people.[22]

Geras's critique here relies implicitly on the Hegelian critique of Kant and the notion that the very positing of a limit signals that one has already passed beyond it. Indeed, the very *idea* of progress that Rorty espouses already presupposes a universalism: to refuse this presupposition is basically to concede failure in advance. This is, indeed, one of Geras's best points. By unearthing the universalist dimension of particularity, he is able to end up insisting on a vision of the Holocaust in which social conditions do not account for everything. This allows him, among other things, to challenge—as an avowed socialist—the more "vulgar" Marxist account of Fascism and the Holocaust.[23]

At first glance, the Rorty-Geras debate appears to be a productive instance of universality and particularity in conflict. Rorty's interest in ridding of us of more generalized motives for action (or inaction) clears the way for "detailed historicosociological explanations." This has the advantage of clarifying the inadequacy of explanatory notions such as "inhumanity" or "hardness of heart" or "lack of a sense of human solidarity" when it comes to accounting for a failure to act morally. In *Contingency, Irony, Solidarity*, Rorty contends that such notions are, in the context of the Holocaust, *not* explanations but instead "simply shudders of revulsion" (191). But before this unearthing of the parochial beneath the universal ends up legitimizing particular enclaves of solidarity, and before it confines discussions of motive solely to particular historical/social conditions, we can turn to Geras's insistence that we ought not dispense altogether with a notion of universality. For Geras, everything cannot be reduced to the particular—nor should it. Such a reduction is part and parcel of what, to cite the title of his more recent book, Geras terms "the contract of mutual indifference."[24] By now, my own preference for Geras's commitment to something universal—and his sense that Rorty's progressively bigger parochialism is in fact a universalism—should not be surprising. The problem in Geras's argument crops up, however, when we begin to see what he finds beyond social conditions moving subjects to act. I refer here to Geras's persistent defense of a common human nature—a "natural make-up" characterized by a "motivational range" comprising both admirable qualities and repugnant ones. Contending that "the claim that there is no human nature at all is at best a thoughtless exaggeration, one that it is impossible to uphold with any genuine lucidity of mind," Geras insists instead on a view of human nature that is "intrinsically mixed."[25] And this means that the stakes of political struggle (and ethical conduct) involve trying to reach that point at which our good impulses triumph over our bad ones.[26] The amelioration of social conditions and the consolidation of political institutions would aim precisely to "block" (but never finally eradicate) troublesome tendencies and impulses—what Geras deems the "space of potential evil."

This claim for a good and bad *nature* beyond the social, however, risks betraying Geras's best insight. On the one hand, Geras wants simply to foster our good nature and block our bad nature, but in what sense can we speak of nature as already good or bad? Is not nature, strictly speaking, that which is *prior* to good and evil? And in the observation that all cannot be reduced to the social, are we not rather noting the *freedom* of the Hegelian subject—the fact that it has *already* negated its nature? Indeed, when Hegel speaks in *The Phenomenology* about the actuality of an ethical act, he refers to *our* capacity for displacement and disssembling when we take this act to be evil. In any case, these questions ultimately undo the projects of both Geras and Rorty, since for both of them, the motives of rescuers are rid of their inexplicable or *unconscious* dimension. If both admittedly rest their theses on the statements of the rescuers themselves, they do so in order to arrive at a point of consensus concerning the meaning and larger political relevance that these desires portend. Their understanding of the rescuers rests critically on the assumption that they are not split subjects, that they are in fact in a kind of seamless communication with themselves, with their surroundings, and with what moves them to act.[27] From the standpoint of psychoanalysis, however, this seamless communication could only be possible if such individuals were, in fact, entirely natural beings—that is, were not desiring at all. In Hegelian terms, we would have to say that such rescuers *had no spirit*.

The Impasse Between Motive and Act

Herein lies a fundamental contradiction within Geras's and Rorty's projects, a contradiction that pertains to liberalism as a whole and its socialist critique: Geras and Rorty aim to figure out what the desires of the rescuers are, and to do so, they accept what it is that the rescuers think and claim about their own actions. But the very radicality of their actions entails that a clear symbolization of motive is necessarily unavailable, since, as I have said, to act *in the present* in a radical way is to forsake the transcendent position of Spirit where things can be thought and discussed. In short, Geras and Rorty aim to get in touch with the desire of the subject. At the same time, however, they treat the subject as if he or she were in touch with their own desire—as if he or she were whole—and thus as *not* desiring in the first place. Their disagreement is thus one between two left-leaning understandings of meaning and the constitution of the subject. Even though they disagree at the level of the content of their narratives, both share a similar aim: to take from the Holocaust a symbolic lesson capable of redeeming the rupture—the structural trauma writ large in historical trauma—represented by the Holocaust. Both emplot the enigmatic quality of the desire of the Other in order to disavow its split, and either way, there is nothing unavailable concerning the desire of the Other, no trauma. What they thus end up with is a way to *redress* certain tendencies they see leading to the commission of evil: Geras proposes an ethic of mandatory care rooted in the duty to bring aid; Rorty advocates an ironist culture whose citizens are more and more sensitized by novels and ethnographies to the pain of others. But both fail to see that the very form of seeking redress itself already partakes of a kind of causality that leads to the commission of evil. This is why, at some level, it *makes no difference* if the rescuers acted out of particular or universal interest: the deeper (Hegelian) point to grasp is that there is something about their interest that is unavailable to us, and that this can become the basis of a Holocaust ethic that takes up the Other's split. To understand properly the liberal component that underwrites both of these positions, we might return here to the figure of Oskar Schindler and to Spielberg's

Schindler's List. My claim here is that the film's treatment of Schindler's desire operates on levels consonant with both Geras's *and* Rorty's narratives. On the one hand, Spielberg's film begins with the Rortyean deconstruction of any universal motive moving a rescuer to act. But as the catalyst for the film's narrative, the particularity of Schindler's desire is gradually congealed into a more universally human framework. In this way, particularity *as such* is domesticated and aestheticized and made meaningful—and not encountered. Spielberg's universal is thus a false one.[28] The universality wrought from the story of Schindler and heroic rescue—and congealed into a normative maxim—is ultimately a pacifying one that prevents, in the manner of obsession, the filmmaker (and citizens of contemporary liberal nation-states) from having to consider the genuine parameters of an ethical act. An index of our freedom and of our status as creatures of an unsymbolizable trauma, this is an act that we have, as Hegelian subjects, already in some sense carried out, and it is an act that certain testimonial works of art can lead us to carry out again.

Clarifying the Rescuer's Enigmatic Desire

That Spielberg thinks he can get at the traumatic kernel of Schindler's desire, that he can render intelligible and meaningful the particular as such, is clear simply from his recounting of scriptwriter Steven Zaillian's point of approach in adapting Thomas Keneally's novel to screen: "He approached it as the Rosebud theory—the mystery as to why Schindler did what he did. Why would a German Catholic industrialist, a member of the National Socialist party, a womanizer, a bon vivant and cynic, sacrifice everything he was and all the money he ever made to save Jews? That became the story."[29] In this fundamental statement of the narrative purpose of the film, we can see just what it is about Schindler that functions as the object-cause of the narrative: there is something about Schindler's desire—a pathological stain—that compromises our identification of him as a savior. The figure of Schindler is thus not, as Bryan Cheyette has said, a "tabula rasa" on which Spielberg dramatizes competing inscriptions of good and evil.[30] Schindler has already inscribed on his figure a certain amount of *jouissance* that threatens our identification with him. This is clear in the way Spielberg elects to first present the figure of Schindler cinematically: the ten close shots of his hands engaged in pouring a drink, laying out ties, going through cuff links, and so on, have the effect of separating those hands from Schindler's person, turning them into a kind of partial object. We are not entirely sure *whose* hands these are, or why they are busying themselves in the way that they are. And when the final shot reveals those hands affixing a swastika pin on a lapel, our identification is made even more tenuous. This is the *jouissance* that Spielberg will begin to render intelligible. Far from conditioning one's symbolic identity—that is, from seeing identity itself as fundamentally dependent on a constitutionally "mysterious" dimension of Spirit that cannot be made meaningful—this locus of Schindler's *jouissance* will, in Spielberg's film, ultimately end up guaranteeing a basic consistency to the identity of the rescuer. The split in the subject—that is, the fact that there is always something traumatically senseless about the signifiers that "identify" us—is remedied through a mastery of that split. Schindler's identity is thus predicated on the recovery and domestication of that which eluded Schindler himself, the ambiguity of his desire and pleasure.

In the case of Spielberg himself, the necessity of this recovery is by no means an incidental feature of his attraction to Schindler and his making of the film. If on one level, Spielberg's "Rosebud" theory encapsulates perfectly the enigma that pertains to Oskar Schindler's desire, on a deeper level, Spielberg could almost be said to be making a formal statement about his relation to his own desire as well. Indeed, in the aftermath of *Schindler's List*, what critics of the film have sought tirelessly to discover is the motive for the transformation that *Schindler's List* itself represents in Spielberg's career: Why has the master of make-believe, the master of escapism, the man who has directed four of the ten top-grossing films of all time, now decided to enter the realm of historical atrocity in a serious way? This striking incongruity was manifest in the headlines of popular media, from the *Los Angeles Times*'s declaration of "A Stirring Departure [. . .] Atypical Spielberg" to *Premier*'s questioning of Spielberg's capacity to "shed the habits of a lifetime" in order to give the story of Schindler "the grittiness it needs." As another headline in the *Times* put it, "Grim. Black and White . . . Spielberg?" As was the case with Schindler, it appears that the desire of the hero himself has "become the story." This homology, in my view, is significant for our understanding of the film. More than merely suggesting a fruitful parallel between the questions concerning motivation that pertain to Schindler and Spielberg, a parallel emerges on the level of the answer to the question—an answer not unrelated to an intention apparent in nearly every one of Spielberg's films: to embody, and come to terms with, some alien, presymbolic material that threatens to collapse the minimal distance between self and other on which the consistency of identity depends. (This formless threat takes the shape of a truck in *Duel*, a shark in *Jaws*, of extraterrestrial creatures in *Close Encounters of the Third Kind* and *E.T.*, of the metallic limb in *Hook*, of the dinosaur in *Jurassic Park*, of the Ark of the Covenant or the Holy Grail in the *Indiana Jones* trilogy, and so on.) Why is the enigma of

Schindler's identity so compelling for Spielberg? Why must it be embodied and emplotted within a conventional narrative form? Because it is Spielberg's own enigma as well and because narrative plot affords him the means to stage its return in such a way that it might be defeated/integrated once and for all. Art is thus the site of liberalism's fantasy of progress whereby the traumatic, foreclosed, ontological matter that belongs to the differential structure of subjectivity is converted from being an alienating object to an object of security and pride. Spielberg's consistent linking of the film with his deepened commitment to a Jewish identity speaks directly to this point.[31] If identity was once for Spielberg something inconsistent, marked by the presence of a disturbing, alien, "ethnic" object (i.e., "Jewishness") that is a source of shame, *Schindler's List* changed all that. Indeed, ethnic identity is now for Spielberg an exercise in self-possession, a source of balance and pride.[32] Just as the question of Schindler is only the catalyst for Spielberg's film—and not the object it is condemned to traumatically encounter—so, too, it would seem, is the question of Spielberg's identity as a Jew.

Spielberg's belief in the power of film—"Every time we go to a movie," he has said, "it's magic, no matter what the movie's about"[33]—can thus be read as animated by far more than a disinterested effort to fill out the historical record. What is at stake is precisely the effort to reclaim what, to borrow Lacan's diction, is *in* Spielberg/Schindler *more than* Spielberg/Schindler—to show that the pathological stain is not really a stain. Spielberg's purification of Schindler's desire is perhaps first apparent in the hyperrealism of *Schindler's List*, and in the body of discourse—created initially by those making the film and reproduced by the machine of critics who first received it—that anticipates and cuts off any attempt to note a gap between itself and what it would know. So saturated has this discourse been with talk about the need for and the triumph of the film's strict realism, certain undiscussed assumptions behind such claims have been difficult to unearth. My own sense is that the entirety of this discourse has in fact grasped, if from the wrong end, the crux of the film, since the hyperrealism of *Schindler's List* can be read as having coordinates in the obsessional economy characteristic of Hollywood film form's unwillingness to deal with the matter of desire, attempting instead to work on the empirical exigencies of desire in such a way that the arrival at meaningful narratives of identity is always achieved. If desire and the genuinely ethical act entails ambiguity, circularity, and ultimately the forsaking of a transcendental position of knowledge, Hollywood realism is almost always about well-framed certainty, linearity, and the maintaining of a consistent social reality.

This point becomes clear if we stop thinking transcendence spatially, as having something to do with height, and see it instead as implying the particular transformed into an intelligible, consistent reality. In this light, even when Schindler's camera proceeds from a "transcendental" vantage point above Krakow *down into* the fray of the liquidation of the Jewish ghetto there, even where he is most faithful to the particular, historical lives of his characters, his realism reveals a holding fast to transcendence. As I have suggested, this realism is of a piece with the effort to render Schindler's (purified) desire as realistically as possible. The problem with Spielberg's treatment of history is thus identical to the problem of his treatment of Schindler: in both cases, what has been foreclosed is the possibility of the traumatic encounter with Schindler's desire and with an instance of historical trauma like the liquidation of the Krakow ghetto, between one's form and one unrepresentable dimension of the Holocaust that forms cannot reach. On the one hand, Spielberg admits the breach and his evasion of it. In the liquidation of Krakow, for example, the SS threw live babies out of windows and shot them like skeet, but says Spielberg, "I wouldn't show that in the movie. Not even with dolls."[34] This is true not just of Spielberg's treatment of the babies, but with the routine hangings in Plaszow that are left out of the film, with Oscar Schindler's dealings with the Jewish Underground also left out (a move that minimizes his connection with other—perhaps Jewish—resistance and rescue movements already organized), and with the consolidation of several different figures into the character of the accountant, Stern. (This was the result of a key rewrite that pushed the work more in the direction of a "buddy" film.)[35] What these departures from the historical record plainly reveal is the extent to which there are parts of the historical record that take us inevitably to a more structural trauma—a trauma against which hyperrealism can function as rampart.

Spielberg's elision of the genuine stakes of grasping historical particularity, however, is glimpsed not just in these fudgings. A move to the empirical becomes ideology not just when it acts selectively on its own research, but when it refuses to recognize that it can never be empirical enough. The failure of Spielberg's film, in the last instance, is that it embodies just this refusal. Those who made the film continually expose this deep-seated sentiment: "We built Plaszow to be as realistic as possible," production designer Allan Starski says. "The location is fully built so Spielberg could shoot from any angle, any corner."[36] As I have already suggested above, Spielberg has articulated a sense of the discontinuity between, on the one hand, knowledge, realism, and representation and, on the other, history, particularity, and horror. What we can refer to as

the enigmatic desire of the Other has seemed, to him, to warrant something new in terms of form: "I didn't want a style that was similar to
anything I had done before. First of all, I threw half my toolbox away, I
canceled the crane. I tore out the dolly track. I didn't really plan a style.
I didn't say I'm going to use a lot of handheld camera. I simply tried to
pull the events closer to the audience by reducing the artifice."[37] When
Spielberg says that he "tried to be as close to a journalist in recording this
re-creation, more than being a filmmaker trying to heighten the suspense
or action of the pathos,"[38] he merely testifies to his commitment to the
journalist's fidelity to the particular. And yet from the comic relief/kitsch
accompanying last minute rescues (and the interviewing of secretaries) to
the beauty of its black and white, from the breakthrough design of skull
caps that allowed Spielberg to simulate the situation of women in a gas
chamber to the momentum of affirmation that leads to a denouement
that has superimposed itself on the material reality itself, we can see I
think a betrayal of the particular in the belief that the universal has
grasped/purified it.

   The formal structure and content of the film also has as its aim an
attempt to domesticate the desire of the Other, to purify it in order to
neutralize it. Some of this is clear in the very transcendental position
occupied by Spielberg at key moments of the film in order to provide a
kind of "disinterested," objective resolution. To communicate a truth
capable of cementing a charter for the well-ordered society—exemplified
by the film's key syllogism: the list is Absolute Good, the list is Life, Life
is Absolutely Good—that truth requires a form and a content willing and
able to cleanse desire of those operative factors at odds with the Good.
Good, of course, requires a purity of vision, and the increasing strength
of this vision is what characterizes the narrative progression of Spielberg's
film. This becomes clear simply from tracing the trajectory of Schindler's
desire through the course of the film, and the gradual substitution of one
form of *jouissance* by another. If this first form strikes us as pathological
given its immediate contexts—for example, Schindler regales Nazi Party
officials in order to profit from war, Schindler's sexual pleasure is unin-
terrupted by the destruction in his midst—the film works to provide us
with a conversion predicated on the renunciation of the first source of
jouissance and the redirection of it to a second source. We might trace four
scenes/segments in which this formal progression is executed. In a memo-
rable scene in the cellar of Amon Goeth's villa built above Plaszow in
which Schindler comes on Helen Hirsch—Goeth's maid—we see and
hear Hirsch recount her first beating at the hands of the commandant
(she had thrown out some chicken bones that Goeth wanted for his dog).
The mise-èn-scene here is significant—there is a covert eroticism that

works against the backlighting: the form is the subtext of the scene's content. "I know your sufferings, Helen," Schindler tells her, leaning over to kiss her forehead. The maid flinches, and Schindler says, "It's not that kind of a kiss." Coming as it does in the wake of the beginnings of Schindler's attempt to save Jews, it is easy to detect here a gesture toward clarifying the motivations behind it. Were the film true to Schindler's desire at this point, it might perhaps have let us see the pathological stain that is his desire: it would have revealed Schindler's kiss of Helen Hirsch to be *that kind of a kiss* and thus have become a dramatically different film. What in fact ends up resonating in this scene is its unintentional gesturing toward the formal requirements of the obsessional desire, which wants always to remain at one remove from the desire of the Other. Schindler's desire, from this vantage point, gets transmuted into a blessed kiss—just the sort of kiss conducive to obsession.

The framing of the liquidation scene continues this progression. Out for a ride on their horses, we see Schindler and his mistress travel toward a point overlooking the city of Krakow; at the same time, the trucks and troops of Amon Goeth enter the ghetto and prepare for its liquidation. After a second shot of Schindler, the camera takes us down into the ghetto itself and its horror: a family eats its jewels in little balls of bread, a hospital staff poisons its patients, men are summarily executed, a boy who tries to run away is shot, families are separated by sex, corpses and suitcases litter the street, and so forth. Handheld camera shots capture the speed of fear. After twenty or so minutes of harrowing images, we are returned to the couple on horses and their looks of anguish. This marks the most authentic moment of the liquidation sequence: a sequence of subjective shots depicting both the hallucinated "real"—the "red toddler" who moves through the ghetto, at times invisible to the Nazis around her—and the look of horror on the face of those doing the hallucinating. (In the exhuming of the bodies Spielberg's camera does hallucinate the reality of this child again, but that is the last formal move of this kind, and clearly not the direction in which the film moves.) The sequence ends with the girl hiding under a bunk and Schindler's simultaneous riding away—a stricken look on his and his companion's face. This is, of course, the moment of conversion lifted directly from Keneally's novel, when, as Keneally puts it, Schindler qua "implacable judge" emerged from "behind the playboy façade." Keneally recounts Schindler's reaction to the liquidation and more important, the sight of the liquidation in full view of the "scarlet child" and without shame: " 'Beyond this day,' he would claim, 'no thinking person could fail to see what would happen. I was now resolved to do everything in my power to defeat the system.'"[39] Just as Keneally secures Schindler's desire at this critical junction in his historiographical novel of Schindler qua rescuer, Spielberg aims to secure Schindler as a specular image of wholeness—the exemplar of a duty-bearing maxim whose terms will soon become explicit. Thus, at the close of the entire liquidation sequence, Spielberg's camera returns to the vantage point of this critical moment of Schindler's conversion. After the Nazis, with flashlights and stethoscopes, root out those who are hiding; after the corpses are looted; after a disheveled Goeth says, "I wish this fucking night were over," Spielberg returns to Schindler's position overlooking the city in order to capture metaphorically the position it must align with Schindler—a position on safe ground that is always *beyond* the struggle and mystery of desire.[40]

The obsessional's concern to domesticate the vicissitudes of desire gains perhaps its most stark expression in the momentum of the film's final ten or so scenes. As so many critics of the film have pointed out, these scenes exploit all the conventional opportunities for affirmation and the reconstitution of symbolic identity—marriage, religion, nonproduction, leadership, friendship—so that the arc of the film can be realized. Schindler returns to church—in Cracow, it was only a place to arrange black market purchases—this time to reconcile with his wife, to give her the promise that before he could not make: "No doorman—or maitre de—will ever mistake you again." Schindler tells Stern he wants the shells his factory is now producing to be defective (the war-profiteer has now turned pacifist, uninterested in production). Schindler restores lived Time and its rituals to the Jews in his employ: the same man who survived the scene with Goeth and the defective gun and who, probably not coincidentally, Spielberg has made a rabbi, is interrupted at his post and told by Schindler that it is Friday afternoon and that he should be preparing for the Sabbath (Schindler has a bottle of wine for him, and in the next scene, we see a service). He even restores to German military personnel a sense of honor and manhood in his speech informing them of their country's surrender (though they still need the orator to tell them what to do). And finally, as Schindler prepares to flee, he is presented with a ring inscribed with the Talmudic saying, meant already to be taken as the definitive *interpretation* of Schindler's actions: "Whoever saves a life, saves the world entire."

Moving chronologically in fictional time where quickly accumulated scenes can build to the redemptive moment Spielberg's film is building toward, *Schindler's List* does not break with such time even when the film enters what it imagines to be "real" time. "You have been liberated by the Russian army," a man on horseback tells a crowd of Jews sitting on the ground in Brinnlitz.[41] "Where shall we go?" he is asked. "I wouldn't go East," the officer replies. "They hate you there. I wouldn't go West either."

"We could use some food," one of the Jews says. After the Russian officer, pointing to his left, says, "Isn't that a town—over there?" the countershot transports us immediately to present Israel and to a chain of *Schindlerjuden* walking in a line toward the viewer. In the move from the huddled Jews sitting on the ground, to the human chain up and walking together, the connection is clear: for Spielberg, this food is as much spiritual as actual. This chronological closure is buttressed not only by its implicit link to the Judaism practiced in the opening scene that frames the film—a scene of Jewish observance of the Sabbath—but by the closing subtitles also. A tree planted in Schindler's name on the Avenue of Righteous Gentiles outside Yad Vashem, we are told, "grows there still." In this way, Spielberg's film joins in elevating Israel's statehood to the status of redemptive sign.[42] In the burst of the film into color, Spielberg announces and endorses this return, giving history back to a nation whose focus on heroism (and politicization of the Holocaust) seems aimed at never, in the future, to have to contend with a missed act—that is, with having to represent an act regressively.

As stones are placed on the grave of Oskar Schindler by the actors in the film and their real-life counterparts, the film thus ends with the prospect of Jewish desire qua satisfied. Its only blemish—Amon Goeth— is not to be seen at the end, though we are given a final, distant, beautiful shot of Schindler's figure, the darkly dressed Liam Neeson. In this way, the liberal message of the film is secured: from the standpoint of satisfied desire, which is the standpoint of no (self-interested) desire, we see only the Good—only Schindler and not Goeth. In disallowing the enigma of desire, the split in spirit that *is* its identity, Spielberg's film has the effect of getting rid of desire. This is its unfortunate underside and the under- side of liberalism more generally: in attempting to secure a kind of con- sensus around the Good and thus mastering desire, it might just end up unleashing it in ever more violent forms.

3

Hysteria as Deferral

The White Hotel and the Idea of Death

Hysteria as Protest and Premonition

My discussion of *Schindler's List* in the context of debates about the meaning of Jewish rescue aimed to show that both the film and the larger discourse of which it is a part are symptomatic of an obsession with an effective act of intervention that liberal democratic political regimes themselves did not manage, at the time, to execute. Narratives of rescue that represent the desire of the rescuer thus function almost synecdochically in order to produce a mobilizing ethicopolitical maxim that basically gets us to feel satisfied with liberal political ideas and institutions. The lesson of the Holocaust then becomes one aligned with a notion of universality rooted entirely in consciousness and in a renewed identification with meaningful ethicopolitical norms. One automatic response to this liberal identificatory stimulus would obviously be to try to make more ambiguous the relationship between the subject and such norms. To put this in terms of Hegel, one would have to insist here on introducing a gesture of negation that would challenge the self-evident authority or meaning of the maxim gleaned from the behavior of rescuers. This gesture of negation is precisely the traumatic split that *founds* spirit—the means by which, as Hegel never tired of repeating, spirit comes to appear *to itself*. Negativity or trauma is thus the means by way of which a given subject even comes to have identity in the first place. So, if the obsessional disavows the necessity of this traumatic kernel for all identity and is thus able to fashion more or less straightforward, realistic, and chronological narratives of history, we might say that in the interest of producing an encounter with trauma, the obsessional (to borrow the terms of psychoanalysis) must be

hystericized. For psychoanalysis, this is what must happen for analysis to
proceed. Hysteria's progressive possibilities lie in the fact that, rather than
solving (in the manner of obsession) the enigma of the Other's desire,
hysterics at least are never satisfied with the maxims said to symbolize
that desire. It is now a commonplace within psychoanalysis to see the
protean symptoms of hysteria as exemplifying just this—the subject's protest
against his or her symbolic identity. Elisabeth Bronfen sums up this view
when she argues for reading the self-fashionings inherent in the performance of hysteria "as a language that allows the subject to voice both
personal and cultural discontent."[1] The symptoms of hysteria, in other
words, bear witness to a radical uncertainty left entirely out of the liberal,
obsessional view and the ethicopolitical maxim it proffers for our
prereflective identification (e.g., "Whoever saves one life, saves the world
entire").

Because such symptoms bear witness to a kind of discontent with
respect to *who* the subject must be for an other (or the Big Other—the
social order at large), they also stand as so many phenomena in danger of
being reduced to singular conceptual frameworks, to analytic discourses
aimed at classifying (and thus subjugating) the hysterical subject. On this
reading, hysterical symptoms stand as a means of bearing witness that
seeks to contest universalizing tendencies, even as medical and psychiatric
discourses arise that seek to bring such symptoms back into universalizing
interpretive paradigms. The problem with such tactics is that they risk
replicating the very gestures hysterical symptoms are out to challenge.
This is perhaps most obvious in the doxa concerning Freud's interpretation of hysteria as linked exclusively with dissatisfied feminine sexual desire,
and the sense that Freud is at his Hegelian worst in securing the univocity
of psychoanalytic meaning by such an interpretation. The questions posed
urgently to this version of Freud are thus: What if the hysterical symptom
in fact bears witness to something else entirely? Might not an ethics of
bearing witness to history gain profitably from a taking up of the hysteric's
protean performances? This is what poststructuralism has in mind in its
replacement of fixed identities with plural, discursively, and performatively
produced subject positions.

Because these are the very rhetorical questions that underlie its
radical wager that the hysterical symptom of a female analysand of Freud's
in fact announces the particular bodily fate of that analysand in the massacre at Babi Yar, I'd like here to turn to D. M. Thomas's *The White Hotel.*
Thomas's novel is essentially the story, told from several different perspectives, of Lisa Erdman, a fictional analysand of Freud's in the 1920s.
The initial two sections of the novel—one in verse, the other in prose—
are presented as having been authored by the novel's protagonist herself

and they involve a sometimes explicit rendering of her erotic fantasies, which transpire at a white hotel atop a mountain that is beset by corpse-producing disasters (fire, flood, etc.) and that include violence and the phenomenon of falling. The third section is a scientific case study Freud published concerning Lisa, which traces her symptoms back to the primary narcissism interrupted by the death of her mother. In the fourth section, we get a broad account of Lisa's life between 1929 and 1936: this realistic narrative sets up the circumstances surrounding her coming to live in Kiev, and it includes a series of correspondences between Lisa and Freud in which Lisa contests some of the meanings Freud has given to her symptoms. The novel's final two sections bring us to the massacre at Babi Yar on September 29, 1941, and its aftermath. In the first, several of Lisa's earlier bodily symptoms are literally enacted in her very murder; in the second, Lisa and her fellow victims are, in a kind of magically realistic rendering of a hereafter, transported to a "camp" peopled by "immigrants" that is clearly identified with the territory of Palestine/Israel. Here, Lisa speaks with her father on the telephone and is reunited with her mother, who, in a replay of Lisa's childhood, offers Lisa her breast and who decisively fills in the gaps in Lisa's past, thereby putting it to rest.

My consideration of Thomas's novel in the following pages will show the extent to which Thomas replaces the obsessional's linear narrative and arrival at a meaningful ethicopolitical maxim with a series of narratives that offer for our consideration a plurality of historical truths derived precisely from hysterical dissatisfaction and its protean performances. As I suggested in chapter one, hysteria is here formally inseparable from a certain deconstructionist sensibility. In the *absence* of any clear ethicopolitical maxim capable of arresting the signifying chain and thereby securing our identity when confronted with the Holocaust, it seems that all a novelist can do is to proliferate and disseminate narratives that run the gamut of the generic spectrum. *The White Hotel's* pastiche of the epistolary, the verse epic, the private journal, the psychoanalytic case study, and social realism (to name just a few of the forms the novel takes) would seem to suggest that Thomas has at least understood that the trauma of history places historiography in a crisis that cannot be obviated by unself-conscious narratives that arrive at a singular historical truth. But, as my reading of Thomas's novel argues, the move toward self-conscious historiography can, by sticking to the deconstructionist logic of proliferation and dissemination, work to defer the encounter with trauma. And in so doing, it can also clear a space for apologetic or ill-gained redemptive representations. No longer claiming to be *the* narrative of History, the latter concede their status as *one* of many that can rightfully claim a seat at the table of historical inquiry. This touches on the troubling issues taken up by Saul Friedlander's *Probing the Limits of Representation* that I mentioned in my introduction pertaining to the way postmodern multiplicity has "seemed to test implicit boundaries and to raise not only aesthetic and intellectual problems, but moral issues too."[2]

Let me begin by returning to Thomas's interest in contesting the universal Truth at the heart of the obsessional economy. This is, for Thomas, without question an ethical project with coordinates prior to the Nazi extermination of the Jews. The centrality of Freudian historiography in a novel dealing with the Holocaust can be explained in no other way. The presence of that historiography renders explicit the notion that the lowercase truths of history depend on a struggle that is essentially structural and epistemological, having to do with how meaning is made of phenomena. By saving the hysterical symptom from a certain totalizing, historiographical effort—Freud's—Thomas suggests that the ethical lesson of the Holocaust must arrive ultimately at the antipluralistic, philosophical basis of Nazi political power. Thus, though Freud is literally absent from the scene of extermination in Thomas's novel, *The White Hotel* places him there figuratively—and not on the side on which he would have found himself in actuality. In the prefatory note to the novel, Thomas may distinguish between the "myth" and the "scientific validity" of psychoanalysis, claiming that it is not his intention to put the latter into question. But the novel's penultimate arrival at the massacre at Babi Yar strikes me as a visit for the purpose of adding (symbolically) one more body to the infamous ravine. In short, *The White Hotel*'s phantasmatic identification of Freud with the site of mass murder suggests that Freud *belongs* to the historical epoch marked by mass murder—not so much because, as a Jew, he belongs among the persecuted, but because he and the analytic discourse he authored are in league with the perpetrators. "The Sleeping Carriage" section of Thomas's novel, indeed, is a scene that forcefully gives back to Freud and Freudian psychoanalysis that which both refused to privilege: what actually happened and not what has merely been remembered, the sociopolitical and not the sexual, the particular and not the universal, peasants and not *petit bourgeoisie*. Babi Yar, in the words of one of the novel's narrators, is an "afternoon that was no conceivable part of time,"[3] and the "conceivable part of time" is precisely the net Freud is seen to throw at and around the neurotic symptoms that he encounters.

For Freud, the human order of time is at the heart of the very meaning or intelligibility of such symptoms: they are, quite literally, inconceivable outside of time. This is in fact one of Freud's best insights: the symptom often bears witness to the psychical struggle to exist within time, to maintain an intelligible identity. As Freud puts it, "In general symptoms are only formed to escape an otherwise unavoidable generating of anxiety."[4] The source of this latter anxiety is precisely the prospect of libidinal unemployment, that is to say, the inactivity that would accompany libido's complete and total satisfaction, the traumatic acquisition of its ultimate fantasy object—the end of time, existence itself. This final drive is libido's last, because the satisfied libido would have no more need for objects. "We are so made," Freud says, "that we can derive intense enjoyment only from a contrast and very little from a state of things."[5] The subject who desires, in other words, depends fundamentally on a contrast, a tension wherein appetite for satisfaction always exceeds the meeting of core demands or needs. The pleasure principle itself, insofar as it is the initial direction taken in the life of desire, depends on this tension, which is one reason why the fundamental goal of the pleasure principle is to regulate its own dissatisfaction. Satisfaction, because it presents the prospect of libidinal unemployment, here entails a loss of the world in its entirety. It is a state, Freud says, "before which the efforts of the pleasure principle break down, a 'traumatic' moment [. . .] which cannot be dealt with by the normal rules of the pleasure principle."[6] This is why Freud insists on the need for libido to experience some frustration, why he insists, in other words, on the "normalcy" or "necessity" of some form of neurosis. As the fictive Freud of *The White Hotel* tells Lisa Erdman, the gain of psychoanalysis lies "in turning your hysterical misery into common unhappiness" (149).

For D. M. Thomas, however, the method that discovers the source or cause of the symptom always and only in the "conceivable part of time" blinds itself to the premonitory function believed to inhere in some symptoms—that is, their pointing to some inconceivable part of time: the future, purgatory, Eden before the Fall, and so on.[7] (All of these dimensions crop up in *The White Hotel*.) As several readers of the novel have noted, Thomas's thought on this matter owes a debt to Jung, who insisted on the need for "not only a present-day, personal consciousness, but also a suprapersonal consciousness which is open to the sense of historical continuity."[8] This "suprapersonal consciousness" is of the order of religious belief: it is a divine consciousness that knows or is believed to know that which is prior, and also superior, to temporal existence. It is this consciousness—this "vast outer realm" in Jung's words—that Freud is said to have sacrificed in giving primacy to the inner, or sexual, realm. As Jung put it, " 'The strange thing is that man will not learn that God is his father.' That is what Freud would never learn, and what all those who share his outlook forbid themselves to learn."[9] What Jung understands here is a certain ontological disjunction that separates the human and divine realm. To his credit, Jung sees that the eye of the subject is not all-seeing—that is, he acknowledges the limited access by which the individual subject or psyche, bound by temporality, is constrained in its access to the whole of the cosmos. In the limited nature of this access is the barrier between self and object, self and history, self and other. Freud accounted for this barrier—observed with his own eyes on the world stage and in the trauma wards of Vienna's hospitals—by positing a "beyond" to the pleasure principle, by noting the persistence of the pleasure principle's failures.[10] If the pleasure principle was once, as Freud puts it, that which "we have hitherto ascribed dominance over the course of the processes of excitation in mental life,"[11] it is now seen to be opposed by something equally dominating: a compulsion to repeatedly experience unpleasure that points to the existence of a deeper, "death" drive. Jung (and Thomas), however, does not remain at this impasse. Instead, he entertains a solution to it: the limited eye of the subject can turn around and confront the larger eye that is behind it, the eye capable of comprehending the whole of the temporal order itself, the eye of the divinity so to speak. And more than just confronting this larger eye, some subjects can even occupy its position: they can, as it were, become Cassandras, effectively effacing the difference between the human order of time (which they inhabit) and the order of time that belongs to the Gods. They can, in other words, begin to see themselves from the place outside the temporal order from which they are seen. My approach of Jewish rescue from the standpoint of Hegel in the preceding chapter aimed to show that the effacement of this difference can only be said to transpire in the genuinely ethical *act*. For Jung, however, this effacement can be carried out from a position of knowledge. This is exactly what deconstruction tries to do as well (despite its claims never to occupy an undeconstructable moment), and it is how, in *The White Hotel*, the symptom is given the power of almost literal premonition as the bearer of alternate *meanings*. Taken as the perceiver of the entire temporal order from the standpoint of knowledge, Thomas hereby elevates the survivor of trauma to the status of visionary.

The possibility of stitching up the divide between the limited vision of the personal and the full vision of the suprapersonal—given the "sense of historical continuity" thereby produced—is significant for two reasons. First, it maintains an inviolable framework capable of assimilating, after the fact, any merely temporal experience. Second, it holds out the possibility of a literal ability to see the (again merely temporal) future. It is on this second score that Freud, in Thomas's novel, is especially indicted, for the key to dissolving symptoms like those of Lisa Erdman's—symptoms whose dissolution might have literally saved her from perishing at

Babi Yar—requires precisely a transcending of the temporal, a mythic sensibility that Freud's systematic, Enlightenment rationalism is seen to depreciate. In his memoir *Memories and Hallucinations*, Thomas writes, "Mythologically, hysteria was associated with powers of premonition— the Delphic oracle and Cassandra. Might not some of the hysterias treated by Freud have been caused by apprehensions of the future rather than suppressions of the past?"[12] Freud's insistence on phenomenological time here involves him in suppressions that are for Thomas evidence of a rationalist bias, seducing and seductive:

> Gradually two aspects of the case histories impressed themselves on me. First, they followed the classical structure of Greek drama: ignorance suddenly and painfully banished by a blinding flash of light. I wondered if the discoverer of the Oedipus complex hadn't sometimes imposed his own aesthetically pleasing resolution. Secondly, these studies were Viennese seduction stories. A troubled young woman came in and lay down on a couch; Freud, his cigar flaring, got to work on her, striving to strip her naked. Day after day the struggle went on, behind locked doors. Her powerful resistance made it all the more exciting. At long last, and quite unexpectedly, he broke through, drawing blood from the hymen.[13]

The violence in these two aspects are not unrelated: the kind of formal closure that Freud's case histories enact is intricately linked with patriarchal power and sexual violence. And the overarching link that Thomas draws is with Babi Yar and the Holocaust, for as the novel's epigraph from Yeats suggests—"We had fed the heart on fantasies,/The heart's grown brutal from the fare"—such instances of mass murder are not just events that bring psychoanalysis into contact with persons and events that exceed its ways of knowing; on the contrary, Freud's "science" of mental life—that is, its phenomenology, its ways of knowing, its feeding of fantasies—is itself complicit in the events themselves.

Jung and the Lure of a "New Realm of Objects"

This notion, of course, is part of Jung's sustained critique of Freud, the markings of which are evident in the "great midsummer mist" that Sandor Ferenczi mentions in the letter that opens the novel: in that mist, Jung senses the existence of some "prehistoric monster," while Freud can only tease him "for being a Christian and therefore mystical" (4). (Ferenczi reports that mysticism is a plight that Freud sees Jews as having avoided.)

Already in Ferenczi's letter we see what is apparently the link between a repudiation of the mystical and indifference to future eventualities: Freud does not care an iota about the prehistoric, mummified "peat-bog corpses" that Jung says have been found buried in northern Germany, and he reproaches Jung for talking obsessively about them. A Freudian rejoinder to "the Jungian critique" here would center on precisely this obsession, specifically, the desire to "fill out" symbolically, or iconographically, the suprahistorical space that conditions mere historical reality. The elision of philosophical logic in this enterprise is significant. What are the fruits of this obsession if not a way of getting around the entire Kantian problematic of knowing the transcendental object that determines the present (e.g., the prehistoric past, God, the future, etc.)? The basic thrust of the first *Critique* is that because our knowing is always bound to space and time, there is no way for us to *know* objects as they would exist beyond space and time. There is thus no way for us to know the transcendental object. This is why all objects of knowledge are, for Kant, appearances. When Kant speaks of the Understanding's "vocation," he refers precisely to its recognition of this fact. Ultimately, all that the Understanding knows is that it is unable to encounter the limits of sensible cognition in a sensible, understandable form: "If we want to call this object noumenon," Kant writes, "because the presentation of it is not sensible, then we are free to do so. But since we cannot apply to it any of our concepts of understanding, the presentation yet remains empty for us."[14] The restriction thus placed on the Understanding is implicitly ethical. As Kant warns, the critique of pure understanding "does not permit one to create a new realm of objects apart from those it may encounter as appearances, and to stray into intelligible worlds—not even into the concept of them."[15] The religious traditions of Freud and Jung respectively would appear to fall astride this ethical maxim, with Judaism insisting on a virtual ban on pre- or posthistorical iconography and Christianity manifesting an abundance of it.

The case against Jung here, then, requires complicating Freud's own disavowal of mysticism, for Freud's disavowal is not of the mystical experience per se, but of that experience when it claims to have apprehended temporally and spatially a transcendental object/Other in itself bearing a message capable of being integrated into the sociohistorical world. The communication of this message then stands to remedy the traumatic conditions of possibility for a sociohistorical world. It is this latter experience that is reproduced in the abundance of positive images that "fill out" the entirety of the mystical realm. Instead of gesturing toward that realm—in a way that maintains its thoroughly enigmatic status—these images have the effect of eliminating our uncertainty apropos the beyond. It is precisely this uncertainty that another conception of mysticism—and another set of "mystics"—preserves. The Jew might be the first of this set, for he knows that God is his Father, but this only acquaints him with a place that is beyond the pale of icons: the place of God's desire, the *effects* of which we are clearly subject to, but whose ultimate design remains inscrutable. What the mystic, in this sense, preserves is the unknowability of this beyond: that the mystic is subjected to its whims does nothing to secure its identity. Lacan makes this plain when, referring to Bernini's statue in Rome of Saint Theresa, he claims that the "essential testimony of the mystics consists in saying that they experience it, but know nothing about it."[16]

The mysticism of the Jews and of Freud (and of Lacan) here is clearly not Jung's. In their refusal to elevate the mystical to a position greater in stature (and equal in positivity) to the temporal, both of their worldviews are seen to practice violence against the larger fields of which they are only a part. The Jewish people's rejection of the miracle of Christ—his virgin birth, his resurrection—and Freud's rejection of a concrete extratemporal realm are in this light homologous. It was Jung who saw in the refusal of these particulars the seeds of anti-individual, totalitarianism. As Rowland Wymer, citing Jung, points out, "In one sense at least, Freud's 'scientific' investigation of his patients can be paralleled to the Nazi terror, which in so many ways is its complete antithesis: 'Overvalued reason has this in common with political absolutism: under its dominion the individual is pauperised.' "[17] According to Wymer, this view is, if tentative, Thomas's, and the dominion Jung mentions is that which the novel attempts to break apart. The novel wants, in other words, to depauperize the individual. This "dominion" gets its fullest expression in the form of the first half of the novel, culminating in the "Frau Anna G." section that for Thomas no doubt marks the triumph of the seduction—that is, Freud's writing up of Lisa's case history, his perforce articulation of the etiological link between hysteria and sexuality, his "drawing of blood from the hymen." For this reason, it must be drastically undercut. Freud and his method must be shown in their inadequacy, for this method is but the "little eye," and it must turn back toward, in order to occupy, the place of the big eye whose eyesight is all-encompassing. Someone else, it appears, will have to take up the matter of Lisa's hysterical symptoms and the realm to which they pertain: a different, less pauperizing, form is required.

At least initially, we can read the multiple narrative forms of *The White Hotel* as participating in the larger attempt to retheorize (i.e., desexualize) hysteria. Thus its seeming affinity with a certain feminist project. The aim of this project has been, of course, not only to depathologize the female figure who is seen as "naturally" hysterical, but to cast a critical light on the visual basis on which hysteria itself is grounded. These displacements are on two counts analogous, on the level of form, to ones performed by Freud: first, his initial transfer of hysteria to women from the group wherein the Viennese medical establishment had seen and located it, Jews; and second, his rejection of the nineteenth-century belief in the ontological representation of disease. These two displacements are not unrelated. As Sander Gilman puts it, Freud's "rejection of Charcot's mode of 'seeing' the hysteric [was] also a rejection of the special relationship which the Jew has with the disease. . . . The face of the Jew [had become] the face of the hysteric."[18] What Freud attempted to counter, even as he remained embedded in it, Gilman says, was that "diagnostic system rooted in belief of external appearance as the source of knowledge about the pathological. For the 'seeing' of the Jew as different was a topos of the world in which Freud lived."[19] In Thomas's novel, these displacements are mobilized against Freud himself. Herein, for many readers of the novel, lies *The White Hotel*'s radical insight. Laura Tanner, for instance, writes, "Clearly, Freud's psychoanalytic perspective precludes his recognition of the very categories of experience on which Lisa's situation is based; Freud's limited forms of understanding lead him to read Lisa's suffering as a symbolic manifestation (rather than a literal demarcation) of a past event (rather than a future occurrence)."[20] David Cowart argues that the "ultimate level of [Lisa's] truth concerns not her body or her mind but her soul, her spiritual reality. This level, inaccessible to her doctors, yields up its secrets only to an artist: the creator of *The White Hotel*."[21] For Cowart, Thomas's achievement lies in the novel's suggestion of that "larger, external, divine order" that Freud rejected. And Mary Robertson sees Thomas as showing "that Freud's larger failure to put himself in dialogue with real history is symptomatic of the failure of prominent analytical languages to make the world better by understanding what happens in history."[22]

In the novel's move, first from the "analytic hour" and its pseudonymity to the actual history of Lisa Erdman ("The Health Resort"), and from there to a principle scene of the Holocaust ("The Sleeping Carriage"), Thomas is said to perform the formal act that these critics indict Freud for having failed to make:

> Most of the dead were poor and illiterate. But every single one of them had dreamed dreams, seen visions and had had amazing experiences, even the babes in arms (perhaps especially the babes in arms). Though most of them had never lived outside the Podol slum, their lives and histories were as rich and complex as Lisa

Erdman-Berenstein's. If a Sigmund Freud had been listening and taking notes from the time of Adam, he would still not fully have explored even a single group, even a single person. (294–295)

This is, in the words of Wymer, a sign of Thomas's understanding that "every one of the nameless names who died at Babi Yar was a uniquely precious individual, possessing an inner life rich and complex enough to defy rational interpretation."[23] Implicit in this claim is the notion that Thomas, in a way Freud does not, respects the nonrational experiences of the human subject. Many of the central theoretical questions at the heart of this book reemerge here. Insofar as *The White Hotel* narrates or represents or gestures in words toward the lives and fates of the victims at Babi Yar, it is not at all clear to me that it has moved outside the realm of rational explanation, since such instances of symbolization already entail a negation of the nonrational, the particular. Indeed, the very corrective Thomas offers is no less guilty of having missed the particularity of the nameless who perished in the Holocaust. But this is not a reproach meant to imply that there is a way to avoid it. What one representation misses, another is free to complement. But this plurality cannot be sorted into the categories of rational and nonrational, where "rational" denotes overweening universality and "nonrational" denotes fidelity to particularity. Nonrational here appears identical to the noumenal, and thus equally bound to Kant's critique. Eluding any attempt to apply our concepts of understanding to it, its presentation, Kant insists, remains empty for us. And we cannot simply imagine it as a new world of objects, cannot, when it comes to bearing witness to the past, recover the dead by straying into intelligible worlds. Since the nonrational is that which conditions all symbolization, it cannot be encountered within it; moreover—and this is, in my view, Thomas's crucial misstep—it cannot be said to *signify* in a way that is readily interpretable. As another "rational" (i.e., symbolic) narrative, the "Sleeping Carriage" is another universalizing enterprise. The imperative it faces—and ultimately avoids—is to usher us toward an encounter with its particular condition of possibility, with the structural trauma that ought to come on the heels of an attentiveness to an event such as Babi Yar.

This last point is important given the formal shift that marks the novel's final, "purgatory" section. The documentary realism of Babi Yar, we are told, has "nothing to do with the guest, the soul, the lovesick bride, the daughter of Jerusalem" (298). What follows is the Jungian solution to the trauma of limited eyesight, the trauma of human time: the symbolizing of a pre-Oedipal or Imaginary realm, a sort of weigh station of the afterlife where mothers and daughters offer up to one another their

breasts, and the Holocaust dead keep pouring in. On one level, this section of the novel is manifestly consistent with Thomas's "postmodern"
(anti-Hegelian) delegitimization of rationalist historiography—that is, with
his refusal to grant authority to one form of writing or knowing history.
We should, however, be wary of hailing these manifestations of the
poststructuralist dimension of Thomas's narrative structure[24]: its decentering of narrative authority, its commitment to multiple viewpoints, its
intertextuality, its contesting of the coherent "humanistic" subject, its
"stereoscopic rather than monocular" vision of the psyche and of history,
its dramatization of "how we produce meaning in fiction and in history."[25]
The point to be made concerning these formal shifts is not that Thomas
"put[s] himself in dialogue with real history" by including perspectives
heretofore absented from it; it is not that history and the psyche are to
be seen "from all sides." On the contrary, the formal logic of *The White
Hotel* is more properly described by the dynamic Thomas himself locates
in Freud: "the classical structure of Greek drama: ignorance suddenly and
painfully banished by a blinding flash of light. I wondered if the discov-
erer of the Oedipus complex hadn't sometimes imposed his own aestheti-
cally pleasing resolution." The point here is simply that, in terms of the
function certain forms are being asked to carry out, there is in fact *only one
truly formal shift*—not several—and it occurs in the break from Freudian
analysis after the "Frau Anna G." section. This is why the difference
between the "realistic" section at Babi Yar and the "fantasy" section of
purgatory cannot be adduced as further evidence of the novel's multiplicity. On the level of form, they are homologous: both are part of an
attempt to rid us of a certain ontological disjunction by securing that
inconceivable referent—the referent of *ontology*—said to be occluded by
Freudian rationalism. What appears to be narrative multiplicity is in fact
a function of the novel's controlling logic, a logic determined to infinitely
postpone the encounter between temporal, discursive beings and tempo-
rality/discursivity itself. Deconstruction keeps insisting that this encounter cannot take place, but the inescapable truth of the matter is that it is
taking place in each of their meaningful propositions.

   The point then is not that Thomas's novel refuses to privilege fantasy or reality, and is thus able to destabilize any achievement of fictive
closure. (It is true that Freud reappears in purgatory, but as a beaten man
with a heavily bandaged jaw and a cancered mouth that has been reduced
to the smallest of holes: this image hardly provides a basis for arguing for
the provisional or indeterminate nature of the novel's interpretation
of him.[26]) There is in fact another axis that guarantees the consistency of
Thomas's narrative, and it is the preservation of this axis—the
extratemporal—which has attracted Thomas to the Holocaust. Those who

experienced it, or "survived" it, are Thomas's hysterical patients: they are the objects of his seduction. What Thomas has in mind, of course, is a reversal of Freud's mistake. In listening to the survivors, he (Thomas) will listen for the future. They are his Cassandras, and what they testify to is not the desperate demand, as the bearers of unspeakable horror, to remain in and for language, but rather the speakers of a representable extratemporal truth. But it is just here that Thomas has missed the real import of Babi Yar: for the thirty-thousand killed there, Babi Yar was not the place of the extratemporal, but rather Time itself. It was the place where the ultimate object—existence itself—was grasped. But only the dead grasped this; surviving requires the frantic attempt not to catch hold of this object.[27] This is the site of Thomas's misstep. From the *sense* that an event like Babi Yar took place outside of time, Thomas has invented the existence of an *actual*, symbolizable referent that is extratemporal. This referent is, of course, the autonomous Jungian psyche, which is no mere empty presentation for the Understanding but is instead "the living force whose sphere of action lies beyond our world of every day."[28] This psyche is for Thomas fundamentally a "guest" in the phenomenal world; it is a consistent entity with consistent properties, and its direct presentation is not only possible, it does not even occasion terror. The violence of Freud and the violence of the Holocaust are hereby linked because both have as their object this "guest." In *The White Hotel*, Freud misses the real import of Lisa's symptoms, and Nazis and Ukranians murder Jews, because neither can account for or accept the collective psyche as a substantial entity. Both enact, it would appear, the failure to heed what Jung called *"participation mystique"*—a higher level of experience and of community. This is why Thomas can say that his novel is not about the Holocaust but about the soul:[29] the soul and its harmonious, pre-Oedipal environs are prior to the Holocaust and the object of extermination in it. The purgatory section is for this reason a trap: the reader who would deny it would replicate Freudian/Nazi violence. Deny the inconceivability of one dimension, the soul in its afterlife ("her mother had not died, she had emigrated" [313]), and one ends up denying the inconceivability of the other: "The world was a world of little children being hurled over a wall like sacks of grain being thrown onto a wagon" (288).

Thomas's endorsement of a substantial, extratemporal psyche on which real community is based, however, betrays a misunderstanding of Nazi ideology. The community preached by that ideology was precisely of the Jungian order; it sought to heal the split between individual and divine vision by believing itself privy to the perspective of the divine; its picture of community was based on the positive realization of something extratemporal: the "one-thousand year Reich," the prehistoric man whose race and features history has polluted. (Jung's obsession with the "peat-bog corpses," in this light, does not appear all that benign.) Hitler is to be taken literally when he speaks of "the racial question" as "giv[ing] the key not only to world history but to all human culture"[30]: world time and human time—the abyss between us and them—were precisely the secrets Nazi racism sought to unlock. The goal proffered by fascism was in fact the achievement of the autonomous psyche or soul—now believed to be absent only because of external or "parasitical" forces. So, what Thomas misunderstands is the source of the violence that is made to link the office of the analyst with Babi Yar: the refusal or failure to heed the communal binds of some phylogenetic collective unconscious. Babi Yar was, on the contrary, a product of an attempt to realize such binds, to realize the fantasy of an organic society rid of the agents believed to be engineering its imbalance. But it is Freud, far from sharing an affinity with the Nazi gesture, who repudiates this attempt. It is Freud, in other words, who insists that the exclusion of the inconceivable does not occasion murder; what does is the possibility—and even desirability—of achieving a state of total inclusion. It is Freud who, in repudiating full human possession of the mystical, respects the necessity of exclusion.

The purported feminism of Thomas's novel has to do principally with the status and the gender of this suprapersonal consciousness that occupies the place of exclusion. *The White Hotel*'s desire to include this consciousness depends fundamentally on an embodiment of it. Given Jung and Thomas's valorization of the feminine,[31] it surely is no accident that Thomas has chosen the body of a woman to mediate the trauma of the Holocaust. It is this body that not only sees the Holocaust in advance, it also survives the literal destruction in order to provide nourishment and images of unity to guide the postwar human world. In gendering this consciousness, Thomas has apparently landed on a positive property that pertains to the sexed body prior to signification: he has materialized some extratemporal substance that exists in (and prior to) the female body. The "inconceivable part of time," it turns out, is gendered, which is why the gender of the novel's central character is so significant. As Mary Robertson argues, "[Lisa's] femaleness is thus indispensable to the theme of the book; this novel could not have had a male hero. Thomas suggests that woman has a kind of knowledge the world could use."[32] This knowledge is linked, obviously, with the somatic symptoms of Lisa's that Freud mis-interprets. These telepathic capacities are for Robertson "feminine" and so unable to get a fair hearing. Simone de Beauvoir, indeed, noted the predominance of somatic symptoms in women[33]—she, too, might have said the novel could only have had a female hero—but if for her these symptoms are primarily a sociohistorical production (the product of woman's "total situation"), for Thomas they are something else. They suggest an ahistorical, prophetic insight.

In this installation of woman in the position of the suprapersonal— their hysterical symptoms understood as literally prophetic—*The White Hotel* appears to be another intervention in the debate concerning feminine sexuality and the source of sexual difference, and specifically, the centrality of the castration complex in Freud's account of sexual division. In the case study Thomas writes for him, Freud interprets Lisa's symptoms as signs of a repressed homosexuality (her wish for her mother's death clearly relies on the Oedipus complex as the determiner of desire), and the fact that this case study gets radically undercut can only signify Thomas's opposition to the normative Freudian account. In a later letter to Freud, Lisa seems to speak for Thomas when she all but accuses Freud of a recovered-memory ruse: "Frankly, I didn't always want to talk about the past; I was more interested in what was happening to me then, and what might happen in the future. In a way, you *made* me become fascinated by my mother's sin [. . . .] But I don't believe for one moment *that* had anything to do with my being crippled with pain" (226). Lisa's letter here, in its contesting of Freud's account, seems to place at loggerheads the castration complex (the source of sexual difference for Freud) and the properties that describe that difference (masculine focus on the past; feminine insight into the future). In siding with the latter, Thomas joins an opposition to Freud that, according to Juliet Mitchell, "saw the concept of the castration complex as derogatory to women. In repudiating its terms they hoped both to elevate women and to explain what women consisted of [. . . .] Woman, so to speak, had to have something of their own. The issue subtly shifts from what distinguishes the sexes to what has each sex got of value that belongs to it alone."[34] Though hardly fascist in itself, this view—and the production and proliferation of signs and qualities unique to each sex that it produces—moves in the opposite direction from that unsymbolizable, structural trauma that determines sexual difference in the first place. For Mitchell, the necessity of encountering this trauma lies at the heart of a radical feminist practice—centered not on the articulation of "what each sex has of value that belongs to it alone," but on a recognition of sexual difference as the point where signification breaks down: a recognition of the stupidity of sexual difference itself, the way sex is simply the means I have for existing at one remove from the ontological domain of unsymbolizable being itself.[35]

It is in this light that the final section of Thomas's novel takes on its real import, for what it signifies—in its valorization of the Imaginary and orality and mother-child identification—is, quite simply, existence not marked by the castration complex, the paternal Law, or the traumatic split at the heart of spirit. This is the explicit thesis of Frances Bartkowski and Catherine Stearns, for whom *The White Hotel* maps through the "itinerary of Lisa Erdman an entry into the symbolic via the name of the mother." For Bartkowski and Stearns, Thomas elucidates "specifically female desires," and for them, "The Camp" section depicts a pre-oedipal stage in which "mother and daughter are able to merge and separate, listen and speak"; it depicts a "culturally repressed image [. . .] mutual recognition between women,"[36] a "way of knowing" predicated on the rediscovery of the mother's body (i.e., the white hotel). This is, however, the very schema that gives to women (and even, presumably, boys) an intersubjective relation marked by the meeting of two complementary beings, a meeting not marred by sexual difference or its foundation: mutual powerlessness in the face of the beyond. There is, in this schema, no object that lies beyond this intersubjective relation that the child desires (and around which revolves the child's relation to his or her desire), no lack within the subject itself. In Lacan's discussions of the castration complex, however, it is the object that is "beyond" the mother, a "beyond" fundamentally outside our control, that is necessary for mother and daughter and son to separate and speak. It is this same "beyond" that initiates the impasse of sexual difference, that gives to anatomical difference a significance that cannot be transcended. *The White Hotel*, however, like the Ukranian soldiers who violate the almost-dead, seems to aim at just the transcendence of this difference. Freud says of the orality and the return to the mother's body everywhere depicted in Lisa's "Don Giovanni" poem that "in the 'white hotel' there is no division between Anna and the world outside; everything is swallowed whole" (135).

One immediate consequence of "residence" at the white hotel here becomes clear: Lisa's exercise of control. As in the game of *fort-da* played by the child, at the white hotel, the thing that threatens one's fantasy of omnipotence—the object that exists out of reach, the object that, in instituting division, creates desire, the object that *is* the posited subject—is brought within one's control. We have here a sidestepping of the castration complex, for, as Jacqueline Rose writes, "Castration means first of all this—that the child's desire for the mother does not refer *to* her but *beyond* her, to an object."[37] This involves, then, a necessary breaking of the mother-child dyad, the dyad to which Thomas, after the Holocaust, wants to return. And it involves a symbolic object that is necessarily always out of reach, always "beyond." Lisa's altruism in giving her body to more than one man—and the mutuality of the white hotel more generally—is actually, in this light, really the opposite of altruism.[38] The fantasies of "Don Giovanni" and "The Gastein Journal" illustrate ways of getting, not giving up, control: "[w]ith her eyes closed and her face buried in the pillow, she could not tell which of them was making love to her, it was all equally rare, tender and full of good juice. She felt happy that part of her body was occupied by someone else. The spirit of the white hotel was against selfishness" (99).

This deep happiness reveals the real underside of the White Hotel's unselfishness. One's own status as object is mitigated by making the encounter that most foregrounds that status a self-willed one. That part of herself that Lisa is not the subject of—that is, Lisa in full possession of herself *in the present*—is, in the white hotel, filled out by the body of mother of lover, and Lisa is able to imagine herself the agent in the experience: "I didn't mind which one of them was in,/the steaks he cooked were rare and beautiful,/the juice was natural, and it was good/to feel a part of me was someone else,/no one was selfish in the white hotel" (29). That these experiences in which Lisa cannot coincide with herself become instances of a *jouissance*-laden unselfishness is crucial, for they point to a dynamic that is the mark not only of Lisa's hysteria but of Thomas's novel as a whole: the event that shatters the subject's, or the work's, ostensible autonomy is transformed in such a way that the shattering is seen to come from the agency of the subject or work itself—thus sneaking autonomy back in through a side door. This is clear in Lisa's consistent eroticization, to be discussed momentarily, of the events that remind her of her utter powerlessness, and in Thomas's decision to write a novel about the Holocaust in which the central character telepathically sees it coming: what is outside comprehension will at least have been prefigured, and an analyst in Vienna, a Jew no less, should have seen it coming.

Eroticizing Horror, Repairing Loss

It must be said that this "beyond" before which we are powerless, this "beyond" that is outside comprehension, is fundamentally the site of nonmeaning, of death: to deny it is to deny death itself. This denial, Juliet Mitchell writes, lies at the center of hysteria: the hysteric is one who cannot effect the transition between "death as an ever-present emotional 'happening' " and death as an "idea," even though, as Elisabeth Bronfen suggests, this is the very idea the hysteric announces via his or her performance: "This conversion of psychic anguish into somatic symptom can be interpreted as the enactment of a message in code. Yet what the hysteric broadcasts is a message about vulnerability—the vulnerability of the symbolic (the fallibility of paternal law and social bonds); the vulnerability of identity (the insecurity of gender, ethnic, and class designations); or, and perhaps above all, the vulnerability of the body, given its mutability and mortality."[39] The "excitation" that the hysteric discharges somatically, rather than deal with psychically, is precisely the affect inseparable from this traumatic "idea"—the conceptual, unreadable knot at the source of our split. According to Mitchell, the hysteric aims to render this knot readable. For the hysteric, "Death is only another thing to be opposed and conquered. The point about death is, of course, that it cannot be conquered; it does have dominion."[40] One obvious link to the purgatory section of Thomas's novel becomes apparent, for what is "The Camp" if not evidence of an artistic consciousness that can accept the bodily occurrence of death—Thomas is certainly not one of those "deniers" who does not even believe the bodily death occurred—but not the idea of death and the ceasing of thought that accompanies it? On this level, *The White Hotel* reveals its own hysteria in the face of history.

The genesis of this hysteria may in fact be located not only in the horror of the end, but in the horror of the beginning as well. Mitchell, for one, traces hysteria back to the child's exclusion from the primal scene of his or her very creation, and notes how the denial of death is strictly equivalent to the denial of this earlier realm of nonmeaning: "Death or its equivalent is the ultimate non-existence of pre-conception."[41] The hysteria of Thomas's own work of art, in some sense, is also the product of its exclusion from its "primal scene," from the historical event it is fundamentally dependent on, but which, in rendering it helpless, triggers its desire for control. We can see something like this dynamic describing Thomas's relation to Babi Yar itself. The eyewitness account of its only survivor (Dina Pronicheva) that he reads in Anatoli Kuznetsov's *Babi Yar* overwhelms him. Its impact on him artistically, however, is indiscernible: he continues his research for a thesis on the problems of translating Pushkin. When the trauma of Babi Yar returns to him, it returns to him in a way that binds the trauma: he links it to a poem written *prior* to his encounter with Pronicheva's narrative (it is this poem that became the "Don Giovanni" section of the novel), and this linkage means only that he has anticipated the trauma and has a form in which to engage it:

> One afternoon, as I was sitting doing nothing in my cell, Babi Yar came back to me, and linked up with the wild monologue *The Woman to Sigmund Freud*, rotting in a drawer at home. There were extraordinary connections [....] I couldn't escape the conviction that the woman of my poem was Dina Pronicheva—or someone very like her.[42]

This telepathic anticipation is one way Thomas would appear to maintain a fantasy of ominipotence after the traumatic irruption of the story of

Dina Pronicheva—the lone survivor and subject of Kuznetsov's narrative—into his artistic identity as poet and translator: he, himself, had already written the first part of Dina Pronicheva's story.

This way of remaining in control in and after the encounter with death is modeled in an exemplary way in the gesture that introduces the "The Camp" section. Thomas takes a condition of helplessness and transforms it into exactly its opposite. Death can be opposed and conquered because it has "nothing to do with the guest, the soul, the lovesick bride, the daughter of Jerusalem." Zion is here the mother from whom we are exiled, but to whom we shall return. The purgatory section, in this sense, takes an Orthodox Zionist view one step further. Concretizing the mythic stature of Israel, and the reality of God's pact with his "children," it stages their return to the land they were promised. In this depiction, there is no finality to loss—not of Israel, not of the mother, not of the promise of return. What Thomas's novel refuses to accept is just this notion of finality: the *idea* of the mother's death, the constitutive helplessness that, Mitchell says, must be recognized—"Accepting one's dependence on someone who is not within one's control, who can go on missing and thus be 'dead,' is to overcome one's hysteria."[43] We have here landed on an articulation of what it means to engage the Holocaust: the dead must be allowed to "go on missing and thus be 'dead.'" The *idea* of their death must be *conceptualized* absolutely, with all of the implications that such a conceptualization would have on our desire to remain in control, to be the subject of our experience. This conceptualization would involve an encounter with unsymbolizable structural trauma—not the suprahistorical, Jungian psyche that might unify us, but the psyche that houses a body of nonabreacted memories and desires. That thousands of "immigrants" arrive in purgatory—they arrive in the same box cars that removed them from temporal history—is clearly, then, not an exercise of absolute conceptualization for the purpose of encountering trauma but rather a sign of the way more and more narratives work ultimately to defer the encounter with trauma. One of Thomas's justifications for this section—that it does not depict a painless, tranquil state of things—misses the critical point: people may still be suffering, but they are still living and speaking.[44]

This moment of, and subsequent flight from, an absolute conceptualization of death is dramatized in the case of Lisa herself. The case study Thomas imagines Freud writing, in fact, reveals Lisa's approach of this critical point—the point at which hysteria is either reproduced or broken from. This is clear in Freud's summary of the "Frau Anna G." section where he reports how after Lisa's wish for her mother's death is granted, leaving the little girl free "to do what every little girl wants, bear a child to her father," happiness does not ensue: "Instead of bringing her happiness, her mother's death brought misery. She learned that death meant being in the cold earth forever, not just staying away for a few more days. Nor was her matricide rewarded with her father's love" (162). In this case, Father is more and more remote because he, too, is faced with an instance of nonmeaning: in light of his wife's infidelity, he does not know if he was present at the point of Lisa's conception. It is here that a wholly contingent act arrives on the scene to give Lisa a way out of these relations that have her confronting the realm of death: her sexual violation at the hands of anti-Semitic Russian sailors: "They spat on me, threatened to burn my breasts with their cigarettes, used vile language I'd never heard. They forced me to commit acts of oral sex with them, saying all I was good for, as a dirty Jewess was to—But you'll guess the expression they used" (221). This episode should be but the third in a series that destroys Lisa's capacity to believe herself in control of her life. Instead, it initiates her first hysterical symptom (breathlessness), a sign of her bringing all three episodes into the teleological reach of her control. Not only is Lisa, in the experience involving the mob of sailors, given explanations that put her in control of the relation to her two absent parents—she learns "that perhaps her mother had deserved to die, for being a bad woman" (162), and also blames her father "for being Jewish" (221)—she also takes up an attitude in the scene of violation itself that stands her in good stead in every subsequent encounter with that which lies outside her control. "Looking back at those fearful events," Lisa recalls in her letter to Freud, "I found them *arousing*" (222). What we have here, it appears, is the eroticization of violence in the service of the hysteric's denial of helplessness, the conversion of traumatic bodily vulnerability to omnipotence.[45] This eroticization of violence makes Lisa the subject, not the object, of the experience of violence, and it explains Lisa's obsession with sex, and the constant commingling of sex and disaster, in the first two parts of the novel that she authors. "If I'm not thinking about sex," she says in her "Gastein Journal," "I'm thinking about death [. . .] Sometimes both at the same time" (96).

The erotic is, for Lisa, a way to bridge the abyss between something and nothing, between meaning and nonmeaning, between herself and death. It is a way of remaining in control and as a speaking being in the same way that the "Postcards from the White Hotel" reveal the manner in which the guests at the White Hotel keep the disaster at one remove. "The dead shall be raised," a Pastor writes in his postcard, "I have no fear of that." A Baker's wife reports that her mother had died in the fire, "But she was an old lady, so we mustn't grieve over it too much." And a salesman's mistress writes, "Luckily it was a wing away from where we are, so our things are all right." What is clear here is the extent to which

Thomas has exceeded the Jungian framework he embraces: the position of the hysteric evokes a truer form of engagement with death than do these postcards. Hysteria, if only initially, signifies the subject's refusal to comply with reality and the identity he or she is being asked to play in it; in other words, that the hysteric "converts" the unspeakable into a sign by way of the symptom indicates his or her resistance to that reality.[46] In this way, Lisa's hysteria stands implicitly as a critique of the dominant mode of dealing with disaster evinced by the other guests at the hotel: they have all acceded to the "reality principle" of disaster. And yet if more authentic than these patently superficial reactions, Lisa's reliance on the erotic is nonetheless analogous to them, and all of them flee the unexplainable. The postcards of these guests reveal a set of people who refuse outright to engage the horror that might be disturbing to them; Lisa engages that horror only in the eroticization of it. The poem written by the Japanese maid killed in the cable car accident—"The plum who marries/an ox can anticipate/great sorrow, great joy"—is for Lisa no consolation and for this reason sexualized: "She did not think it amusing, as her friend did; she found it disturbing, moving, even erotic" (94–95). And in order to bring that which is outside into an even more intimate realm, Lisa fantasizes sexual encounters involving herself that are grounded in masochism. Like her "arousal" at the hands of the Russian soldiers, this has the effect of transforming every act of the other into an autoerotic one: "One of his fingers was in her anus, hurting her, but she wanted to be hurt more" (48). In Lisa's hysterical fantasies, the erotic always has this role: it is the realm in which Lisa is able to preserve her status as agent in her encounter with the (dying) other. In this move, the dying other becomes the other whose death Lisa imagines herself responsible for. If the death of the other threatens to collapse the barrier between herself and the real—if, in other words, it threatens psychic breakdown—it must for this reason be transformed. When Lisa finds herself thrown into the cruel, miserable world from which she is unable to maintain a necessary distance, survival depends on this gesture: imagining herself responsible for the breaking of the barrier.

Rather than having these encounters with death and the dominion of trauma teach Lisa, and all of us, something about the necessary loss of agency—it is the reparation of this loss, not the loss itself, that lies at the heart of so much human cruelty—*The White Hotel* refuses Lisa this recognition. We see this clearly in Thomas's introduction of the mass murderer Peter Kurten, and in the hysterical effect that his arrest and execution have on Lisa and others: "An event from a long way away, which had nothing to do with her personally, tormented her worse than grief" (207). Lisa thinks of Kurten, and Kurten's wife, and Kurten's victims, and is haunted by the arbitrary forces that determine our situations. Her head spins

> with the thought that it was only God's grace, or mere chance, that she was Elisabeth Erdman of Vienna and not Maria Hahn of Dusseldorf! Waking up one morning, full of sweet life, with small bright plans to buy some new make-up or go to a dance . . . falling in with a pleasant, charming man, and strolling with him in the woods; and then . . . Nothing. But even more unimaginably horrible, if she had been born as Peter Kurten . . . To have to spend every moment of your life, the only life you were given, as Kurten . . . But then again, the very thought that *someone* had had to be Maria Hahn and Peter Kurten made it impossible to feel any happiness in being Lisa Erdman. (209)

At first glance, Thomas has brought his heroine close to a structural recognition about the contingencies that prevent us from thinking of the world as a closed, harmonious totality. The problem, however, involves the way this recognition is already elided by a Jungian conception of Kurten's violence as ineluctably fated from the beginning. Convinced that something prevents individual contentment, Thomas here suggests that actual persons are fated to play the role as bearer of violence and evil. Given the terms of the myth, someone has to be the victim and someone has to be the perpetrator. My own sense is that this view warrants the criticism of those who worry that a conflation of historical trauma and structural trauma implies that we are powerless to prevent the former. The proper rejoinder to Lisa's insights regarding the impossibility of contentment, however, would insist that just because the world is the result of a "cause" that cannot completely be rendered intelligible, this does not mean that we must resign ourselves to a world in which we are either murderers, victims, or the readers of stories of murder in the newspaper. Just as the death of Lisa's mother has its coordinates in the *idea* of death that preceded her bodily decease, the story of Kurten and his victims has its coordinates in the *idea* of contingency that precedes his heinous crimes. It is this contingency which means that even Kurten did not have to *be* the Kurten that Lisa imagines he had to be.

As I have said, to accept these ideas would be to begin to deal with the debilitating, free-floating affects that constitute the hysteric's symptomatic "expression" of them. Lisa clearly engages the sufferings of others, but she engages them only on the level of emotional happenings, not on the level of ideas. Engaged exclusively on the former level, they can be "discharged" on that same level. Affect here becomes a principle form

of defense against exercising one's thinking absolutely—a "particular sub-
terfuge, a special trick," as Sartre once put it, for eluding a more fundamental difficulty.[47] What this suggests is that it is the idea of death that
is required for our encounter with the images of death—and Lisa does
encounter these images—to be something more than the occasion for
somatic discharge. That someone "had had to be" Maria Hahn or Peter
Kurten, that mother and uncle died together in a hotel fire, that soldiers
in World War I have been buried in trenches—these are the meaningless,
arbitrary, nonsensical facts that are brought into the fold via the hysterical
symptom. They are phenomena the hysteric struggles to signify. That
thirty-thousand people died in a ravine outside Kiev is *The White Hotel*'s
meaningless, ontological fact, but as Thomas confesses, "I began strongly
to feel it couldn't end there, with thirty thousand corpses in a ravine."[48]
In the economy of the hysteric's theater, a further conceptualization always awaits. Thomas's narrator says that each death, similar in technique,
was nonetheless individual: "it had happened thirty-thousand times; always in the same way and always differently. Nor can the living ever speak
for the dead" (295). Thomas's solution to this impasse is for the dead to
speak: even the dead must be able to signify. Between the living and the
dead, between the will of a nation and the will of God, between mother
and child, there is no separation. This in a novel touching the event that,
in the name of an era that promised not be marred by this separation,
separated mother and child without remorse: separated them irrevocably,
forever and for all time. Only the deferral of trauma, the failure to interpret the hysteric's symptoms *absolutely*, enables us to bear witness to history in a way that continually performs the reversal of this separation.

4

Leverkühn as Witness

The Holocaust in
Thomas Mann's *Doctor Faustus*

Music turns the equivocal into a system.

—Adrian Leverkühn

Mann Beyond Irony

In turning now to Thomas Mann's 1947 novel *Doctor Faustus*, my aim is
to begin to gesture toward a mode of bearing witness that ultimately
rejects the poststructuralist thesis that ambiguity, indeterminacy, and the
proliferation of historical narratives constitute the first and last word for
an ethics of historical memory. My discussion of *The White Hotel* sought
to uncover both the gains made and problems raised when such a thesis
comes to guide a novel concerned with writing (and remembering) the
past. On the one hand, the repudiation of capital-*H* History conceived of
as rational, transparent, and meaningful does challenge unself-conscious,
straightforwardly redemptive narratives of history. I have referred to this
challenge as entailing the hystericization of traditional historiographical
forms (and their purveyors), as a way of introducing a doubt-inducing gap
between such forms and the historical events they presume to capture.
This gap can be instrumental in the effort to begin to reconstruct parts
of the past outside the purview of traditional historiography. On the other
hand, however—as the final section of Thomas's novel indicates—the
perpetual project of partial reconstruction cannot ward off the return of
redemptive narratives wearing the guise of equivocation. Indeed, as the
speakers in Thomas's afterlife make clear, equivocation itself can operate

to defer an encounter between language, history, and its traumatic conditions of possibility.

At first glance, *Doctor Faustus* might seem like an unlikely choice for challenging the hegemony of ambiguity in historiography. As a novel intimately concerned with Mann's own ambivalent identification with Germany as an exile in the wake of its fascist turn, *Doctor Faustus* is in many ways up to its ears in ambiguity.[1] In his landmark study of Mann, Erich Heller sees such ambiguity as the *sine qua non* of what he deems Mann's "moral intelligence." For Heller, virtually the entire Mannian oeuvre is marked by the capture in traditional literary form of contents that contest the very right of such capture. This is nowhere more evident than in *Doctor Faustus*, and it is the index of that novel's moral achievement. In *Doctor Faustus*, Mann may allow the tragedy of Leverkühn's (read: Germany's) absolute damnation to occupy the content of the novel (in a way that Zeitblom, on his own, would never have), but he refuses to permit that tragic disintegration to hijack the novel's form. Opposing an art that takes its liberation from tradition too far, Mann thus rests his moral case on an ironic aesthetic sensibility "resolved to preserve the continuity of form as the symbol and promise of something absolute and indestructible," on the "irony of giving a traditional form to the very experience of its disintegration."[2] My own reading of Mann's novel below does not aim fundamentally to dispute the truth of Heller's thesis. Indeed, I think Heller is right to see Mann as remaining at one remove from the significant, formal impact that Leverkühn's aesthetic sensibility would have for the biographer who would pen his history. What I do challenge, however, is both the extent to which this remaining at one remove constitutes the novel's ethical credentials and the judgment that associates Leverkühn's art with Nazi barbarism. In keeping with the Hegelian theses of this book, we would have to ask here: How does Mann's ironical juxtaposition between form and content work to defer the encounter between form and the structural trauma conditioning it? Is not the ironic position of ambivalence and ambiguity *itself* already a systematized position? Might it not be claimed that *Doctor Faustus*, despite its ironic mantle, is already a Leverkühnian novel?

To pose these questions is already to telegraph the argument I pursue below. In my reading, the novel's ethical credentials lie precisely in the Leverkühnian form *written about* in *Doctor Faustus* but ultimately contained by Mann's (ironic) fidelity to novelistic form. We shall have to await the fourth and final section of David Grossman's *See Under: Love* (the subject of this book's next chapter) for a text that formally exemplifies Leverkühn's aesthetic sensibility. But *Doctor Faustus* does at least provide us with a manifesto or blueprint for how to proceed. Reading Leverkühn's music against the form in and by which it is contained, then, my central contention is that it is fundamentally a music of witnessing. This is the deeper logic linking Leverkühn to the years in which Zeitblom is writing. Because of his (Hegelian) willingness to systematize the equivocal, the biography of Leverkühn belongs to the moment when bearing witness to the murderous Nazi regime becomes imperative—not because he is that regime's artistic prototype, but rather because he bears witness to that structural trauma for which that regime promised redress.

History Inside the Faustian Paradigm

The biography contained within the pages of Doctor Faustus is the work of a former professor of philology at odds with the Nazi regime, begun on May 27, 1943 and completed in April 1945. Though Zeitblom often returns to the scene of his biography's composition, it is the life of his boyhood friend, Adrian Leverkühn, that is the central object of his (and Mann's) concern. Zeitblom takes us back to the origins of Leverkühn's intellectual curiosity growing up on a farm near Kaiseraschern, his place in the order of patrilineal descent that mandates his becoming a scholar (as opposed to a farmer), his academic study first of theology and then of music, and finally, his emergence as a famous composer of his age. Throughout, as Zeitblom struggles with Leverkühn's increasingly antihu-manistic ideas regarding the nature and purpose of art, we are invited at a number of moments to consider Leverkühn as a doomed composer, a damned composer, or both. These moments include an encounter be-tween Leverkühn and a prostitute that leaves the former with a venereal disease; an encounter Leverkühn himself imagines he has had with the Devil; the murder of Leverkühn's violinist friend, Rudolf Schwerdtfeger, for which he feels responsible; and finally, the death from meningitis of his beloved nephew, Nepomuk Schneidewein. Alongside these moments of perdition and tragedy come musical masterpieces that are increasingly heretical and difficult to make sense of. In the company of friends in the early summer of 1930, Leverkühn collapses before even playing a note of his final composition, The Lamentation of Doctor Faustus, and ends up living in madness for ten years before dying in the place of his birth in 1940.

Perhaps the paradigmatic instance of Zeitblom's advancing the anal-ogy between his "damned" friend and his "damned" country comes with his introduction of the crematoria near the end of the novel. It is April 25, 1945, and "a transatlantic general," Zeitblom reports, has forced the population of Weimar to march past the crematories at Buchenwald. As chorus to the tragedy he's narrating, Zeitblom announces that the current situtation is strangely linked with the period that forms the frame of his biography—the last two years of his hero's (read: Germany's) "rational existence" (1929 and 1930) that saw the production of Adrian's "utmost work": the symphonic cantata *The Lamentation of Dr. Faustus*. Those years, he says, "were part and parcel of the mounting and spreading harms which then overwhelmed the country and now are being blotted out in blood and flames." "For Adrian Leverkühn," he continues, "they were years of immense and highly stimulated, one is tempted to say monstrous creative activity, which made even the sympathetic onlooker giddy."[3] The suggestion of fascism in this parallel is not difficult to detect: the "monstrous creative activity" of the composer Adrian Leverkühn (now looking more and more like the devil of the Western imagination) dizzies a sympathetic onlooker such as Zeitblom in the same way the "monstrous creative activity" of National Socialism dizzied, say, the population of Weimar. Zeitblom's analogy—and this is not the only instance of it— directs our reading of the novel in two critical ways: it fundamentally implicates Leverkühn's art in German fascism *and* it turns Mann's novel into an inquiry into the relation, apropos of the criminal, between guilt and grace. Leverkühn's art, in other words, as part and parcel of the domination and extermination, is such that its creator—like the population of Weimar—has reached the point where he must take up the Faustian predicament between eternal damnation or mercy.

There is, for Zeitblom of course, a great deal at stake in having Adrian take up this question, for it is in fact the one he is concerned to take up apropos of Germany. Now that the torture chambers have been broken open and foreign commissions inspect the incredible photographs, is Germany, like Adrian Leverkühn, eternally damned?:

> Is it mere hypochondria to say to oneself that everything German, even the German mind and spirit, German thought, the German Word, is involved in this scandalous exposure and made subject to the same distrust? Is this sense of guilt quite morbid which makes one ask oneself the question of how Germany, whatever her future manifestations, can ever presume to open her mouth in human affairs [. . .] all that is German now stands forth as an abomination and a warning. (481)

Of crucial importance in this response is the way it typifies a certain engagement with history. Zeitblom, it would appear, is less concerned with the pictured victims of Nazism, than he is with the question, or possibility, of German redemption or damnation. Seeing that Germany has "failed horribly in [its] last and uttermost attempt to find the political form suited to [its] particular needs," Zeitblom worries that his nation, hated on all sides, will "have to live shut in like the ghetto Jews," unable to show its face outside (482). Zeitblom's concerns here are by no means an innocent (or inadvertent) facet of his personality, and they speak directly to the underlying motivation for the correspondence he sets up between the career of Adrian and that of Germany. That correspondence enables Zeitblom to displace the actual source of his conflict—Germany's embrace of fascism and its execution of genocide—to a realm once removed from it, to the biography of a bedeviled artist. Adrian's final works, along with the Holocaust itself, here occupy identical positions: those who committed them must pray for their souls, once pure, now defiled. This is the paradigmatic Zeitblomian response to the events that appear to defile. Rather than suggesting a defilement we have always been subject to, they become occasions for the romantic reaffirmation of a soul that exists free from any pact with the devil. (Our birth is but a sleep and a forgetting.) For Zeitblom, the events that defile must be referred to the Faustian situation—that is, must be made the subject of a drama about guilt and grace. For the narrator of *Doctor Faustus*, history becomes this drama, and those who lie utterly outside of it—the murdered Jews, for instance—are the casualty of a crucial elision.

Zeitblom's move from the death camps to the theological problem of Faust is for this reason troubling, and yet the proper response to it cannot be to assign the victims a role as well in the very same drama. Egon Schwarz, for instance, is correct to note the problem in Zeitblom commending Leverkühn and his worshipers to divine mercy while glossing over Jewish victims, and yet his critique, too, transfers the question raised by the places of extermination to the terrain of a positivist religious problematic. "Are the Jewish outsiders," Schwarz asks, "included in the plea for mercy or must they stay outside once more? That is the question."[4] Schwarz suggests here that Zeitblom's "exclusion" is the anti-Semitic act par excellence; in true German fashion, according to this reasoning, Mann's novel "once more" relegates Jews to the status of outsiders. Schwarz's critique, however, rests on the common (mis)perception of anti-Semitism as that which designates and maintains the Jew as outsider. At the most obvious level of anti-Semitic ideology—the level of its slogans— this is clearly the case: the Jew is regarded as the "eternal blood-sucker," the "parasite" attached to an otherwise pure and sound social organism.[5] At a deeper level, however, these slogans serve an opposite function, which is in fact the deeper ground of anti-Semitism: the Jew is made the outsider so that the foreclosed place outside the social order can be known and given a body, so that the "real" outside not be traumatically

encountered as the place of matter bereft of meaning.[6] If this second level
is in fact the level of the real anti-Semitic act, then to include Jewish
victims in a larger petition for grace would be to perform a gesture
analogous to it, because both have their source in the need to mitigate the
encounter with the place of that which is outside the symbolic order and
the meaningless body that happens to occupy it: the emaciated and inscrutable Jewish corpse, for instance. To return to Zeitblom's failure to
memorialize the Holocaust, the point is not that his plea for mercy is not
comprehensive enough. It is instead that the very discussion of mercy—
or damnation, for that matter—in the context of the Holocaust represents
an attempt to save an ordering system in the face of the catastrophe that
shatters it, to bring inside that which is outside. At stake for Zeitblom is
precisely this system—the very category of grace and the Being who
might bestow it—and one way of preserving it is to keep it alive in the
form of a problem. Herein perhaps lies the enduring appeal of the Faust
legend, or of the very attempt to allegorize German history along Faustian
lines: regardless of its variations with respect to outcome,[7] in raising the
question of grace (divine or otherwise), it tacitly maintains the existence
of a force that deals in damnation and mercy, and in so doing, links us all.
Mann himself experienced this appeal—he responded sharply to those
who did not see the novel's "Christian character"[8]—and that experience
points to the deep formal need the Faustian drama meets. This same need
drives Zeitblom to turn "*Das Leben des deutschen Tonsetzers Adrian
Leverkühn*" into an examination of a soul "sold to the devil." In this turn,
Zeitblom is able tacitly to maintain the existence of an angelic soul
(Adrian's/Germany's) *prior* to its corruption, and to incorporate more easily
into his (and Mann's) symbolic universe, then, the unspeakable dimensions that constitute that corruption—that is, one can, if only for a moment, feel connected to Adrian Leverkühn; one can, at least, "pray" for
his soul.

   To incorporate the victims of the Holocaust in the Faustian drama—
to speak of including them, too, in a plea for mercy—would be to grant
ourselves as well the comforts of such prayer. For Zeitblom, these fruits
are not insignificant. As the novel's ultimate line of prayer makes clear—
"God be merciful to thy poor soul, my friend, my Fatherland!" (510)—
the petition for grace enables Zeitblom to salvage a felt connection to his
country as much as to Adrian. This feeling is one of the payoffs of the
Faustian application, and even the Holocaust is caught up in it, enfolded
within a rationalism that must maintain, it would appear, a unified "we"
at all costs: if "we" were once the land of poets and thinkers, now "we"
are the penitent who must pray. Zeitblom's anxious predicament is the
one Mann felt in exile—how to retain a kind of love for German culture

and history in the face of the terrifying German atrocity?—and what becomes clear in it is the way a humanism charged with salvaging this love slips into a form of nationalism. In this feeling of community lies the shared basis of Zeitblom's humanism and German nationalism. Zeitblom must incorporate the two singlemost threats to this feeling—Adrian Leverkühn and the murdered Jews—into the decidedly German drama of Faust because his feeling of connection can survive only within this more nationalistic focus. It is precisely the nation qua "natural" entity that is at stake in the Faustian application.

Such an entity yields a feeling of belonging that is its raison d'être. The guarantor of this feeling is of course the imagined auditor of Zeitblom's prayers, the Big Other, which grants consistency to his life, his teaching, and his understanding of history. Zeitblom here reveals in an exemplary way the hidden underside of prayer, namely that we never pray *for* those we say we are praying for. We pray, instead, for the Third Party without whom we cannot imagine our lives, and without whom consistent identities (like "teacher," "German," "scholar," or "father") are impossible. Zeitblom's prayer for friend and Fatherland is precisely *for* this Third Party, and it fulfills two critical functions. It brings the deeds of both Leverkühn and the Nazis into a framework that maintains positive notions of a transcendent essence, and more important, it maintains Zeitblom's *fidelity* to the injunction inherent in that essence—to obey. In this light, the entire project of *Doctor Faustus* might be seen as Zeitblom's steadfast attempt to remain loyal to the dictates of this essence, to reap the enjoyment, the consistency of identity, of "doing one's duty." The self-doubt he evinces with respect to competency, the fear and dread and horror he invokes to explain his " 'faulty' technique of narration" (286), is nothing but Zeitblom's feeling that he may not be able to write Leverkühn's biography and be obedient at the same time. The conflict between the "daemonic," which Zeitblom says he has "at all times found utterly foreign to [his] nature" (4) and Zeitblom's core disposition (rooted in moderation of mind and body, in the piety of culture, and in the tenets of classical humanism) is in fact the conflict between duty and desire. To the end, Zeitblom refuses the risk entailed in the latter.

Despite his *public* act of disobedience then—Zeitblom has resigned his post in a German university—despite the destruction of his country and the destruction of European Jewry, Mann's narrator still carries on his life *for* the cosmic force that he imagines links us all. Throughout *Doctor Faustus*, dutifulness delivers what it always does: a way to sustain the real existence of some unifying principle before which we experience essential solidarity. Although his humanism may not entail traditional belief in God per se, the unifying principle to which Zeitblom clings serves the same (God/Father) function; were it not there, there would be no one to obey. This is precisely why obedience must be made universal: *no one should see that it is not there, that this transcendent, unifying principle does not, in fact, exist. And more important, God himself should not see it.* Indeed, the unifying powers of this principle, as we have seen, are at their highest when this principle is conceived of as necessarily empty. One critical way of maintaining the illusion of plenitude lies in the subject's assumption of guilt itself. Simply put, guilt unifies, and in so doing, preserves the essential identity of a unifying principle. The feeling of guilt is, to use one of Zeitblom's phrases, "religiously productive" (272); it provides a core consistency on which community depends. All the more reason, then, to emplot Leverkühn and Nazi Germany within a long narrative of "original" German sin. As Etienne Balibar points out, in the historical production of the people, or of national individuality, the constitution of a new unity depends on a model of unity that must be seen to "anticipate" that constitution—the Faustian personality for instance in which "we" Germans have always been "at home."[9] This is the source which, Zeitblom would have us believe, supposedly illuminates the link between the Leverkühnian and Nazi catastrophe: both are derived from some Faustian urge, some originary guilt for having made a pact with the devil. Zeitblom reflects on just this source when he says that one would be hard-pressed to see the "blood state" of the Nazis as something forced, or as "foreign to our national character":

> For was this government, in word and deed, anything but the distorted, vulgarized, besmirched symbol of a state of mind, a notion of world affairs which we must recognize as both genuine and characteristic? Indeed, must not the Christian and humane man shrink as he sees it stamped upon the features of our greatest, the mightiest embodiment of our essential Germanness? (482)

I think we can see here that the notion of a kind of "national" original sin that establishes essential guilt carries out a clandestine mission. Far from destroying the notion of a Big Other who has "chosen" Germany for some solidifying task, the Faustian urge as "essential" (or "original") German sin keeps it alive. It is one way of refusing to permit history to put one at risk. The connection not to be missed here pertains to "original sin" more generally, and the way it serves to mask the Big Other's nonexistence. As Slavoj Žižek has claimed, "The sense of man's 'original sin' is precisely to spare Him [God] the existence of his 'inexistence' (inconsistency, impotence) by assuming guilt. The logic of 'original sin' is therefore again: better for me to be throughout guilty than for Him to learn about His death."[10]

Several questions here follow. Is not this the "logic" that describes Zeitblom's response to Nazi barbarism? Are not all of Zeitblom's explanations concerning his "nature"—his open embrace of what he calls the "high-minded realms of the *humaniora*" where one is "safe from impish phenomena" (20)—are not these explanations the explanations of a man who quite simply wants to spare this unifying force, this Big Other, the news of its nonexistence? Is it not here that his engagement with the Holocaust is most suspect? If at first glance Zeitblom's humanism—his belief in the legitimacy of man's self-reverence—seems to waver in his indictment of Germany for its fascist crimes, it does *not* do so in another more critical sense. Zeitblom may indeed feel guilt and shame hearing news of the atrocities—he ratifies Eisenhower's declaration that the people of Weimar were as "guilty" for Buchenwald as those who actually administered the camp—but it is still guilt and shame of a *dutiful* nature.[11] It is guilt and shame *for* the Big Other still capable of conferring a patriotic feeling, however perverse, and a consistent postwar German identity. It is, we might say, guilt and shame *for* Eisenhower (and for the Allies), thus Zeitblom's esteem for the latter and for the "community" the latter unwittingly creates in which Zeitblom is able to participate.[12] In other words, Zeitblom does not think Eisenhower's action is unjust because the performance that follows from it gives Zeitblom a chance to join with his countrymen: "Was that unjust? Let them look. I look with them. In spirit I let myself be shouldered in their dazed or shuddering ranks" (481). His humanism, in other words, has become the inverse of itself: only the content of his conception of obedience has changed; formally, it remains the same. If before, the Big Other was one before whom we revered ourselves, it is now one before whom we feel disgraced and dishonored.[13]

It is precisely here in the context of this inversion that a connection emerges that crystallizes *Doctor Faustus*'s incisive insight into fascism and into a way of orienting ourselves as rememberers of the Holocaust and history. I am speaking here about the crucial feature that *Zeitblom* and National Socialism have in common: the need to continue to act obediently for the Big Other, and the need to organize and/or eliminate those in their midst who suggest an ontological void in the very place of that Other. It is a need to turn every contingency into a *meaningful* sign. Both the perpetration of the horror and the attempt to bear witness to it thus have this in common: the disavowal of the traumatic kernel of nonmeaning at the heart of the human world. The odd man out in this equation of course is the artist who forces himself toward an encounter with—who *bears witness to*—this traumatic kernel: Adrian Leverkühn. It is Adrian who understands the stupidity or the silliness—recall here his laughter at would-be meaningful orders—of believing in a Big Other who possesses

the truth of our desire, and for this reason, he must be seen not of the
fascist's party, but rather as anticipating a manner of bearing witness to
that party's victims. By orienting himself toward the place of trauma, by
bearing witness to the unsymbolizable dimension of murder and human
suffering, Adrian appears to be the one who truly understands perhaps
the most significant cause of the genocide—the desire to identify and
eliminate a body responsible for the symbolic order's constitutive instability, to find in history a reason for our historicity. Adrian's encounter
with that which conditions the finite, temporal world, however, is not—
as it is for fascism—a way to secure this world, and this is why it exemplifies
an ethics of historical memory. In short, Adrian "goes all the way" in the
attempt to bear witness to what is unsymbolizable; rather than remaining
within the confines of a subject position constructed by language, Adrian
risks his very place within language.[14] Despite the "obvious" import of his
statement of intent then,[15] what Mann has given us—unwittingly or otherwise—is a character who, prior to the Holocaust, already exemplifies a
manner of bearing witness to it that arrives at the structural conditions of
any particular historical moment. That is to say, Leverkühn *qua artist*
risks his very place in the symbolic order in order to testify to the place
of the real that lies outside of it—a place that need have been occupied
neither by the anti-Semitic caricature of the Jew nor (more genuinely and
tragically) by the bodies of exterminated Jews. My claim here is that
Leverkühn already knows what a number of contemporary representations of the Holocaust, on both the left and the right, continue to disavow: that we live in the world at the mercy of a kind of senseless chaos,
and that any attempt to order and make meaning of our relation to that
chaos that does not acknowledge its utter contingency or "stupidity," is
already affiliated with the fantasy of fascism.

Illuminating the Stupidity of Order

This recognition of Adrian as a kind of anticipatory, exemplary witness to
the trauma of the Holocaust reverses radically the critical *doxa* on the
mythical composer. That *doxa*, following Mann's own statements and
Zeitblom's analogizing, almost religiously links Leverkühn's career with
fascist Germany in order to establish the artist's barbarism and guilt.
Patrick Carnegy sees Adrian, for instance, as "errant Germany." Gunilla
Bergston says that "Germany becomes Adrian Leverkühn." Erich Heller
argues that Leverkühn is Mann's way of showing how artistic freedom "so
easily deteriorates into [...] an alliance with the very powers of evil."
Donna Reed sees in Leverkühn's life and music the "prophesy in cultural

terms [of] the political holocaust to come." And Herbert Lehnert, in claiming that Leverkühn's "anti-conventional pride translates into removal of his art from human concerns," contends that Adrian's "imposition of artistic order is represented as an analogy to totalitarian power."[16] (For Lehnert, Zeitblom is not in the novel to be distrusted; he is there to balance a "radical cultural pessimism.") The mistake in these "obvious" readings of Mann's novel lies in their inability to note Adrian's fundamental recognition of what both Zeitblom and Nazism never recognize, of what I have said is crucial to our efforts to bear witness to the Holocaust: that there is always something arbitrary and utterly senseless about our ways of experiencing and ordering our existence in the world, that the nonexistence of the Big Other is a truth of our human condition that leaves us frail and constitutionally incapable of completion, that there is a kind of logic to the traumatic conditions of history's possibility that resolutely resists historicization. The point to be made apropos of Adrian's "imposition of artistic order"—Arnold Schoenberg's twelve-tone system of composition to be discussed shortly—concerns precisely this logic and what it entails: both the impossibility of a complete, fully meaningful social order and the necessary "stupidity" or "silliness" of those forms that enable there to be order in the first place. By exaggerating the very act of ordering, Adrian's art demonstrates itself to be utterly antithetical to the workings of totalitarianism. Far from an act of hyper self-reflection, Adrian's theory of art not only paves the way for the production of new, pathbreaking music; it also puts into question the very expressive function of artistic communication. His response to the horror of the human situation—that is, we live at the mercy of an "imbecilic" order or else we do not live at all—could not be more different than that of German fascism. He furthers the imbecility of order, and laughs; Nazism posits a pure, natural (Aryan) order, and sets out to exterminate those believed to be in the way of its achievement.

I would like here to return briefly to the interpretation of Mann offered by Heller with which I began this chapter, since Adrian's commitment to an "imbecilic" order goes to some of the central artistic pitfalls Heller's Mann is credited for having avoided. According to Heller, Mann never bought a notion that Proust, Joyce, Rilke, Musil, and Kafka did—that art *begins* with the impossibility of thinking and speaking coherently any more. These writers, Heller contends, may have tried to forge a new and complex manner of literary coherence from this impossibility, but in so doing, risked having only "designed and built inspired monuments at a dead end."[17] Mann's rejection of the priority of incoherence is aimed at avoiding the moral danger implied by this dead end, at refusing an artistic practice increasingly and obsessively autoreferential. To summarize Heller's

claims on behalf of Mann: the more art concerns itself with structural/
logical matters, with technical mastery, aesthetic purism, and pure contemplation, the more it risks losing its connection to "real life" and ultimately courting silence. Here, then, is the explicit indictment of
Leverkühn, according to which an art aimed at illuminating the systematic "stupidity" of all ordering paradigms signifies a removal from properly human concerns. If this is Mann's indictment, then he has, I think,
underestimated the capacity of Leverkühn's music to orient us toward a
trauma whose disavowal has, historically, had disastrous human consequences. In short, he has underestimated precisely the *human* stakes of
thinking philosophically about "real life," about the fact that (to borrow
the terms of Hegel) *consciousness* of real life is already the *grave* of real
life.[18] Moreover, it is not as if Adrian begins simply with this assertion.
Indeed, following the method of the *Phenomenology*, Adrian moves through
a series of forms, arriving only at the end at the recognition that has
implicitly structured the entire journey.

So, in my own reading, the recognition of order's "stupidity" signifies
not a removal from human concerns, but an approach of them at their
deepest level. Far from animating a project of extermination, this recognition confronts Adrian with a kind of constitutional impotence that no
activity, artistic or otherwise, can cure. This is an impotence that the
genuine artist embraces; as the devil says to Adrian, "We, thou and I,
lever prefer the decent impotence of those who scorn to cloak the general
sickness under colour of dignified mummery" (238). Adrian's composi-
tional activity for this reason escapes the obsessional economy that so
often guides the work of technical invention: he does not act in order to
maintain the meaning and the sense of the Big Other. The "works" that
Adrian sees as frauds—the self-sufficient forms of traditional art that Adrian
can see only as the result of game-playing—are those of an obsessional
economy: they are the result of so many little acts that hold out the
possibility of an essential meaning for its constructions, sacrificing themselves to the project of concealing an abyss. This sacrifice is part and
parcel of Zeitblom's ethic of obedience;[19] and it is this ethic—in refusing
to permit the place of the void to interrupt, or render senseless, our
experience of harmony in the world—and not Adrian's, which partakes, at
the level of fantasy, of fascist ideology. Leverkühn himself, it would appear, must be invoked to save himself from his interpreters (and his own
creator).

In refusing this sacrifice, Leverkühn's art points beneath itself to the
abyss for which it stands. It is of course Adrian's art that again and again
exposes the "stupidity" of those systems that attempt to fill out the void
that marks our relation to nature and to history and to ourselves. The

very progression of the forms he develops and employs is determined by the desire to expose, at the level of technique, the arbitrariness of one's choice of technique. This dynamic, of course, is what gives the lie to the self-sufficient work of art, and to the entirety of the symbolic universe, which is why the artist who would expose it is akin—as the devil puts it— to the criminal and the madman. "Do you ween," the devil asks Adrian, "that any important work was ever wrought except its maker learned to understand the way of the criminal and the madman?" (236). About composers more generally, the Devil says, "Every composer of the better sort carries within himself a canon of the forbidden" (239). Before taking up directly the formal shifts that mark the telos of Adrian's musical compositions, we can see this "criminality" or "madness" in an exemplary way in Adrian's astronomical and oceanographical investigations, and in the reaction they elicit from Zeitblom. Adrian has been reading the work of a certain Professor Ackercocke, and Zeitblom sees nothing in the ocean deeps or in the perpetual explosion of our galaxy capable of stirring one to the feeling of God or moral elevation. " 'Admit,' said I to him, 'that the horrendous physical creation is in no way religiously productive. What reverence and what civilizing process born of reverence can come from the picture of a vast impropriety like this of the exploding universe?" (273). Horrendous for Zeitblom are those statistics—for example, a light-year as equivalent of six trillion miles—that defy human understanding, statistics before which we stand utterly alienated, statistics that speak the terrifying otherness of the object world. Adrian's trespasses in this extrahuman realm, in the brute facts of the universe's vastness, threaten Zeitblom's pleasure in the face of the ungraspable. The real source of the pleasure Zeitblom gets from doing his duty here becomes unmistakable; it lies not just in performing some sort of tribute to an actually existing God, but in the possibility— if everyone does his duty, too—of experiencing the pleasure of belonging in a meaningful way to the "family" of living species:

Piety, reverence, intellectual decency, religious feeling, are only possible about men and through men, and by limitation to the earthly and human. Their fruit should, can, and will be a religiously tinged humanism, conditioned by feeling for the transcendental mystery of man, by the proud consciousness that he is no mere biological being, but with a decisive part of him belongs to an intellectual and spiritual world, that to him the Absolute is given, the ideas of truth, of freedom, of justice; that upon him the duty is laid to approach the consummate. In this pathos, this obligation, this reverence of man for himself, is God; in a hundred milliards of Milky Ways I cannot find him. (273)

It is only under the aegis of this higher principle, this "Father"—in Zeitblom-ese the "transcendental mystery of man"—that Zeitblom can achieve the impossible: that Wordsworthian bliss of a sense sublime of something far more deeply interfused, that feeling of *connection* to every other thing in the universe, that reverence of man for himself. His belief in this unifying "ideal signifier," and more specifically its incarnation in the nation, is evident in Zeitblom's final appeal with its invocation— still!—of a Fatherland.

Herein lies Zeitblom's real objection to Adrian's scientific inquiries. It is not just that Adrian's "sublime objects" do not, as Kant said they should, increase our estimation of both ourselves and our minds in our relations with Nature.[20] It is not just that Adrian's examinations do not work to inspire romantic-humanistic feelings of reverence (for his own "enthusiasm for size," Zeitblom is here the exemplar of Kantian "judgment," mentioning three other more traditional sites of encounters with the immense: the Pyramids, Mont Blanc, and the dome inside St. Peter's); it is instead that they expose the *formal* principle that organizes that experience in all of its stupid, arbitrary, nonsensicalness:

> Adrian did fling himself into the immense, which astro-physical science seeks to measure, only to arrive at measures, figures, orders of greatness with which the human spirit has no longer any relation, and which lose themselves in the theoretic and abstract, in the entirely non-sensory, not to say non-sensical. (266)

This is, though not for Zeitblom, in fact Adrian's achievement: he makes the descent to that deep place where we most experience the utter nonsensory, nonsensical nature of the nothingness at whose whim we live. It is Adrian who unmasks every single conceptual framework that wants to pass itself off as something other than a fraud, every single conceptual framework that believes it actually possesses the goods to fill out the terrifying abyss and lack of connection that marks our relation to the universe. *And thus it is Adrian who exemplifies a way of bearing witness to the real of history without recouping something symbolic from such an act.*

Zeitblom refers to this as his friend's "itch": "Adrian spoke of the itch one felt to expose the unexposed, to look at the unlooked-at, the not-to-be and not-expecting-to-be looked at" (268). What Adrian discovers in looking at the thing not-expecting-to-be-looked-at is that the thing is actually the place of a void, an emptiness that one attempts to "fill out" with artificial notions of the transcendental mystery of man and of duty. (Adrian's "journey" with Akercocke thirty-six-hundred feet beneath the sea in a two-ton hollow ball—essentially a trip into the void—is another instance of this project.) For Zeitblom, there is a feeling of indiscretion bound up with such investigations. What disturbs him about Adrian is the sense of nonchalance or indifference with which the latter has taken up this task, the sense that Adrian has "derived his knowledge not simply through reading, but rather by personal transmission, instruction, demonstration, experience" (272). This is in fact the case in a way Zeitblom cannot imagine, because Adrian is one whose actual experiences—his reading, his visit to the brothel, his meeting with the devil—only make explicit what has been experienced implicitly all along: one's being at the mercy of the nothingness just named. His experiences, in other words, do not have him trying to maintain the existence of some different, discrete identity or value *prior* to the experience. On the contrary, they have him understanding all the ways that very "prior" identity was always, all along, marked by the experience now being encountered directly. This is why the devil tells Adrian not to pretend that he has not been expecting him, and it is also why it makes little sense to locate the precise point of Adrian's perdition. Such an effort appears always to be a nostalgic one, hearkening back to an imagined/imaginary time not marked by lack or loss—that is, by damnation. Marguerite De Huszar Allen is right to note that Adrian "is damned long before he officially encounters the Devil," but this insight becomes merely the occasion to propose an earlier encounter as the actual point of damnation. "Adrian's true pact," Allen writes, "occurs in the form of an amorous union with a diseased whore called Esmeralda."[21] This reading, however, risks participating in the long misogynist narrative of the Judeo-Christian world—the proud spokesperson of which is Zeitblom himself—in its positing of Adrian's "health" against the backdrop of Esmeralda's disease.[22] Zeitblom's report, in typical fashion, lays the castration/contamination at the doorstep of Woman: "His [Adrian's] intellectual pride," he writes, "had suffered the trauma of contact with soulless instinct" (146). Such a report makes plain Zeitblom's investment in Adrian: Adrian as the exemplar of innocence who underwent a "Fall."

The point to be made here is that the kind of innocence Zeitblom relies on is always retroactive. This realization, were Zeitblom capable of it, would collapse his entire investment in the Faustian drama. If Man is never, strictly speaking, innocent, then there is no actual moment of perdition, no "true pact," no classical Faustian situation, only moments that indicate to Adrian that he never enjoyed the kind of innocence he, or Zeitblom, might have thought he had. That is to say, he has been without this innocence from the beginning. Each "true pact," then, only makes explicit a truth that Adrian has felt implicitly all along—the ontological experience of his own loss or damnation. Damnation, in other words, does not come afterward, because as Hegel once argued, the Mind capable of conceptualizing damnation is staked on the very division damnation expresses. "We must," Hegel says in the lesser *Logic,* "give up the setting of incident which represents original sin as consequent upon an accidental act of the first man. For the very notion of spirit is enough to show that man is evil by nature, and it is an error to imagine that he could ever be otherwise."[23] As Hegel sees it, the story of humankind's "Fall" belongs entirely to an understanding that proceeds in terms of "everyday, finite consequentiality"—an understanding that enables the conclusion that the "first state ought not to have been relinquished." But the very consistency of consciousness, Hegel reminds us, depends necessarily on the "Fall" into consciousness: one only comes to know nature after having been severed from it.[24] The state of health that Zeitblom would have us believe Adrian lives in prior to the contaminating contact with "soulless instinct" is thus entirely Zeitblom's fantasy, and it is this fantasy that stands in the way of a more genuine recognition of the constitutive inadequacy that pertains to the relation between subject and history. The division of which Hegel writes, and on which damnation is based, is, in other words, both essential for all symbolic representation—and thus for the representation of history—at the same time that it "damns" such representations to incompletion. In disavowing Hegel's truth concerning the primordial aspect of this division, Zeitblom is thus able to continue to believe that the symbolic order was once, in fact, complete, that language was once (and might once again become) one with the real.

The original five-tone series Adrian employs—"B, E, A, E, E-flat," spelling (in German) the code name for Esmeralda—must be seen in the light of a pursuit to become explicitly what one has been implicitly all along: as the attempt, on the level of technique, to embrace the "stupid" force accidentally encountered. For Adrian, this ideal signifier is contingent—or "stupid"—in a way Zeitblom's "Fatherland" is not. If for Zeitblom, the organizing principle signifies a destined, meaningful community, for Adrian, the five-tone series is derived from the accidental consequence of a prank. We should, therefore, not be tempted to see any actual, positive meaning in the series: it is but the clasp of arbitrariness. That is, while Zeitblom sees a necessary totality looming behind its signification, Adrian recognizes the relationship between sign and signified as not logically dictated (to evoke Hegel once again), but as arbitrary. Adrian's understanding of the fundamentally arbitrary nature of this relationship is apparent in his letter to Kretschmar detailing his decision to become a composer. Adrian's disgust—he declaims the "robust naivete" (132) that he sees everywhere in the artist—is precisely for those works that apparently testify to the adequacy of their own artistic mediation:

"the beautiful, " the "surging feeling, the Ah-h-effect" that the order of a musical composition "naturally" arrives at. The stuff of art, for Adrian, lies beneath what these compositions so decorously sing of within a domain that Adrian refers to as his "fear and concern." In Adrian's view, art "passeth far beyond the pattern, the canon, the tradition, beyond what one learns from others, the trick, the technique. Yet [as he says to Kretschmar] it is undeniable that there is a lot of all that in it" (132).

Toward an Ever More Arbitrary Form

What Adrian here understands is the utter necessity of a pattern—he says later that "organization is everything. Without it there is nothing, least of all art" (190)—and yet what he despairs of is the insipidity with which the pattern produces works marked by beautiful, unequivocal, harmonic triumphs. And given the "the complete insecurity, problematic conditions, and lack of harmony of our social situation" (180), these works, for Adrian, have no legitimate relation to the world: they are, he says, a lie. The despair that follows from this gets its first expression in *Ocean Lights*, which Zeitblom sees correctly as the work of an artist giving his best to the conventions in which he no longer believes. *Ocean Lights* is but the demonstration of conventions for the purposes of parodying them. (This is why it has seemed to Adrian as if the methods and conventions of art are *"good for parody only"* [134].) Carrying with it what Zeitblom calls traits of the "intellectual mockery of art" (151), it signifies the initial point of the Leverkühnian trajectory: an understanding of the ironic.

Adrian's genius, however, lies in his next step—in his recognition of the *formal* implications of this understanding: the need to eschew ironic distance. The beautiful, self-sufficient work may be a fraud, but it is not enough that one merely content oneself with the task of ironizing it. The reason for this is clarified by Zeitblom himself, for whom the ironic becomes a way to maintain allegiance to the Big Other.[25] (Irony serves just this function in Zeitblom's response to another of Adrian's ironic works—the thirteen Bretano songs.) Irony is the "out" Adrian will soon make increasingly difficult to draw on (even as the novel's author continues to rely on it). He will not merely continue to "fill up" forms in which he no longer believes. He will expose, instead, in the form of the work itself, the nonsensical meaninglessness of the imposition of form at all.[26] We have now arrived at the twelve-tone method of composing whose origins are to be detected in the subject of one of Kretschmar's lectures: Johann Conrad Beissel. Responding to the artificiality of the chorals coming over from Europe, Beissel does something novel: he develops a theory of

composition that is *even more artificial:* "An ingenious and practical theory
of melody was swiftly and boldly resolved on. He decreed that there
should be 'masters' and 'servants' in every scale." The result of this arbitrary system is, surprisingly, the democratization of musical composition.
Adrian's description of Beissel makes this clear: With chord-tables for all
the possible keys, anybody could "write out his tunes comfortably enough,
in four or five parts; and thus he caused a perfect rage for composition
in the community" (65). Fueling this democratization, however, is the
demonstration of the utter contingency underlying one's symbolic identity as artist or composer. We have here a key reversal of the more romantic, New Age encouragement to discover the artist within all of us,
for what we discover when we recognize ourselves as artists, are simply
the stupid, daily acts of ordering that maintain the ontological consistency of our being in the world. Beissel's theory reveals this existential
insight by foregrounding the very arbitrariness of musical form, by refusing to allow us to recoup something meaningful from the activity of
artistic production. This is why, Kretschmar says, it sank into oblivion
when the sect of German Seventh-Day Baptists ceased to flourish (it was
"too unusual, too amazing and arbitrary, to be taken over by the world
outside" [66]), and it is also why at this point Zeitblom's and Adrian's
respective aesthetics part ways. Zeitblom cannot defend "such a ridiculous and dogmatic arrangement," whereas Adrian insists that he can "do
with him [Beissel]. At least he had a sense of order, and even a silly order
is better than none at all" (68). The syntax of Adrian's claim here evokes
Hegel's line concerning Spirit in the *Phenomenology:* "even reveries are
better than its own emptiness."[27] No line, however, has been more invoked to prove Adrian's protofascism and the protofascism of his absolute
form—the twelve-tone method of composing.[28] Mann's novel has in fact
been read as uncovering the close connection between the twelve-tone
method and Nazi suppression of irrationality. According to Fred Chappel,
Zeitblom is correct to note the way Adrian's maniacal rationality threatens to transform that rationality into its opposite. Like the Nazis, this
thoroughgoing rationalism has its source and origin in the most irrational
of impulses. Chappel writes, "Mann is careful to show over and over
again in his novel that Leverkühn's coldly rational and highly mathematical means of expression has been constructed upon a basis thoroughly
romantic and primitive."[29]

   As is no doubt clear by now, my own reading is out to correct the
perceptions informing these judgments. Adrian's recourse to the primitive
is not for the purpose of achieving a self healed of fragmentation, a self
in total control. It is one motivated instead by a desire to take up the self
absolutely *in order to bear witness to the "real" source of the subject's fragmen-*

tation—that is, the real of history that is outside all symbolization. Adrian acts on the fundamental phenomenological insight of Hegel: that everything thought is already universal, and that only in the gesture of unapologetic universalizing is thought itself opened up to what it is not possible to think.[30] By taking thought itself to its extreme, Adrian thereby sets the stage for the ultimate opposition of something and nothing.[31] For Adrian— and for those trying to bear witness to the unsymbolizable dimension of history—this is the only opposition that matters. This is perhaps the light in which to regard the important distinction between Zeitblom's and Leverkühn's respective conceptions of the arts: Zeitblom opposes words and music, culture and barbarism—an opposition between *something* and *something*—while Adrian repudiates this hierarchy by accepting and including the barbaric. The importance of this distinction for Mann, as Marc Weiner points out, lies in the direction of democratic politics: Mann wants to replace "Zeitblom's cherished aesthetic polarization and the elitist sociocultural hierarchy it suggests" with an art which—by virtue of its inclusion of the barbaric—will "function within a community in such a way that all of its members have familiar and intimate access to aesthetic enjoyment."[32] Leverkühn's art, Weiner suggests, functions in *Doctor Faustus* as an emancipatory tool, but it can only do this by "recover[ing] from its status as culture, that is, from its alienation in the modern age, and by implication from its use as an aesthetic mask hiding the reality of social inequality and political domination."[33] Mann's desire may indeed have been to try to forge a way toward what Weiner calls a "postcultural community,"[34] but we must be clear, even if Mann is not, about the extent to which the democratic possibilities of this "postcultural community" depend on that community's refusal to regard its inclusionary ethos as redress for its fundamental estrangement or incompletion. Staked on the opposition between something and nothing (which is where Leverkühn's art insists that we stake it), the achievement of this postcultural community would mean simply the achievement of a sort of togetherness in the face of a more constitutive instability and anxiety. (Given the fact that for most people the raison d'être of community is precisely the resolution of such instability and anxiety, I can only second Weiner's lack of optimism concerning the sort of collective Mann might be trying to forge by way of Leverkühn's art; the most "inclusive" community, in other words, would in some sense be the most precarious yet.)[35] Leverkühn's return to the primitive, then, must be seen as *a return to this estrangement*—where the failure of omnipotence is perhaps most marked. His use of the absolute is for the purpose of exposing its defects, a purpose that cannot be confused with Hitlerism because the community promised by fascism never consisted of a return to some constitutive estrangement.[36] Contra fascism, the primitive is for Adrian not the realization of Imaginary relations, of harmony and balance and perfect unions. Whereas the Nazis posit such relations as a desired goal—even as they invent obstacles to it (i.e., the more the Jews disappeared, the more potency they were imagined to have)—Adrian is nothing but honest about just how horrible its achievement would actually be. How else is one to explain, at the onset of his "madness," Adrian's suicide attempt after hearing of his mother's imminent arrival? How else to explain the "isolated occurrence" Zeitblom mentions after Adrian's breakdown, the "outburst of rage against his mother, an unexpected seizure" (508) on the train ride north into central Germany? What is this if not the expression of a certain horror at being trapped within the Imaginary, a certain horror at suffering the loss of the ability to speak and desire? The true horror lies not in the Symbolic Law to which we are subject, but in life without this law at all—that is, life without the ability to speak at all.

And yet its achievement is precisely what the artist must risk in order to communicate our fundamental estrangement. In a certain sense, the radicality of Mann's artist for historical memory lies in his taking at its word—his overidentification with—fascism's desired goal of a society not beset by unsymbolizable forces. He risks what they never would: its actual realization. This risk, admittedly, entails an asocial act, but this is far from a sign of that risk's barbarity. Far from being an example of the totalitarian impulse, Adrian's "rigid" or "strict" creations expose the fundamental antagonism that discussions of personal or national unity would conceal, the unsymbolizable dimension in relation to which we live—utterly estranged. Promises of a messianic Reich are part of a different sort of strictness. Herein lies the unsurpassable accomplishment of the dododecaphonic principle that Adorno, in *Philosophy of Modern Music* notices: "the correctness of twelve-tone cannot be 'heard' and this is the simplest name for the moment of meaninglessness in it."[37] This "correctness," for Adorno, is part of a necessary change in the function of musical expression. The communication of a series of disjointed blotches designed to challenge music's facade of self-sufficiency, is not a matter of content but of form: "Structure as such is to be correct rather than meaningful. The question which twelve-tone music asks of the composer is not how musical meaning is to be organized, but rather, how organization is to become meaningful.[38] Adorno would here follow Beissel: the problem of organization is to be addressed by even more organization, so much so that subjective expression itself is resisted. In this denied expression, however, something is, if only on the level of form, after all expressed: "Horror has cast its spell upon the subject and it is no longer able to say anything which might be worth saying."[39]

What is heard instead is precisely a nothingness, the sound that cannot be made to mean, the note that cannot be played. *The artist who would memorialize the dead can do so only on the level of technique, and only in such a manner that technique itself dramatizes the impossibility of transmitting the hell of their suffering, the "real" time of their death.* The devil says to Adrian that art must make its recipients "listen" to precisely this impossibility: "only the non-fictional is still permissible, *the unplayed,* the undisguised and untransfigured expression of suffering in its actual moment" (240). It is the (non-)communication of this moment, this terrible suffering of the negative, that marks Adrian's two expressionistic masterpieces: the *Apocalypse cum figuris* and *The Lamentation of Dr. Faustus.*

In both works, form itself is organized so as to point beneath itself to the unsaid it carries inexorably with it. The first, according to Zeitblom, covers the entire field of the apocalyptic; it works out the most complex of technical and intellectual problems by subjecting such problems to the strictest law. More significantly, Adrian himself, qua artist, subjects himself, in his very being, to this strictest of laws, risking in the process his very contact with reality and the consistency of symbolic identity. Zeitblom can only shudder at these literal risks, "at the legitimacy of [Adrian's] activity, his claim in time to the sphere into which he had plunged" (373). The *Apocalypse* intimidates Zeitblom not just for the terrifying juxtapositions of its parodies, the horror of its loudspeaker effects, the pandemonic laughter of the Pit that sweeps through fifty bars, it intimidates for what it suggests about the actual state toward which his friend leans in order to produce artistic truth. A clear parallel exists between Adrian's conception of the oratorio's end and the toll it takes on his emotional well-being:

> He did suffer a relapse. It was shortly before he got to the end, that frightful finis, which demanded all his courage and which, so far from being a romantic music of redemption, relentlessly confirms the theologically negative and pitiless character of the whole. It was, I say, just before he made port with those roaring brass passages, heavily scored and widely spaced out, which make one think of an open abyss wherein one must hopelessly sink. The relapse lasted for three weeks with pain and nausea, a condition in which, in his own words, he lost the memory of what it meant to compose, or even how it was done. (360)

This is here the condition of the artist that is to be unequivocally articulated in the context of *The Lamentation:* the artist who risks his own annihilation, his own symbolic identity as composer, in the act of creation, in the act of testifying to the Hell of memory. The genius of the *Apocalypse*

lies in just this risk, and in the way it "remembers" what had not even
occurred yet: the hellish laugh that in Zeitblom's description slips indis-
tinguishably into, and then back out of, the sounds of human slaughter.
This laughter—analogous to, and soon to be superseded by, the screams
of the Nazis's victims—is then perfectly juxtaposed with the sounds of
children singing. This strict correspondence—which Zeitblom contains
by turning it into a sort of Leverkühnian aesthetic signature—is not to
the work's discredit. As aesthetic signature, Zeitblom is able to praise the
work's essence: "Everywhere is Adrian Leverkühn great in making the
unlike the like" (378). And yet he does not want to go further than this,
though he does say that in the chorus of children is "the devil's laughter
all over again" (378):

> The passages of horror just before heard are given, indeed, to an
> indescribable children's chorus at quite a different pitch, and in
> changed orchestration and rhythms; but in the searing, susurrant
> tones of spheres and angels there is not one note which does not
> occur, with rigid correspondence, in the hellish laughter. (378–379)

This formal correspondence, Zeitblom says, constitutes Adrian Leverkühn's
"profound significance," though his gloss is a paradigmatic mystification:
"calculation raised to mystery" (379).

This is characteristic Zeitblomian misreading. It is not Adrian's
"calculation" that is mysterious as much as what Lacan (after German
idealism) would call *das Ding*, which all calculation seeks to flee, and
which finally might take from one the ability to calculate at all. This is
the effect that Adrian's final composition, the symphonic cantata *The
Lamentation of Dr. Faustus*, has on its creator—it should be the effect on
us as well—and with it, Mann's novel reaches its culminating insight:
artistic creation testifies to the hell of history only in its own drive toward
symbolic death, in its renunciation of its very symbolic function, in the
senselessness of its form. In his overidentification with the arbitrariness of
life and death—Adrian sees his life continuing *at the expense of* little
Nepomuk's—Adrian culminates the "symbolic suicide" first manifested in
the encounter with Esmeralda: a "taking back" of Beethoven's Ninth
Symphony. We are here directly back into the domain of the Holocaust,
for what Adrian risks, in his "revocation," is not just his place as esteemed
composer in the symbolic circuit of meaning, but the very investiture of
music within that circuit.[40] The radicality of this act lies in the way he
refuses the lure of totalitarian paranoia in bearing witness to that place
soon to be occupied by the Jews and gypsies of Eastern Europe. Before
the fact (but not really, given the period in which *Doctor Faustus* was

written and published), he is already the one most committed to their memory, to the place outside the symbolic circuit of meaning in which they exist. In my view, this points up the ethical significance of bearing witness to a structural trauma, a significance whose articulation necessarily takes the form of a paradox: if, when remembering the victims of particular historical traumas, we are led to a more structural traumatic encounter, we are in a sense, at this very instant, "remembering" future victims *before they have become victims*. My own hypothesis is that this "remembering" can play a vital role in arresting the production of victims. This "remembering" leads to the following ethical conclusion: let us have no more victims in the name of seeking redress for structural trauma. To return to Mann's own novel—began during the War and published in 1947—I think it is plausible to see it (even if unwittingly) as a kind of lament that this sort of witnessing did not take place *before* the violence that produced the Holocaust commenced.[41] Only those of Zeitblom's camp would speak here of Adrian as having, in retrospect, "gone too far." The radicality of his risk resides precisely in his rejection of a future vantage point from which he might gauge his present undertaking. What is rejected is in fact the very guarantee of symbolization, because symbolization oversees all the ways we have of dealing with the trauma of the Holocaust and our historical situatedness.

It is for this reason that the most authentic work of art that would have the Holocaust as its subject be one that refuses the inherent affirmation of symbolization. And more radically, it is for this reason that the most authentic act of bearing witness to the Holocaust be one that places in question the very ability to symbolize. Adrian's *Lamentation* lands authentically on both of these scores. Technique has here become even stricter; there is, Zeitblom reports, "no longer any free note" (486). Submitting every note to the most arbitrary of laws, Adrian has perfectly revealed the fugitive disposition of all symbolization. Thus, the identity between the angelic choir and the hellish laughter encountered already in the *Apocalypse cum figuris* is carried to its furthest extreme: that identity, Zeitblom tells us, has now become "all-embracing." In this way he achieves freedom: "by virtue of the absoluteness of the form the music is freed" (487–488). At its end, the chorus of lament passes into a movement purely orchestral: "it is, as it were, the reverse of the 'Ode to Joy,' the negative, equally a work of genius, of that translation of the symphony into vocal jubilation" (489–490). The horror to which Adrian must testify is that which cannot be spoken. For this Faust (Adrian), the thought of being saved has become the bait held out by the Tempter. This is crucial, of course, because it turns Zeitblom—and more generally, Thomas Mann—into the figure of the Tempter. At least this was the implicit judgment of

Adorno, for whom any hint of consolation or redemption or regeneration smacked of a wished-for affirmation that art could not, in good conscience, deliver.[42] The cello's high G, which is given as the last word, as it were, of Adrian's *The Lamentation of Dr. Faustus* must be seen in the light of this context—not, as Zeitblom would have it, as a sign of Adrian's "conversion," and not, as Hans Rudolf Vaget would have it, as "Leverkühn's most desperate plea."[43] It must be seen, instead, as Mann's own last-minute flight from Adorno's insistence on unequivocal negativity: the echo of the high G, for Zeitblom, "abides as a light in the night" (491). What Mann apparently could not give up was precisely this symbolic, light-giving function of art. Against it, we must set Adrian himself who despises the tradition that might "save" him, and who insists on exposing the consolation that symbolic identities and symbolization itself affords. (Consider, here, Zeitblom's pleasure at Adrian's seeming assumption of symbolic identities—e.g., "suitor" of Marie Godeau, "father" to Nepomuk Schneidenwein, composer, etc.) The experience Adrian wants us to have is the experience of being outside symbolization, even though the risk is that—like Adrian—we might remain there.

This is, of course, the path of a properly traumatic memory. What we must undergo is our own disappearance, the risk of losing everything, for it is only then that the act of memory is allowed truly to change us. We have perhaps now reached the point where we can understand the novel's epigraph from Dante: "O Memory who wrote down what I did see/Here thy nobility will be made plain." For Adrian, memory lies somewhere beyond the human world; its "nobility" lies in the lesson it teaches us about time and the way our finitude divides us in two, into the division of which Hegel wrote. There is not a time for us—in the world of our relations with others—in which we are not damned. With this recognition, there is no imaginary left to motivate our violence and cruelty, no scenario in which what plagues the consistency of the social order is given a name and a body, no fantasy that promises the possibility of wholeness. If we have risked our very being within the symbolic order, if we have peered into the void, if we have occupied without reserve a totalizing position, we have, then, *borne witness to the real*. And though, in so doing, we reveal the arbitrary, the "stupid" nature of the form that that testimony takes, we nonetheless thereby bespeak the trauma of history that is the irrecuperable trauma of our selves and of our world. It is a trauma we can do nothing about, a trauma for which there is no redress. Conceived of in these terms, the act of remembering the Holocaust does after all work to combat those occurrences that partake of its repetition.

5

History as/and Paranoia

David Grossman's *See Under: Love*

Eclipsing Self-reflexivity

My reading, in the preceding chapter, of Adrian Leverkühn—the "damned" composer at the center of Mann's *Doctor Faustus*—argued for an ethical trajectory to his artistic progress that ultimately makes his art an art of the witness. Such an argument was, admittedly, one that runs counter not just to Mann's intentions in the novel and the critical consensus regarding the historical and political symbolism involved in Leverkühn's damnation, but also to those within Holocaust studies who would no doubt like to see more clearly delineated the specific historical trauma to which Mann's composer is bearing witness. By most accounts, including his own, Mann is said in the last instance to have clung to Christianity over nihilism, tradition over experiment. And few would find enough in the *Apocalypse*'s "passages of horror" (sung by a children's chorus) to link that work with the children killed in the Holocaust—never mind the historical anachronism involved in such a link. My own reading concurs with these accounts, but draws different conclusions from them. Indeed, one of my central contentions is that Mann's novel ought to be credited for its outline of precisely the artistic practice that he sees as soliciting and warranting damnation. The warrant for such credit, in my view, is twofold. First, the aesthetic memorial strategy Mann gives to Leverkühn in 1947 is, in the biography of the composer's life proper, developed and practiced well *before* the execution of Nazi aggression. It may well be that Mann is trying to plot historically the philosophical and artistic contexts for Nazism, but it is also incontrovertibly true that Leverkühn's staging of an encounter with structural trauma is both prior and antithetical to the *execution* of historical trauma. Second, Leverkühn's totalizing method constitutes an eclipse of the ironic sensibility and self-reflexivity of postmodern historiography. I have dealt with the problems raised by this sensibility for Holocaust memory both in my discussion (in chapter 1) of a Derridean-inspired historicism that prohibits and defers any synchronic moment of language and the structural encounter with trauma it entails, as well as in my reading (in chapter 3) of the plurality of narrative forms in Thomas's *The White Hotel*, which prepares the ground for its equivocally redemptive final scene.

These problems are the recurrent object of critique in the first three sections of the novel to which I now turn—David Grossman's *See Under: Love*. In that novel's first section, entitled "Momik" (so named for the novel's protagonist, Shlomo Efraim Neuman), Grossman tells the story of a nine-year-old child living in Jerusalem in 1959 who tries literally to incarnate, in the basement of his home, a "Nazi Beast" responsible for the posttraumatic symptoms evinced in his parents and in virtually all of the adults in his neighborhood. The second section, entitled "Bruno," depicts the adult Momik's attempt, in 1983, to commune with the murdered Polish writer, Bruno Schulz, in order to recover a lost novel of Schulz's that outlines an imminent messianic age. The third section, entitled "Wasserman" (and still set in 1983), has Momik attempting to recover the last installment of the "Children of the Heart" serial adventure story for which his grandfather, in the 1910s and 1920s in Europe, was famous (Momik imagines this last installment as having been narrated orally by his grandfather to Herr Niegel, the Camp Commander at Treblinka). Momik's difficulties in materializing the Nazi Beast in the first section telegraphs thematically a point reflected formally in "Bruno" and "Wasserman," which are quintessentially self-reflexive texts that return the reader repeatedly to the very scene and difficulty of their composition.

As I shall show in my reading below, however, despite the formal advance to self-reflexivity in the second and third section, a deeper unity joins all three. In my reading, the uncovering of this unity sheds some much-needed light on the paranoia that persists in the approach to the Holocaust that prohibits any totalizing narrative gesture. The prohibition of such a gesture, as I have suggested, animates the prevailing memorial practice today, in which proliferating particular narratives must stage their failure to reach a putative universal position of knowledge believed to be safe and complete. I say "persists" because the poststructuralist turn to irony, self-reflexivity and particularity no doubt has as its initial target the unspoken "paranoia" of empiricist or positivist historiography. However, the prohibition of such a position of knowledge implies that it is, in fact, possible—and that fascism names the political corollary of the realization of such a possibility. As I have already made clear, my own understanding of fascism points in a different direction toward its conservative character, toward the refusal of the constitutive conditions of an already-universal order of language and consciousness. The ethical practice informed by poststructuralism—the spawning and dissemination of self-reflexive narratives that must all foreground their textuality/particularity—partakes of the same refusal by postponing indefinitely what the taking up of a universal position would, in fact, entail. For me, this is the radical formal achievement of the fourth section of Grossman's novel ("The Complete Encyclopedia of Baby Kazik's Life"): it repudiates, in the name of witnessing, this postponement. In *See Under: Love*'s final section, Grossman's writer-hero no longer stages his failure to tell Wasserman's story, but rather tells it *completely* by way of one of the most totalizing forms available—an encyclopedia. The reading that follows aims to elucidate the precise ethical dimension of this move. In order to do so, I shall have to take up the novel's first three sections in turn. By reading the way these sections link the disavowal of structural trauma (in the attempt to memorialize a historically specific trauma) to the perpetuation of the vicious and destructive circle of history, we can, I think, illuminate Grossman's ethical wager for our post-Holocaust moment: when overrun by paranoia, the antidote to history lies not *in* history and in a categorical pledge to historicize, but rather in the encounter with that which can never become history, with the traumatic particular—in *See Under: Love*, the life and death of a baby in Warsaw compressed to a single day (May 4, 1943). It is this encounter that catalyzes our memorial efforts and constitutes their ultimate contribution to an ethics aimed at preventing deadly repetitions.

Paranoia and the Problem of Subjectivity

The arrival of Anshel Wasserman on the first page of Grossman's novel— "It was like this, a few months after Grandma Henny was buried in her grave, Momik got a new grandfather"[1]—sets up the crisis of authority familiar to Holocaust writing and representation. As a survivor, the terrible (and disjointed) story that Momik's new grandfather has to tell is a story that no novel can render summarily. It is a story of Treblinka, and of watching one's wife and daughter disappear in a line filing toward the gas chamber, and of watching new arrivals do the same. As we have seen, this problem is never strictly epistemological. Indeed, in Grossman's novel, his hero's inability to write his grandfather's story reveals the extent to which the crisis-inducing epistemological limit is always experienced as an ontological problem. For as long as Momik cannot decipher the code of his grandfather's speech, he is faced quite simply with the feeling of not knowing, with any certainty, who he is. One of the achievements of *See Under: Love* lies in its staging of the way historically specific traumas render explicit our self-division, getting us to feel that a loss vital to our full sense of self has taken place. For Momik, this is the feeling (as he puts it) of "being unable to understand my life until I learn about my unlived life Over There" (109). Even as a boy, Momik suffers the manner in which historical trauma makes wholeness impossible. This is why, when he washes his face in the bathroom of his house, Grossman has him "[holding] his head exactly where the long crack runs down the middle of the mirror" (47).

See Under: Love, however, does more than just stage the subject's split in the face of historical trauma. Indeed, each of Momik's attempts to learn about his "unlived life Over There"—by way of a mythical Beast in section 1, of the murdered artist Bruno Schulz in section 2, and of the last "Children of the Heart" tale told by his new grandfather Anshel to a Nazi in section 3—are in fact Momik's attempts to treat entirely as a matter of historical knowledge a decisive aspect of what actually existed Over There. These attempts illustrate some of the (covert) benefits reaped from conceiving specific, historical traumas in an exclusively historical way: when so conceived, the problem of the subject's own constitutive split is held likewise to be a historical matter. In this way, *See Under: Love* dramatizes the prevailing form for coping with the inability of identity to come full circle, the psychological operation whereby a problem of being *is turned back into* a problem of knowledge—that is, the paranoid construction. Paranoia is here the "solution" to the Hegelian subject, and to the "defect" implied by the disparity that exists in consciousness between the "I" and the historical substance that is its object. As I have said elsewhere, for Hegel, this disparity is the *soul* of subjectivity and the object world: it is, says Hegel, "that which moves them."[2] In short, this "defect" conditions the emergence of the order of language and consciousness—implying necessarily that neither this order nor the subjects interpellated within it can ever presume supreme autonomy or insight. But for the paranoiac, the case is otherwise. In his view, no defect is structural or constitutive. What Hegel deems "the negative in general" is, for the paranoiac, an already intelligible exemplar of alterity responsible for having taken our autonomy from us. The paranoiac is thus self-evidently a creature of superior intelligence: he is able to detect the "real" reason behind what only appear to be inexplicable, contingent phenomena.

Having recognized that our relationship with the object world is governed by the aforesaid disparity, the paranoiac correctly registers the fact and implications of our split, but imagines the possibility of its reversal. For the paranoiac, the ultimate locus of causality that eludes the symbolic order and that is crucial to self-understanding is not the logical condition for nonpsychotic societies and subjects. On the contrary, the existence of some One or some Thing is posited that, if recovered, eliminated, or both might make it all clearer. How does one cope with the subjective experience of irretrievable loss and instability, of the feeling that a critical part of the world has vanished? Grossman displays with striking clarity, in the "Momik" section of the novel, the paranoid response: one tests the old frameworks that might have once managed to deliver a satisfactory explanation, and when that fails, one copes by declaring war on the imagined thief—that is, the Nazi Beast.

As a psychopolitical phenomenon, war is, of course, one of Grossman's fundamental ethicopolitical concerns as a writer. In addition to appearing throughout *See Under: Love*, it is, literally, the novel's last word. I shall have occasion below to engage the historicist reading of *See Under: Love*, which aims at establishing its subtextual link with Grossman's more popular works critical of Israel's politics vis-à-vis the Palestinians in the West Bank and Gaza.[3] But for now, I would like simply to note that Grossman's dramatization of the motives for war *do* unearth some striking, transhistorical parallels. Momik's war against the Nazi beast, for instance, is in its basic outline, formally homologous with the Nazi war against the Jews: the Beast/Other/Jew has stolen something vital from me, the Beast/Other/Jew *really* does in fact exist, the Beast/Other/Jew must be eliminated. This sort of war always meets a crucial need for the subject who declares it. In Momik's case, it eases a central tension that pits his birth in Israel as a putative "new man" against his inheritance of a particular cultural and familial history that ties him to the Eastern European experiences of his parents, grandfather, and neighbors.

Those readings that have noted the proximity of the year of Anshel's arrival (1959) to the capture and Jerusalem trial of Adolf Eichmann (1960), and which situate Grossman's novel in the context of the confrontation between Zionism and the Holocaust, are no doubt pertinent here.[4] For the "new men" of Zionism, the capture and trial of Eichmann proved that the older, diasporic exemplars of Judaism could not be eclipsed so summarily. Indeed, we might say here that Momik's difficulty pertains to the (arbitrary) signifiers disseminated by Zionism in Israel believed to name and establish a Jewish-Israeli identity fundamentally different from the one associated with Judaism in Europe. Offered up for the subject's identification, Grossman shows how such nation-making identifications were always already marked by a kind of gap. In this light, Momik's incarnation of the Nazi Beast for the purpose of domesticating it can be read as an allegory for Zionism's confrontation with the return of the repressed, with the history and practice of Eastern European Jewry that had been largely rejected and denied in Israel's formation and emergence as a state. When, with Eichmann, the repressed returns, the Zionist confrontation with the Holocaust aimed by and large to conceive the gap as a removable obstacle capable of being overcome, or subsumed within a larger collective, affirmative narrative. Yael Feldman has referred to this as the triumph of ideology over psychology.[5] What the successful incarnation of the Nazi Beast would mean to Momik involves precisely a convergence of the individual and the social, of personal knowledge and national myth: in the presence of a verifiable Beast, Momik would be able to write the story of the Holocaust without feeling that he has not really written it, and he would be able to identify with a triumphantly Zionist, Israeli identity without feeling that something has happened that gives the lie to that identity. In any case, for Momik, the "curse" of the Nazi Beast becomes the force that unites a multiplicity of disparate miseries and inscrutable signs, lending a singular purpose to his existence:

> The really big prophecies are for Momik alone, there's no one he can tell them to, like spying on his parents, and all the spy work to put together the vanished land of Over There like a jigsaw puzzle, there's still a lot of work left on this, and he's the only one in the whole wide world who can do it, because who else can save Mama and Papa from their fears and silences and krechtzes, and the curse, which was even worse after Grandfather Anshel turned up. (18)

The Beast, we might say in light of the discussion of the anti-Semitic construction of the Jew in chapter 1, is Momik's Master-Signifier, his *point de capiton:* it is his way of applying a proper name to a number of heterogeneous elements for the purpose of consolidating them.[6]

The stories Momik invents, his earliest efforts to make history exist by fitting it into forms that might make sense of it, are attempts to make the stupidity of this proper name give way to a literal meaning it is imagined to contain. About his father's nightmares, for example, Momik explains:

> The screaming is certainly weird, but what do we have logic and brains and Bella for? When we examine the screaming in the light of day, it turns out to be quite simple. It was like this, there was a war in that kingdom, and Papa was the Emperor and also the chief warrior, a commando fighter. One of his friends (his lieutenant?) was called Sondar. (28)

In the grim humor of Momik's attempt to mythologize the *sonderkommando*, what is clear is that the heroic forms of popular adventure stories so abundantly at the boy's disposal—forms that tell of kings and armies and magical escapes, spies and detectives and secret signals, time travel and Snow Queens and "submarines like in Jules Verne" (47)—these forms cannot comprehend the events of Over There. The defining feature of paranoia, however, is its refusal to be discouraged by particular failures at comprehension, by *particularity as the site of comprehension's failure*. Indeed, the phenomena these forms cannot accommodate, far from destroying Momik's entire conceptual approach, end up invigorating it. In true paranoid fashion, Momik merely attributes consecutive failures to external causes—that is, to the mysterious power already believed to inhere in the object of his paranoia—and resolves on more extreme measures. Thus, Momik's inability to feel content with the versions of history in which everything acquires a benign simplicity. Momik's central recognition—"So much was missing. The main thing was missing, he felt sometimes" (29)—reveals the impossibility of his project even as it functions as that project's driving force. Momik's other efforts, culminating in the attempt to "raise" the Nazi Beast in his cellar, perform a similar function, and in the process exemplify the way the Holocaust itself can be made to deliver a solution to the very anxiety that occasioned it. His "commando invasions" into the heart of Grandfather Anshel's story (among other things, he reads aloud various combinations of the numbers tattooed on his grandfather's arm), his acting out of the ritual from the Sholem Aleichem tale, his systematic means for naming and comprehending infamous phrases of history ("I killed your Jew": two fists, four fingers; "like sheep to the slaughter": five fists, no fingers)—all are part of an effort to achieve, within the universe of meaning, formal relations with that which is radically Other. For Momik, this Other is rightly taken as the ultimate locus of causality: it has taken from him a brother, and has given him a hundred names;[7] it makes his father scream in his sleep, and forces him to write everything down in his spy notebooks. Momik's mistake, however, is to think of history in purely historical terms, to think the unique and horrible particularity of Nazism as surviving the passage from Event to History in an entirely intelligible form.

That this horrible particularity does not in fact survive the passage plagues every one of Momik's attempts to have his narratives of the Holocaust correspond to its imagined essence and to have his narratives of himself correspond to the real of his identity. His father as Emperor-in-exile, Grandfather Anshel as the only fighter who would not surrender, himself as spy/detective/Theodor Herzl–like savior—all are part both of

the objectifying mind's obsession to make something heroic, or sentimental, or sublime, of the nothingness of history and of self, and of another
inadequate fictional paradigm. Nothingness is precisely what the romantic
imagination of the nine-year-old boy sets out to transform; this is its gift:

> Momik has this gift, a gift for all kinds of languages no one under-
> stands, he can even understand the silent people who say maybe
> three words in their whole life talk, like Ginzburg who says, Who
> am I who am I, and Momik understands that he's lost his memory
> and that now he's looking for who he is everywhere even in the
> garbage cans . . . oh yes, Momik can translate just about anything.
> He is the translator of the royal realm. He can even translate noth-
> ing into something. Okay, that's because he knows there's no such
> thing as nothing, there must be something, nu. (35)

Aimed at keeping the signifying chain in motion, Momik's task as translator is perpetual narrativization: no image or phase can arrest the linking
of words together into a story. It is not surprising that Ginzburg is here
invoked to demonstrate Momik's feats of translation, for Ginzburg's
identity-question is the one at the heart of the ontological deadlock that
ultimately characterizes the subjectivity of the witness: Who am I for this
history? for the lost Neumans whose names I listen for on the radio? for
my trapped parents and my trapped grandfather and my trapped friends
on the park bench? Who am I, in other words, *for* those who experienced
the Holocaust? I want to return more fully to Ginzburg's function in the
novel below, but his appearance here as a figure whose idiotically repeated
identity-question, for which Momik must furnish a context, allows
Grossman to isolate the centrality of the witness' ontological relation to
subjectivity in the impulse to tell more and more stories about history.
Here, I think Grossman shows how this impulse is often acted on in
order to postpone that moment in which the subject *is* nothing but this
question. By having Ginzburg repeat the identity-question incessantly,
the question loses its meaningfully, interrogative status. That is to say, it
no longer can be said to call for a response. In this way, it places front
and center the witness's ontological relationship to subjectivity in which
we experience an abyssal uncertainty as to who we are.[8]

The critical, ethical consequence of this abyssal uncertainty has to
do with the warrant for redress lost therein. If bearing witness to history
leads us to experience the removal of the identity-question from the
ordinary call-and-response circuits of speech, then we are already beyond
the fascist trap, since the question in this form is the question fascist
ideology works to forestall at all costs.[9] In short, when memorializing

history means encountering the word or image for which there is no story, the implications of this encounter for the "story" that is the witness's subjectivity are significant. These implications are at the heart of Grossman's poignant parody of the romantic imagination's fundamental project—its ability to "discover" and thereby symbolize the desire of the Other by way of the keener sensibilities of the poetic vocation. The terms of this vocation dictate that there can be "no such thing as nothing," that even the most recalcitrant cipher of nothingness ultimately has a story to confess and that the best poet-visionary-translator is ultimately only the most receptive. Today, we tend to credit romanticism for at least acknowledging, even if only partially, the projections involved in the discovery of the object world's truths (recall here Wordsworth's remarks, in "Tinturn Abbey," apropos the poet's eye and ear in nature—"both what they half create/and what perceive").[10] And yet romanticism remains within the orbit of something *already there* that the poet merely receives. This is certainly the case with Momik. In his particular encounters with the bearers of alterity, the explanations Momik finds there are not understood as his own, sometimes desperate, concoctions or translations but rather as already and actually there in the object. Momik's "gift" depends on precisely this illusion, for it implies that he has only "found" the language in which the genuine object/other answers, and not created this answer in the first place. The very reference to his activity as translation implies the actual preexistence of the original. As poet-visionary-translator, he believes himself to have discovered in the royal realm of the object a meaning and an order—that is, a sensible *something*—that has only the appearance of nothingness, a something that has either duped those around him, or sworn them to secrecy (if they know the languages Momik does, they certainly are not letting on; he thinks they have perhaps taken some sort of oath).

It is because these stories fail, because the "answer of the real" is really an instance of the subject's own positing, that Bella's accidental mention of the Nazi Beast captivates Momik in the way that it does. The existence of an actual Beast is for Momik "the biggest clue of all" (30), because it gives him a way holding out the literal possibility of incarnating the force he imagines as the possessor of history. To establish a genuine historical relation with this force would be, as it was in his attempts at storytelling, to establish a genuine relation with the real of his own Jewish identity. As Grossman demonstrates again and again, these projects are inseparable for the subject engaged in them; what the boy, in his struggle, wants from history is something more than history can give him: an identity unsullied by inconsistency and lack. Momik's desire is to know the traumatic particular(s) of history and of his own desire—that unsymbolizable surplus which, once and for all, would make Momik a "real" Jew, and not a boy plagued by the feeling that he has merely been acting the part. Were the Beast actually to appear in the cellar as a creature of consciousness, Momik would not just be able to authenticate the "curse" that has frozen everyone he knows from "Over There" into the equivalent of tiny glass animals (his analogy), it would also authenticate both his status as "Jude grandson" and his investiture as storyteller. This authentication relies on the gaze of the (actual) Beast.

It should thus not surprise that after Momik's failed attempts at befriending the Beast—to "tame it and make it good, and persuade it to change its ways and stop torturing people" (30)—the "raising" of it depends more and more on the ability to "raise" the genuine Jew in the process. If the Nazi Beast, as the nine-year-old boy believes, is an essence, so too is the "real" Jew he believes is required to draw it out. Momik's attempt to produce a Jew "real" enough in order to get the Beast to show its face is part and parcel of the paranoid solution to an ontological difficulty: the desire to reproduce the Nazi Beast is not merely the desire to gain full knowledge, it is the desire for that ultimate object supposed to confer on him full being. It is this that explains Momik's determined research—"Momik worked like a combination scientist and detective" (68)—into various traits believed to inhere in the "real" Jew. Copying pictures from library books and making notes from his own encounters with Jews, Momik hopes to detect the substantial meaning behind what only appear to be contingent features—for example, "how a Jew looks at a soldier, how a Jew looks when he's frightened, how he looks in a convoy, [. . .] how a Jew krechtzes, how he screams out in his sleep, and how he chews on a drumstick, etc." (68). When the taking on of these traits fails, when his repeated parading in front of the Beast fails to elicit a response from it, Momik does not recognize the ontological coordinates of his project's empiricist assumptions, clinging instead to his belief in the existence of a Genuine Jew qua set of positive, substantial features. Here, we might do well to recall Hegel's categorical insistence that the "spirit" of a people (in this case, the Jews) can never be seen in its immediacy, and that performances of the body are not *expressions* of a prior, intelligible, meaningful, signifying reality.[11] Interpreting the Beast's recalcitrance as having to do with his own faulty impersonation, Momik concludes that the Beast "could probably tell the difference between a real Jew and Momik suddenly trying to act like a Jew" (74). Thus, Grandfather Anshel is enlisted for a trip to the cellar:

Wave your hands too! And Grandfather waved his hands the way he does, and Momik watched him closely to make sure he was really trying hard and doing what he was supposed to do, and he glanced at the cages and the suitcases and the torn mattresses and silently cried, Jude! Jude! Here, I brought you the kind you like, a real Jude that looks like a Jude and talks like a Jude, and smells like a Jude, a Jude grandfather with a Jude grandson, so come on out . . . (80)

In his attempt here to elicit a performance of authentic Jewishnesss, I think we can see the way the Holocaust can work to ratify a physiological or characterological link between Jews. For Momik, Jewishness is not already a weapon of the aggressor, but rather something that can be *won back* from the aggressor. In short, the recovery of the real spirit of the Jews *awaits a war*.

Grandfather's Anshel's failure to elicit the Beast only intensifies Momik's sacrifice in the service of his war. Momik sings songs in Hebrew and Yiddish, he recites prayers from his father's High-Holiday prayer book, he even takes to covering the far wall of the cellar with pages torn from his copy of *The Diary of Anne Frank*. When the Beast still refuses to come out, Momik brings down all of the neighborhood survivors from Over There and commands them to "be so Jewish it [the Beast] won't know what to do with itself" (83). In this instant, Momik is brought face to face with the point of the collapse of his paranoia. What Grossman makes clear is that the miracle promised by his interpretive model is not going to come: "He raised his arms and begged, Enough, stop it now, he raised his arms as if to surrender, like a boy he saw in a picture once, but a terrible scream escaped him, the cry of a Beast" (84). This cry renders obvious the object lesson at play here. In trying so hard to elicit the source of evil and violence, Momik becomes the thing he is out to defeat; in the attempt to bear witness to the victims of the Holocaust, Momik ends up victimizing the survivors in his midst. In the absence of the Beast, Momik remains angry at himself for not having been more precise, more scientific in his approach. But there is an alternate recognition looming beneath the text at this point that telegraphs the recognition Grossman's novel grants his hero in the book's final section: the most ethical of sacrifices are those made for that which cannot be symbolized, for that which, in a given universe of meaning, appears as *nothing*.[12] If the scream signifies that Momik has, in a sense, *become* the beast he is trying to defeat, his subsequent reaction misses this truth in a fundamental way. Faced by stories that defy conventional narrative form— "the kind of story you always forget and have to keep going back to the beginning to remember" (84)—Momik ends up regarding storytelling as a sign of the survivor's (and by extension, the diaspora Jew's) disgusting fecklessness:

Shut up already, enough already, we're sick of your story, you can't kill the Nazikaput with a story, you have to beat him to death, and for that you need a naval commando unit to break into the room and take him hostage till Hitler comes to save him, and then they catch Hitler and kill him too with terrible tortures, they yank his nails out one by one . . . and you gouge his eyes out without an anaesthetic, and then you bomb Germany and wipe out every trace of Over There, every good trace and every evil trace, and you liberate the six million with a spy mission the likes of which have never been seen, you turn back the clock like a time machine, sure, there must be someone at the Weizmann Institute who could invent something like that, and they'll bring the whole world down on their knees, pshakrev, and spit in their faces, and we'll fly overhead in our jet planes, war is what we need, screamed Momik. (85)

In this breathtaking passage, Momik essentially posits aggression as the solution, before and after the letter, to the problem of bearing witness to trauma. In the choice between stories and war, Momik casts his lot with the latter, believing that the war has not really ended and that liberation or victory is still possible. For Grossman, the implications of a memorial method that ends up arriving at war warrant serious consideration.

Redoubling Paranoia

I have been arguing that the larger point behind Momik's poignant and desperate attempts to heal or free those he loves is that history ends up surviving as paranoia. Moreover, this paranoia is of a piece with violence and the vicious circle of hatred and suspicion. Before moving directly to the "Bruno" section of the novel, I would like to clarify this point by tracing a couple of threads that cut across the novel's four sections. I will begin by returning to the figure of Ginzburg, and specifically, by comparing Momik's encounter with the Beast to Grossman's depiction of the encounter between Ginzburg and the SS interrogator, Fritz Orf.

The "aesthetic pleasure" Orf gets from using his tools of torture is tied directly to the objective certainty he thinks he is getting from the screams of his victims. Orf views his work as Art because it has all the properties of Aristotelian theater (e.g., "fixed rules of interrogation," "predictable stages and moments of tension and climax," catharsis, etc.). Strictly speaking, the enjoyment he gets from his work lies not in the actual suffering of his subjects (he himself says as much), but from the formal enjoyment of his trade, its ability to eliminate difference. His affinity for electrodes attached to the sex organ and nipples of his prisoners suggests as much: "Torture made everyone alike in the end" (319). In Grossman's diagnosis of Nazi torture and degradation, what Orf imagines he has gained access to is the Other's calcified essence—"the truth about the people behind the posters," the "real" Jew. The Jew, for Orf and for Nazi ideology more generally, is the body conceived as the material expression of the Other's alterity, an expression capable of being *known*. When Ginzburg answers Orf's first question, "Who are you?" with the question, "Who am I,?" Orf can barely contain his pleasure now that someone else, too, is interested in finally knowing who the Jew is. That the extermination of the Jews only intensified for the Nazis the unknowable quality of the Jew—hadn't they been instructed again and again who the Jew was?—uncovers the extent to which murder in the clutch of paranoia will never be enough to eliminate the feeling of instability that drives one to murder. Even in victory, the Nazi would search for the "last Jew" after his or her death.[13] As Ginzburg's question survives the worst imaginable torture, the split between German and Jew (and the split within Orf himself) is revealed as irreducible. Here, the real reasons underlying Orf's behavior are exposed—the paranoid construction rather than Sartrean nausea: "He [Orf] lifted Ginzburg up and supported him till he could stand on his feet. This took quite a while, and the touch of the Jew was almost unbearable" (322). The body beneath all of its dissembling is but a lifeless, dead thing. What is unbearable is the fact that no answer to Orf's incessant question is forthcoming. Ginzburg's answer—repeated idiotically, over and over again—*is* in fact that answer, insofar as its mechanical repetition keeps the question a question.

The link between Momik and Orf is not unintentional. But there is a middle term: Momik's parents. Their silence (i.e., their trying-so-hard-not-to-talk-about-it) is not just the result of fear and horror in the face of a particular experience of the Holocaust—they have lost a son, for example—but with the fear and horror that they no more "possess" history than the hedgehogs and ravens and cats and suitcases their son has been collecting in their cellar. One way they have of owning history lies in their obsession with the catastrophic. This is clear not just in the Mother's response to Anshel's arrival ("Mama said . . . what happened? And the fat driver smiled a big fat smile and said, Nothing happened, why are always people expecting something happened" [5]), but also in their suspicion of Momik's potential playmate (Alex Tochner), and in their furtive scouring of the house when they fear Momik has contracted polio. Related to this obsession is the silence they maintain about their past, about, in Momik's mother's words, "things that are no more and shouldn't be mentioned" (8). Only by keeping their history under lock and key are they sure that it is there. Their enjoyment lies in fortress building and in fortress maintenance—that is, the guarded life—and this inevitably means that they are not so much guarding the Holocaust as they are their own status as guardians. When Momik literally enacts one of his father's child-hood memories of the *shtetl*—lighting his way home with a radish and a candlestick—his father reacts by swatting the candle to the ground and saying, "Enough of this nonsense" (63). By refusing to engage the trauma of their past, however, they replicate the paranoia responsible for that trauma in the first place. As I have been arguing, this is, for Grossman, how the Holocaust continues, how history is transmitted. For Momik's parents, the Nazism and catastrophe *is* the secret truth of alterity, which is exactly what they communicate to their son instead of something about the possibility of love.

To his own son, Momik communicates something similar. His rela-tions with Yariv are the exact inverse of his parents' relations with him in terms of the particular historical contents he transmits. On the level of form, however, they are identical. If for Momik's parents, Fate was some-thing vague and terrible and not to be mentioned, for Momik, there is no limit to its actual manifestations, no scene irrelevant to the preparation for its arrival. Foregrounding the violence and cruelty of the world, Momik trains his son for war in order to certify that there is a method to history's madness. The traumatization of his son on the playground is but part of a fantasy of wholeness in which every eventuality might be accounted for. (With his son wailing at the top of the slide, Momik wonders how, if they were caught in a bunker with soldiers looking for them, he would have to shut him up.) If Yariv is to know anything, Momik imagines, he is to know the truth lurking in the deepest recesses of history. This is a truth that ultimately crowds out any notion that history (because contingent) is radically open, and that such openness means that human affairs (both personal and sociopolitical) can and may take other forms—such as kind-ness or love. If violence is, indeed, the Law of history and social relations, then violence need be the only thing that structures Momik's relations with his son.

The embrace of this substantial Law performs a sense-giving func-tion for a number of nonsensical factors. For one thing, it retroactively underwrites a way of coping with the "obedient" march of the victims to their death—that is, in Momik's view, the so-called sheep led to slaughter were simply ignorant of the Law, and for Momik, this is not a mistake that is going to be made twice. For another thing, it guarantees that which is impossible to guarantee: Momik's "protection" of his son, the complete elimination of fear in the core of Yariv's being (which is really a projection of Momik's own fear), as if the effects of (or participation in) an eruption of historical trauma were really only a matter of preparation.

Momik is constantly "getting ready," so that when (he says) the convoys come again, "unlike the rest of you, I will not be shocked or humiliated. And I won't suffer the pains of separation" (151). This is, of course, a goal never reached—or reached only at the cost of all attachment. Only the individual who attaches himself to no one elides the possibility of this pain. The Law thus becomes a way of avoiding the contingency of attachment (the contingency of Law itself), the feeling Momik gets, for instance, at the sight of his son sleeping peacefully:

> Evening. Yariv is asleep already and I go in to look at him. He's lying on his back. I feel shivers up my spine. "You feel it, too?" asks Ruth quietly, and her face fills the room with pleasure. I want to say something nice to her, to make her happy, to show her that I really do care for him, but my throat contracts. "It's a good thing he can sleep through all the noise," I say finally. "He may have to sleep with tanks passing in the streets someday. Or on his feet, trudging through the snow. Or in a crowded cell block, maybe, with ten more like him to a bunk. Or on a—" "Stop it," says Ruth, and leaves the room. (149)

If Momik's feeling of tenderness places him on shaky ground, he must for this reason refer this feeling to what, in the wake of his investigations into the Holocaust, is *most certain:* a conception of human history and existence as nothing but an endless cycle of violence and killing, in Momik's words, "a death machine" (151). This is, I think, probably one of the places at which Grossman is referencing the contemporary political situation in Israel. By this I mean that Momik's view of the world here is more or less an exaggerated version of the one held by Jews in Israel and in the Diaspora that sees the hostility of Arab nation-states and the Palestinians toward Israel as simply an instance of the perennial hatred of Jews. In Ruth's diagnosis of Momik's behavior, however, Grossman suggests that such a view is part of a politics that cannot again open itself up to the risk of encountering alterity after Nazism. Ruth says to Momik, "it isn't places you fear, it's people" (150).[14] And what he fears about them is what he cannot know: what they want from him, their spirit, their desire. As I have said, throughout the novel, this question dominates Momik's actions: What does the Beast want of me? What do my parents want from me? What does Schulz/the Sea want of me? What does Wasserman want of me? And all of his attempts to answer this question are attempts to discover a consistency, a self-identity, to his desire. If it is the case that Momik takes on fascist characteristics, it should be plain that this involves much more than simple "identification with the aggressor." Grossman indicates, on the contrary, that the real point of "identification with the aggressor" lies *beyond* the aggressor: it is an identification with the umediated relation the aggressor is imagined to have apropos his desire.

Orf's torture, Momik's parents' silence, Momik's raising of the Nazi Beast, Momik's own parenting—all are part of the duplication and redu-plication of paranoia that Grossman sees as perpetuating the violence of history. The intent of *See Under: Love*, of course, is to present these paranoid encounters for the purpose of arresting the cycle that oversees their reproduction: so that the Holocaust does *not* survive in the form of thinking responsible for it in the first place, so that History does *not* become the perpetuation of the fascist fantasy, so that one does *not* begin to think and act as if there really were a meaningfully calcified essence to the alterity of the other and of oneself. Momik's later realization vis-à-vis the Little Nazi In You (LNIY) makes this clear:

> the real problem, the disease, lies much deeper. And it may be incurable. And it could be that we are all no more than germs. And when here and there the LNIY is signaled, could it be that this is only a sly and cowardly act of blackmail, the goal of which is to reach a general consensus about the things it is convenient and easy to agree upon? That is, to fight whatever can be fought? (292)

I said earlier that I would return to the subtextual link between *See Under: Love* and Grossman's status as a critic of Israel, and this is the point at which to do so. Here, it is tempting to see Grossman participating in the equation of Nazism and Zionism first made most notably in the context of Israel's war with Lebanon in the early 1980s. Momik's attempt to write Wasserman's story is, presumably, being carried out in the wake of this war. On this reading, despite claiming that analogies linking bestial cru-elty, racism, or murderousness to Nazism are wrong (that they "put vigi-lance to sleep, and pave the way for the next disaster" [292]), Grossman nonetheless does find a universal source for human violence and evil. From this standpoint, Nazism is no longer a unique historically specific phenomenon, but is instead an exemplification, a symptom of a deeper disease "at the root of our very nature" (296). And to the list of this disease's *symptoms*, one might presumably add Israel's policies toward, and treatment of, its "enemies."

Though it courts the charge of further polarizing political discourse on this question, Grossman's strategy here is entirely consonant with my own. Grossman is not saying that Zionists *are* Nazis: indeed, for him, this very designation remains at the level of history, and thus paves the way for the next disaster. What he is suggesting is that history and language themselves are, in a sense, symptoms, and that the mistake of any political regime rests in giving this structural disease "a name, an army, workers, temples, and sacrificial victims" (296). In short, the ethics of an encounter with this structural disease lies in *finding no one there to fight*. This is the lesson of the White Room of *See Under: Love* where the missing body of history cannot be recovered. Grossman's refusal of objective omniscience— his "postmodern" disavowal of the seamless relation between writer and character—pertains to this body. This refusal is decisive for the novel's radical insight because in the narrative breakdowns that ensue, the fantasmatic quality of this body facilitates a kind of return of the repressed: the anguishing immediacy of the writing scene itself is exposed as that which artistic Form, and the finished work of art it unveils, too often attempts to solve. Like a number of postmodern thinkers and writers, Grossman repudiates the point of view of God. But this does not, as in the case of D. M. Thomas, lead to a perspectival multiplicity that will admit, as one of a plurality of possible realities, the "success" of a paranoid pursuit—the reacquisition of the lost, ultimate object. On the contrary, for Grossman, the reasons for rejecting the point of view of God apply as well to any particular, "subjective" perspective. The particular is not possible within symbolization, whether or not that symbolization comes within a framework of omniscience or a framework of multiple points of view. This is why even within the multiple stories of Grossman's novel breakdowns occur, why an investment in character and plot is consistently interrupted.

Symbolization is not for Grossman the ultimate province of memory. Indeed, in *See Under: Love* the White Room is the place where one moves from historical to structural trauma—that is, where consciousness arrests its flow of thoughts in order to grasp that very flow itself, and where one is confronted by the realization that the task of art can no longer be to unearth the missing bodies of history. Abandoning the methodological assumptions of traditional historiography, Grossman—in the spirit of liberal pragmatism—is less interested in what is true and what is false. But rather than focus on better mechanisms for coping with reality, Grossman understands that such mechanisms presuppose the consistency of the social order in which the objects of history/reality have meaning. To aim at coping is already to evade the *real* matter of history. Momik's painful realization vis-à-vis the White Room in the next to last break of the "Wasserman" section makes this clear:

In the White Room there are efficient ways to investigate such questions: if something is written down on paper, and must be weighed in order to ascertain whether it is true or not, then a certain person is clearly on the wrong track. But if the procedure is such that it is enough for a certain pair of eyes to close in order for consciousness to return and for a clear reflection to appear on the mirror of the inner eye without recourse to rational intervention— herein lies the fulfillment of the capricious, physio-literary demands of the White Room. (287–288)

The White Room denies recourse to rational intervention, for such intervention carries with it rules of knowledge all its own. But as "home" to that which is radically Other, the White Room contravenes such rules; there, rational consciousness is eclipsed. In the White Room one does not remain entirely with the historical trauma and its memorialization, but instead, risks the danger *for one's own subjectivity* in the act of witnessing. "To enter the White Room," Momik says during an announced postponement of the novel, "a certain amount of forgetfulness and sacrifice is required of one. But again and again the mysterious warning voices were heard: Get out of here. The White Room is too dangerous for you" (278). In the White Room no language is spoken; the word that precedes it is for this reason "BEWARE." The White Room is where being exists prior to its navigation into existence, where the Other does not (yet) exist, where time awaits its primordial birth.

Bruno Schulz and the Lure of Messianic Visions

Momik's imaginative recovery of Bruno Schulz attempts to discover the path to precisely this origin. At this point, however, it is an origin where a language might still be spoken. Schulz's writings for this reason form the perfect companion for Grossman's novel: they explore the possibility of grasping the real of time itself as it pertains to the achievement of full identity. Father's "experiments" in Schulz's *The Street of Crocodiles* and Joseph's paintings in "The Age of Genius" (in Schulz's *Sanitorium Under the Sign of the Hourglass*) both attempt to solve the breach between the life one imagines and the life one actually lives. The similarity of such figures to Momik are clear: the Father, figured as king who has lost his throne, and Joseph, the artist who "should have been born earlier" are both the dispossessed, locked in the prison-house of human time, divided from an Over There believed to have the power to reverse such dispossession. For having created these characters, Schulz is a potential key to Momik's understanding his "unlived life Over There," because both of Schulz's protagonists attempt to recover lost origins: both attempt a regression back to the point of a primary trauma, or at least one they imagine as primary. This is the motive driving Father's laboratory work on Uncle

Edward in "The Comet"—the final story of *The Street of Crocodiles* in which the latter is "reduced" to his core in order to escape the happy/ unhappy dichotomy; and it underwrites as well Joseph's discovery of "illegal and suspect" branches of time that give us access to "illegal" events.

The suggestion of criminality here is apt because what Schulz seems to be driving at is an artistic act, or an artistic age, that would contravene the everyday sense of time and its control of historical events—driving instead toward the "real" or "messianic" time of those very events. Indeed, Schulz's narrator, in the opening paragraphs of "The Age of Genius," seems to paraphrase Benjamin's "Theses on the Philosophy of History":

> Ordinary facts are arranged within time, strung along its length as on a thread. There they have their antecedents, and their consequences, which crowd tightly together and press hard one upon the other without any pause. This has its importance for any narrative, of which continuity and successiveness are the soul.
>
> Yet what is to be done with events that have no place of their own in time; events that have occurred too late, after the whole of time has been distributed, divided, and allotted; events that have been left in the cold, unregistered, hanging in the air, homeless, and errant?
>
> Could it be that time is too narrow for all events?[15]

It was Benjamin, of course, who said that history's sequence of events could not be charted like the beads of a rosary, that history would have to be "brushed against the grain" in order to create a space for the most significant of historical events. The appeal of this enterprise for Momik should not be difficult to detect. Schulz's recognition that the ordinary arrangement of facts is utterly inadequate in the attempt to know what is real is the same recognition that motivates Momik's acts of recovery in each of the novel's first three sections. Moreover, when this recognition is grasped on the level of artistic form itself, the result is an Encyclopedia—a form that repudiates the narrative "thread" by foregrounding the empty space between entries (a space that is not-time) in order to prevent antecedents and consequences from pressing on one another without pause.

Because of these very regressions, however, Bruno is for Momik more than just an "invitation"; he is also a "warning." This is so because Schulz's "Age of Genius," and his lost manuscript *The Messiah*, do not just promise a world disabused of history, a world in which time might be redistributed so that artists need not traffic in "illegal branches" of it; they demand that one begin to ask the question of "I" that is separate from any essential collectivity. The "Age of Genius" and *The Messiah*, in other words, invite Momik to imagine his overcoming of historical situatedness by becoming truly individual: but for a man encouraged by his parents never to say "I" too freely, this is also an invitation that frightens.

This twofold function of Schulz is for Grossman both his value and his limitation. First, Bruno is one who might teach Momik how to constitute himself as subject in a manner different from the paranoid construction of the real Jew that led him to war in the novel's first section. Schulz's own life is evidence of this. As the gifted pupil without friends, the "hypersensitive child, struggling against foes [one] can't begin to imagine" (93), as the inventor of his own language and private mythology (these are just a few of the parallels to Momik's life), Schulz is the artist who in his separation from society testifies to a way of thinking and being that makes contact with that dimension of our experience that is intimate with irretrievable, irreversible loss. Schulz's self-understanding explodes any contract between the artist and the social order; he is, as Momik says of Munch, the artist who "turns traitor," the one whose "dangerous passions" must be—like "The Scream" in the art gallery at Danzig—cordoned off with a red sign warning, "DO NOT TOUCH." ("Idiots," Momik says. "They should have protected the public from the painting, not the other way around" [90].) This is, as Momik recognizes, one way a society has of "cordoning" off the work of art. The work is "cherished": "the scream bursts rudely into your midst [. . .] and they loved Munch all the more!" (92). In this way, the work of the genuine artist is deprived of its disruptive, "illegal" force: what should sunder community in fact works to consolidate it. In the guise of altruism, the artist is one who is always being "looked after"; from this gaze, Schulz too lies in danger:

> Bruno is still running. . . . Look after him, for his sake, and for ours. Don't let his dangerous passions tempt him to forgo your trusty, threadbare words. Do not allow him to write in body code, to a rhythm unmeasured by clock or metronome. And for heaven's sake, don't let him talk to himself in that unintelligble language. (92)

In Schulz is the artistic consciousness that refuses the conventional forms of mediating one's trauma, the jovial clap on the shoulder at a party and the advice to "come out of your isolation and feel 'the pulse of humanity,' the 'sorrows of life,' don't be such a hermit" (138). Schulz was, we learn, the recipient of such counsel, but his manner of mediating trauma was a form that sought not to mitigate it—the development of a rhythm and a parallel time in order to express the trauma of the contingency of our relations with history. The trauma of the particular is thus approached by Schulz in a kind of "rhythm," in the creation of an "unreal" time:

Have you ever heard of parallel streams of time within a two-track time? Yes, there are such branches of time, somewhat illegal and suspect, but when, like us, one is burdened with contraband of supernumerary events that cannot be registered, one cannot be too fussy. Let us try to find at some point of history such a branch line, a blind track onto which to shunt these illegal events.[16]

For Schulz, Munch's painting is such a branch line; for Momik, it is Munch's painting and Schulz's response to it. In this way, Momik joins the group of "weak links"—those who touch this branch line, and whose sense of loss only grows deeper.

This engagement with the "branch line" is thus a sign of Schulz's refusal to disburden himself of artistic insight and despair. His kiss of Munch's painting for mouth-to-mouth resuscitation equates this insight and despair with breathing itself. Schulz's despair, the Sea tells us, is not the commonplace despair that can be solved by insanity or by fellowship. Bruno does "cheat" and pretend at the latter—at parties and in lectures and letters—but his despair is much more individual and existential. Bruno's despair stems from the otherness that exists within himself, and that cannot be mastered:

> the fear of the abyss between one minute and the next, and of what he would discover on the page after it was touched by his magical magnetic pen, which sucked up the magma of ancient truth, that rose steadily upward through layers of caution and self-defense— and then he would stop and scream in fear, because what he had written seemed to come from somebody else. (137)

At this stage, the content of Schulz's prose is not enough to ensure self-possession because that content is still separated from the particular that is incommensurable with words and thinking. This is why Schulz says that his books are merely the scaffolding that surrounds a "creature un-known." As artist, Bruno recognizes that the life he lives has not really been his: "People lived by robbing each other's lives. Before the war, they had at least shown some tact, taking care not to inflict more pain than necessary, with a sense of humor, in fact, but nowadays nobody even made an effort to pretend" (94). That this situation has come to consti-tute normal, everyday life is for the artist part of a horrible fathomless boredom that the work of art must violently uproot. Those who would "cherish thine artist" only serve to perpetuate this boredom, and for this reason, community becomes one of the things the artist fears most. As Momik says after the imagined scene of Bruno kissing Munch's painting,

"Bruno fears neither the SS nor the Polish police, his latest persecutors. He fears only the great searchlights that converge inside and chastise him to be-like-everybody-else, to live the grey life he can never redeem with a touch of his pen" (90). In his utter loneliness, Bruno represents the kind of individual life Momik can only imagine vicariously—with a combination of envy and pride: "Even the dual was too plural for you, and the truly crucial things had to be said in the singular. So you became a salmon" (165).

The actual historical murder of Bruno Schulz in the Drohobycz ghetto in 1942 here takes on significance, because the Holocaust threatens to envelope Schulz in the fate he most feared: mass life and mass death. This is one of the dimensions of the Holocaust that has so traumatized Momik in his relation to the Event. How is one to be individual in the face of the phenomenon that robs one of individuality? This question is the one driving Momik's reasons for trying to recover Schulz:

> the horrible thing for me about the Holocaust is the way every trace of individuality was obliterated. A person's uniqueness, his thoughts, his past, his characteristics, loves, defects, and secrets—all meant nothing. You were debased to the lowest level of existence. You were nothing but flesh and blood. It drives me mad. That's why I wrote "Bruno." (153)

If it was the Holocaust that obliterated every trace of individuality, it is Schulz who sees the process as beginning earlier—as antecedent to language itself: "He heard the rumbling long before anyone else heard it [. . . .] He guessed everything before it happened" (167). What Schulz has guessed is the "murder" at the core of our existence as creatures of language, an "originary violence" that Derrida calls "the mystical foundation of law." For Derrida, this founding or revolutionary moment of law is an instance of nonlaw—that is, it is a purely performative act without sense that does not have to answer to or before anyone. Far from something to bemoan, this originary act founds the whole of our symbolic world: it founds the differential relation on which language is staked.[17] This is why, as Giorgio Agamben has claimed, we must not conflate "constituting power" with "sovereign power," since such a conflation risks taking a category of ontology as a strictly political concept (and thus bolstering sovereign political power).[18] This is the very conflation, however, that Schulz falls prey to in his attempt to do away with founding violence. For this reason, Schulz too models the paranoid response to the split between the universal, symbolic order of language and the real, traumatic particular. Schulz, we learn, wanted to murder language when he was the object of its "originary violence," because he sees no difference between this structural violence and the historically specific instance of sovereign violence that actually took his life:

> even when Bruno was a little boy he understood this, yes, and he longed not merely for a new world but for a totally new language that would enable him to describe it, because even then, long before he came to me, he guessed [. . . .] Bruno, sensitive as he was, had guessed everything years before it actually happened. And for that reason, perhaps, he had begun to write, to train himself in the new language and the new grammar. He understood humanity and knew; he heard the rumbling long before anyone else heard it. He had always been the weak link. Yes. He knew that a language that will admit a sentence like "I killed your Jew . . . In that case, I will now kill," etc., a language where such verbal constructs do not turn to poison in the speaker's mouth—is not the language of life, human and moral, but a language infiltrated many ages past by evil traitors, with one intention—to kill. (168)

Bruno's mistake lies in seeing the capacity of human speech to admit sentences like "I killed your Jew" as a continuation of the corruption of language rather than as part of a project attempting to eliminate that corruption. In other words, when SS officer Karl Gunther shot Bruno Schulz and then said to the man for whom Schulz worked as a "House Jew," SS officer Felix Landau, "I killed your Jew," he is not merely perpetuating that "originary violence" that separates words from things; on the contrary, he is maintaining the essentiality of the Law currently structuring human relations. Unlike the senselessness of "originary violence"— which by its very senslessness is founding and creative—Gunther's act is retributive and as such conservative: it is violence with a ground.

The lessons here for Momik are many—and risky. To write in body code, and to rhythms unmeasured by clock or metronome, is to begin to engage a place in one's experience with which there can be no compromise. For Momik, this would mean regressing all the way back to the point of the crucial affective recognition and repression:

> I had been deeply immersed in "it" almost from the moment I was born, from the moment I began to despair and relate to people as self-understood, when I stopped trying to invent a special language for them, with new names for every object. And from the moment I stopped being able to say "I" without hearing a tinny echo of "we." And I did something to protect myself from the pain of other

people, from other people. And I refused to maim myself: to become lidless and see all. (296)

It is from this point on that Momik has lived the guarded life. The "thin-
lipped" style of his four books of poetry testify to this fact. And it is also
the obstacle to a more authentic relation to the Holocaust: the inability
to concretize the individual death in the sea of the millions. Bruno's
"escape," in the special sense that Momik gives to that word, is a sign of
Momik's movement toward a conceptualization of the individual's relation
to the Holocaust.

And yet this "escape" is also Bruno's limitation. The very questions
Schulz encourages one to ask are also the questions that might lead one
to believe in the substantiality of the parallel time, to overinvest in the
lost work: to believe that it actually contains the great secret: "I want the
big secret from you and I won't take anything else" (168). Schulz, Momik
imagines, has formulated a "final conclusion, the marrow of our existence" (169). These claims suggest a reapplication of the kind of paranoia
that marked Momik's youth. If in the first section we saw Momik trying
to raise a Monster, we see him here trying to raise a Savior. (It is no
accident here that in the "Bruno" section, Schulz and the Sea are
indissolvable because both function for Momik as repositories of prime-
val/primordial forces. Both are imagined to share a pure relation to language and to time.) The apparent allure of Schulz's envisioned Age of
Genius then would lie in the fact that the very possibility of paranoia has
no place in it, for all Otherness has therein been eliminated. The Age of
Genius would be a world without neurosis because, in it, there is no
dissatisfaction. In this vision of the world, no one would need to mate-
rialize that "excess" or "surplus" that plagues our relations in the world
because there would be no Otherness experienced anxiously. This is clear
first in Schulz's story "The Age of Genius," when on a beautiful, Easter-
time, spring day, Shloma, just released from a winter in prison for "brawls
and follies" (i.e. "wars") finds himself alone with the artist Joseph in
Trinity Square. Alone, Joseph imagines the possibility of the Messiah's
arrival:

We could have divided it between us and renamed it, so open,
unprotected, and unattached was the world. On such a day the
Messiah advances to the edge of the horizon and looks down on the
earth. And when He sees it, white, silent, surrounded by azure and
contemplation, He may lose sight of the boundary of the clouds
that arrange themselves into a passage, and, not knowing what He
is doing, He may descend upon earth. And in its reverie the earth

won't even notice Him, who has descended onto its roads, and people will wake up from their afternoon nap remembering nothing. The whole event will be rubbed out, and everything will be as it has been for centuries, as it was before history began.[19]

In this vision of Schulz's narrator, there will be no more mass life or mass death, no change, only true individuals without the ability to say words like *murder* because the word is contrary to the most basic precepts of life. Schulz, with his Promethean-like Messiah, here perfectly represents the romantic conception and recovery of language: words return to their roots, to their presupposed Original Sense. There is no division between signifier and signified:

> And not only the thought of murder, my Shloma: any thought bearing the bitter traces of decay and putrefaction, destruction and fear. No one will be able to understand such thoughts, just as in the old world you could never really understand a person coming back to life, or the backward flow of time. Because I am speaking to you about a totally different life, about the coming phase of human evolution. (179)

Bruno's words appear here in Momik's rewriting of Schulz's story, and this time Joseph's companion, "Shloma" (i.e., Momik, whose adult name is Shlomo), will not miss the moment of the arrival of the Real Thing. (In Schulz's story in the *Sanitorium* collection, Shloma refuses the role of the New Adam, looking away from Joseph's discovery of "The Original," and instead to the fetish object—the patent leather shoe of Adela, the servant girl.) It is precisely this grasping of the Thing that eliminates time, and returns the world to some realizable primordial unity. Individuals become *truly* individual. Schulz, however, has radically underestimated the cost of this realization, because for the individual to remain in and for language, the moment of the Messiah must be missed. In this recovery, Grossman reveals the Messiah to Momik for what it is: another historicizing of a structural trauma carried so far that it merely recapitulates the paranoia that marks his relations with history. At the end of time and of language, in the return to a prehistoric or preverbal existence, Bruno imagines a world returned to art: "We are all artists, Shlomo, only some of us have forgotten that" (180). And those too afraid to become creators, who cannot understand their call, are disintegrated; they are, for Bruno, "second-hand souls"—those who cannot bear the freedom the Messiah delivers, "the chance to live anew" (177), those who must die because they never really were alive.

The problem with all of this is clear, and it is registered in Momik's reaction. This notion of art begins to strike Momik as barbaric. The "freedom" imagined in this recovery has an immediate appeal ("otherwise we're statues trapped from birth till death" [177]), but the appeal is inseparable from a kind of terror. The Messiah performs nothing if not the task of the dictator, delivering to them control over the real of their beings. Agamben's theorization of the *homo sacer* might be pertinent here, since the subjects of such sovereign power are, at least for Schulz, made to revel in the sacralization of (their) bare life: "The fact of their existence had suddenly become a palpable reality to them [. . .] Life itself was pungent, a provocative pleasure" (178). In Bruno's imagined conception, "creation in the fullest sense of the term" eliminates history. There is no longing for the past, but there's no remembering of it either ("They're forgetting," Bruno beamed. "They're forgetting!" [172].) Only Momik here understands the implications:

> my thoughts turned gloomy. Why, in fact, it had failed already, it had all been a colossal disappointment, and no force in the world could prevent these things from being used for the vilest ends. And I asked myself in a rage, were Roosevelt and Churchill the "good"? Against evil we pit our tanks and planes and submarines, and we set up a different evil. (179)

The point to be made about the Messiah is that if we are in fact to go beyond good and evil, we will have to go beyond symbolization. Any promise of a harmonious community always involves the sort of violence Joseph's scenario contains. The encounter with that which would give us full being must be a missed encounter: in a sense, we must, like Shloma in Schulz's story, *look away* toward a substitute object. The "Original" hinted at in Schulz's story cannot be reproduced—not without suggesting that the paranoiac is in fact correct: that traumatic particulars can be accessed within language, that the human community might again enjoy a pure relation to objects, an unmediated relation between words and things. In the retelling, Schulz is not just one who thinks that there's an other to the Other, he believes he has actually found it. He believes that a world, a reality, can survive the reversal of the fundamental deception practiced by the symbolic order.

Thus, Bruno as embodiment of the artistic subject—"The power of his *ning* was good for a shoal of one only" (161–62)—is an embodiment Momik must incorporate and surpass. The options might be as Bruno describes them—the Messiah or prison—but there is more than one way of living in prison, and it is, besides, still a place in which one actually has a social identity. Messianic time is not the time of the object, no more than a nine-year-old boy can raise the Nazi Beast in his cellar. Time, or storytelling, is too narrow for all events, and must—for us to have time or storytelling at all—remain so. This is precisely why Momik cannot apply Bruno to the story of Baby Kazik in the "Wasserman" section: were he to do so, there would be literally no story. The story exists only insofar as there are obstacles that stand in the way of its completion. Momik voices this realization:

> Bruno doesn't solve a thing for me in the day-to-day. Bruno is a nice dream. But he's more than that too. What he revealed to me was very frightening, and I felt a tremendous resistance to it. I can feel it even now, when I get stuck in the story of Wasserman and the German. I feel I have to defend myself against what Bruno showed me. (153–154)

The way of Bruno Schulz must ultimately be negated for that way appears most horrifying of all: both story and subject risk a suffocating immersion in the oceanic. In losing that which prevents us from gaining true possession of ourselves—from being truly human and artist—we lose our individuality altogether. How does one, then, tell the story without, literally, losing one's self? This is the question that interrupts Momik's attempt to retell Grandfather Anshel's last story.

Beyond Affirmative or Tragic Endings

The new artists (or "partisans") enlisted to help tell Wasserman's story indicate exactly the extent to which full recovery of The Book, The Orginial, *The Messiah*, and so on, is part of a paranoid project. Malkiel Zeidman, the biographer, is perhaps the best demonstrator of this, for what Zeidman makes clear is that the "real" link between book and history would produce a book that cannot be read. An obstacle is a strict necessity for there to be a story at all. Overcoming the barriers between people, Zeidman is the site where the impossible occurs: genuine intersubjective relations. Zeidman is in some ways the Book every book desires to be, within himself able to experience the Other's feeling as the Other feels it:

> I at least can wander freely . . . contain everyone . . . send a wordless greeting at least . . . I am a hostel of sorts, the mute translator of numerous strange languages, because they can say the words, for

instance "misery" and "agony," "hope" and "longing," ah, but only I
know what you mean by them [. . .] only inside me do they acknowledge themselves to each other in all their depth . . . A dictionary I
have become, a person-to-person dictionary, but there is no one to read
me, because I myself am not able to read, I am only the pages. (344)

Zeidman's initial articulation of the positive benefits of his ability—"increasing in however small measure the love and compassion that exists
between people, because, well, we are all so lonely, locked up in our
boxes, deaf and dumb and blind all" (344)—echoes a conception of art,
wherein the ability of a writer to know his characters from the inside is
presupposed. "We have to know others!" Zeidman says, "From the inside!" (340). For Zeidman, there is no discrepancy between himself and
the people his art is able to invade, no uncertainty as to what these people
want from him. The crucial exception, however, are the Nazis guarding
the Warsaw ghetto; in radical evil, Zeidman encounters a force that cannot be incorporated into his purely literary world, the bearers of an alterity
that resists symbolization. These figures do more than just undermine his
claim to have achieved intersubjective relations—the foundation of traditional fiction and its authorial investment in character—they also establish themselves as the thing on which the readability of a book depends.
Zeidman confesses as much when he admits that as a truly intersubjective
book, he is just mere pages, with no one to read him. In Zeidman, the
representative of a form endowed a priori with the ability to capture the
life of Others, Grossman articulates the problem of Momik's childhood,
the problem that drives his appeal to Bruno Schulz, the problem that
comes to a climax in the "Wasserman" section: the impossibility of
intersubjective relations between character and writer, and character and
reader. What Zeidman reveals is that an art staked on the achievement of
these relations betrays its own very conditions of possibility. Such an art,
strictly speaking, would have no audience. The novel about the Holocaust
that actually captured some of its traumatic particularities would have no
readers to read it.

    This explains the struggle for authority between Wasserman and
Shlomo in the rendering of Wasserman's tale told to Neigel. Wasserman's
"Children of the Heart" stories are stories imagined to be fully present
to themselves. Wasserman's empirical research is designed precisely to
foster this illusion; the data he collects serves to authenticate the placement of his characters in the various historical situations in which they
find themselves. In these moves, however, Wasserman conceals the a priori
assumption of intersubjectivity that underwrites his storytelling. This
section of Grossman's novel, however, is not just a telling of Wasserman's

story, it is a *re*telling of it—and this gives Shlomo the space to reflect on the relation between writer and character, and the "beyond" of the character that is often the writer's real source of identification and fascination. This fact is evident in Shlomo's musing on the world of his own character: "Anshel Wasserman lives totally in a world of words, which means, I imagine, that every word he utters or hears has for him a sensual quality which I cannot perceive. Is it possible, then, that the word 'supper' is enough to satisfy his hunger? That the word 'sore' cuts his flesh? That the word 'living' enlivens him? These thoughts, I admit, are a bit over my head" (283). As a pure subject, Wasserman would enjoy a relation to language without rift. And yet the pure subject is one—by this time of the novel, after what Joseph has shown him in the "Bruno" section—Shlomo can only contemplate from a distance. Between Wasserman and Shlomo there can be no intersubjective relation, no relation of complementarity. For Grossman, the characters one creates are no different from the dead one cannot ever completely memorialize, or the baby son you bring in to the world. They are, in other words, another Other before whom Momik faces the question of all questions: What do you want from me? This question is so unsettling because it designates once again our crisis vis-à-vis the act of bearing witness: when we cannot know *their* desire, we cannot know our own. This is nowhere more clear than in Shlomo's discovery that Wasserman has "tricked" him by bringing baby Kazik into the story. The source of the novelist's anguish is cystallized in Shlomo's response to the trick: "I don't understand what the baby wants from me. It's hard enough with my first baby" (154). Narrative authority, for Grossman, is not that which permits the artist to steal with impunity across the frontiers of his characters. For the genuine artist, characters arise from the netherworld of the imagination carrying an inscrutable—and for that reason threatening—claim. Narrative authority cannot "read" this claim.

To give the novel to Wasserman is to give oneself over to the illusion of intersubjectivity, and to the project at the core of this illusion: to infect oneself and one's audience, through the telling of a story, with humanity. This is Wasserman's project vis-à-vis Neigel, and it depends fundamentally on the illusion of a story capable of capturing the Otherness of history. Neigel's love of the simple story, and Wasserman's desire to "infect Neigel with humanity" are both part of a conception of art that seeks and carries out the integration of Otherness. This explains the fantastic popularity of Anshel Wasserman's children's stories. The intersubjective relation between writer and character caters precisely to a way of reading which wants to "identify" with the characters who carry out the greatest good in history. Unity of time and place and action fosters this identification, which is why such readers object to violations thereof. (Neigel distinguishes himself as just this reader in his remark that "modern" writers are misanthropes, who have "ruined" Art.) In the intersubjective relation, no one cannot be known from the inside. In this aspect, the inability of liberal humanism to counter the fantasy of fascism is again illuminated, since both desire the impossible community—that is, the community in which consensus can be reached. To put this in other terms, we might say that both desire a central role in novels. That is to say, they want to be available to the full representational abilities of artists in order to represent themselves to themselves. This perhaps explains Neigel's—and then after Neigel's suicide, his assistant Staukeh's—desire to retain the storyteller as House Jew. In some sense, this desire to retain the Jew is analogous to gassing him. At stake is a representation of oneself that would confirm that you are who you think you are. The nightly story or the nightly transports can function as just this representation. The point is that even the murderers want to be presented fully—that is why they have murdered in the first place: their act of murder is an act that gives body to the other in themselves by externalizing, concentrating, and then exterminating that other. This explains Neigel's rebuke of Shlomo for having yet to take pains to present Neigel more fully in the story Shlomo is writing: "Isn't it true," Niegel asks his creator, Shlomo, at one point, "that writers are supposed to enter all the way into their characters?" (280).

Neigel's question here joins his conception of art with Wasserman's. Their differences notwithstanding—Neigel prefers a simple, entertaining story; Wasserman says there are no simple stories anymore—both share a formal belief in the ability of the story to survive, in the pure passion of telling and listening. In their desire for recognition and reputation, both indicate, as well, how impure such passions really are. Both believe in the learning that takes place when one "gets outside oneself"; this is precisely where Neigel wants to be in his tenure as camp commandant, and it is precisely where Wasserman leads him. The characters of Wasserman's story have aged, but their narrative, their "universal theme"— the triumph of good over evil—remains essentially the same. In the words of the serial's hero, Otto Brig, this is "the only war there is." For Wasserman, no discrepancy exists between the form of the Children of the Heart tales and the actual events of history. Armenians before their genocide, African-Americans during slavery, Navaho poverty, England's poor in the time of Robin Hood, even Beethoven—all are amenable to the serialized saga detailing the battle against "disaster, disease, and deformity, injustice, ignorance, and blight" (195–196). For Wasserman, "every meeting between two people is a wonder and a mystery" (199). The standard deconstructionist point bears repeating here for the truth is that Wasserman's "Children of the Heart" tales are as self-referential as the novel in which they have been placed. They are, quite simply, about the ability of the story to be adequate to, and to triumph over, the realities of history. On the level of form, they answer the slogan repeated before each mission: Is the heart willing? *The heart is willing.* Come what may? *Come what may.*

These slogans only conceal, however, that what is to come has been decided a priori. It is this a priori that permits Wasserman to stage the defeat of evil in the world, but it also involves Wasserman in perpetuating that evil, since humanity is not a calcified substance capable of being injected. As we have seen, there is something *prior to* humanity against the backdrop of which the injection is desired in the first place. The humanist inventor of fairy tales is here linked directly with the Nazi; both have "missions" to redeem the world that depend on the recovery of certain substances and the elimination of others. Liberal democratic programs aim at a substance crystallized around universal human rights. And the metaphors of Nazi ideology almost universally communicate the notion of Jew as substance—recall here Hitler's idea of the Jew as the tuberculosis of nations, and Goebbels likening of the task of the Third Reich to surgery. Both visions might be part of the same constellation containing Wasserman's storytelling purposes. Consider this exchange between Wasserman and Neigel:

> "Are certain passages—I mean—do you think any passages of the, um, soul might be reversible?" "You can easily get rid of grief, of compassion, Herr Neigel, and the love of mankind, the wonderful capacity of fools to believe in mankind, in spite of everything. And the operation will be almost painless." "But can you bring them back again?" asks Neigel, his eyes fixed on Wasserman. "I hope so," Wasserman replies, and to himself, or to me, he says these unintelligible words: "After all, this is my mission, Shleimeleh, for this I am staging my comedy here." (239)

Wasserman's transporting of the Children of the Heart to the Warsaw Ghetto is part of this positive "mission." The triumphant narrative of this story's form, for Wasserman, might still prevail. This is one of the reasons Shlomo must eventually declare war on his own character and the baby that character has introduced.

But it is not the only reason. This becomes clear when the liberal humanist and fascist part ways over the fate of the baby. Kazik's birth with Werner's syndrome (rapid aging) clashes with Neigel's commitment

to an art that entertains and educates, but this is not enough to placate
Shlomo. Wasserman's advice—write about the baby—provokes an outburst from Shlomo because the critical dimension of the novel tran-
scends the particular fate of baby Kazik:

> Write about the baby, Shleimeleh.
> No!!!
> I screamed and threw off the soft, warm hand where the story
> streamed in torrents. I flung myself against the smooth white walls,
> across the pages of my notebook, at the mirror, at my soul—there
> was no way out. Everything was blocked. (297)

The insight Grossman develops in this exchange is this: the artistic attempt to tell the story of the Holocaust is not primarily a matter of
whether one chooses to focus on those who will die or those who will
live. The point is not that Wasserman has the guts to "kill" baby Kazik
whereas Neigel wants the baby not to be harmed and to be happy. This
would make Grossman's writing of the "Wasserman" section the story of
the "Children of the Heart" redux. It is instead that *in life or in death*, the
traumatic particular survives, forcing the witness to occupy an ontological
zone for which there is no epistemological map. Whether as survivor or
casualty, there is still and always the impasse as to what it all *means* for
the subject bearing witness. Momik's declaration of war on Wasserman's
story comes, with good reason, *after* Wasserman has already "decided"—
through the plot device of rapid aging—that Kazik must be killed. What
this indicates is that the nature of the dispute between Momik and
Wasserman does not really concern the fate of the baby. On the contrary,
there is a dispute because for Momik the decision regarding Kazik's fate
does nothing to address the fundamental uncertainty that fate ought properly to elicit—an uncertainty with coordinates in Wasserman's (and by
extension, Momik's) subjectivity. The real struggle Grossman is demonstrating never concerned the particular dimension of Kazik's life—his
survival or his death—but the approach of that life from the perspective
of literary form and the question: What does this baby (alive or dead)
mean for me?[20]

The stories written by Anshel Wasserman and read avidly by children like Neigel are precisely those that repress this question, those that
acclimate the child to history as a stabilizing force. They communicate
the idea of history as mission (Hitler is to the adult as Otto Brig is to the
child: the perfect Father), and not as that which is utterly contingent, and
therefore without "mission" (or progressive movement). Even in killing
the baby, Wasserman's story is far from innocent, for it produces the

unconscious enjoyment of knowing that history has been entrusted to someone. Otto Brig and his band fall prey in this sense to the "deeper disease" that Nazism merely names and lends an army, workers, temples, and so forth. This is what Momik must learn in his recovery of Wasserman's story in order to negate once and for all his paranoid approach of history: he must tell the "end" of the story in a form that destroys this enjoyment. This time the object of Momik's pursuit—that is, the Story—will not be rejected because it fails to capture the essence of the Other. Indeed, the story is not rejected in favor of some other form that promises a real within symbolization. The fourth section of Grossman's novel signifies the arrest of this series of rejections. There, Momik does not reject the story of baby Kazik because a nonsensical signifier organizes it; instead, he takes up the non-sensicalness of that signifier and exaggerates it. The most arbitrary or "stupid" of principles—the alphabetization of random words and phrases—will order the telling of the story's events. The declaration of war on the story is, then, not at all like the declaration made against the Beast: it is a declaration of war *against* the declaration of war against the Beast, and the paranoid construction underwriting the second declaration.

Wasserman's Art attempts to put Neigel in touch with his imagination, in order to create a recognition of some essential human-ness. His diagnosis of Neigel makes this clear: "Your main problem Herr Neigel is that you never leave the confines of your own skin! After all, even the powers of the imagination need gymnastic exercise, else they wither and die, heaven forbid, like atrophied limbs" (232). This is, however, a fundamental romantic misdiagnosis of Neigel's problem: the truth one arrives at when one "leaves one's own skin" does not have a meaning that is universal and ahistorical. On the contrary, it is linked concretely with the symbolic network of meanings in which such an act is inscribed. Thus, we might say that Neigel has in fact left the confines of his own skin every time he has pulled the trigger or supervised another incoming trainload to the crematoria. Neigel's problem is far from a simple sort of narcissism, or an atrophied imagination. He "leaves his own skin" for the same reason Wasserman encourages him, to identify at the deepest level of his being with a concrete Other—in this case the dictator of Nazi Germany who guarantees the consistency of his identity. A critique of Neigel must focus on the reward for this identification, not on perceived shortcomings of his imagination. This is clearly the lure of bureaucratic depersonalization—the fact that there is as much enjoyment in the execution of duty as there is in sadism. Though those put on trial after the war—especially Eichmann—tried to find in bureaucracy something exculpatory, their having elected to identify with bureaucracy (to solve a problem belonging to the structure of subjectivity) clarifies their irreparable guilt. The enjoyment Neigel gets is the enjoyment of acting on behalf of the figure who has robbed existence of its contingency: "I live in the new world, the future I was promised by the Fuhrer and the Reich," Neigel says (237). It is at this level that Grossman directs his final undercutting of the Wassermanian mission—by linking the success of that mission with Niegel's vicious rape of his wife Christina. What Grossman suggests here is that in this rape, Wasserman's story has in fact reached the heart of Niegel—and there exposed and abetted its cruelty. Wasserman has told Neigel to carry the story within him, to make it his own, and Neigel has done just this. Wasserman thought he was imparting a nugget of humanity that would work toward positive ends; the heart is for him evidently incapable of being fundamentally rotten. This is his mistake. His story—and the hearts of its recipients as well—appear always at the mercy of the symbolic structure in which it is told. The proper point of attack, as the final section makes clear, is thus the symbolic structure itself, and its nonsensical character.

Encyclopedic Totalizing as Antidote for War

The Encyclopedia form in which Momik elects to tell the story of baby Kazik is itself a way of making plain that the dispute between Momik and Wasserman does not concern the particular fate of the child. The dispute touches instead on the manner in which all narrative potentially partakes of paranoia, and of the possibility of a "real" relation to history within language. In each of the three quests that make up Grossman's novel, we have seen Momik's failure to produce and identify with those figures who would seem to contain the real of history. These failures have had the effect of revealing to us the fundamental finitude that dooms his efforts. As long as Momik is trying to symbolize these "real" figures, his project must fail because of this finitude, since the finite particular is irreducible to the universal order of thinking. A story, then—any story—is thus inseparable from the whole of the finite world (i.e., the symbolic structure) that sustains its meaning. And if Momik wants truly to open himself to the otherness he encounters in the fact of a little boy's death—of an individual victim of the Holocaust—it is at the level of this whole that this little boy's death will have to be faced. The finite is not, as Bruno Schulz might have maintained, what must be eliminated in order to encounter the real, but rather is, as Hegel suggests, to be maintained and made into an absolute. We have returned here to the Hegelian insights discussed in chapter 1 and the relevance of the absolute for memorial purposes. In opting for a form that *overidentifies* with its object, Momik would appear to have reached the point of absolute self-knowledge, which is, in the penultimate line of the *Phenomenology*, far from the experience of self-transparency or self-possession. Hegel writes that when it comes to the recognition of the Absolute, "the self-knowing Spirit knows not only itself but also the negative of itself, or its limit: to know one's limit is to know how to sacrifice oneself."[21]

This is, in fact, Momik's recognition and the crowning achievement of his formal decision in the last quarter of Grossman's novel: his sacrifice is now no longer a process content to take place *inside* the realm of symbolization and *for* a nameable, symbolizable force. This sort of sacrifice, Momik has realized, must be given up because it appears always to be a way of conferring a substantial integrity on the Law or Master that guarantees the consistency of our symbolic identities. If every sacrifice is for a *something*, then the order of signification—the order of the symbolic—truly is comprehensive. This comprehensiveness is the sine qua non of the vicious circle of violence and retaliation, a circle marked entirely (on both sides) by meaningful sacrifices. But if one sacrifices oneself for *nothing*, if that sacrifice cannot be accounted for, cannot be made sense of, then the symbolic is shown to be lacking. Holes in it become visible, and the order of structural trauma emerges. The very universe of meaning structuring the violence, making it appear natural and necessary, is shown to be the paranoiac's ultimate fiction. This is the ethical import of *making structural trauma appear*.[22] When Hegel says that the self-knowing Spirit has learned "how to sacrifice oneself," he points in just this direction: knowing "how to sacrifice oneself" means sacrificing oneself not for any mere symbolic entity, but for the real itself. Momik's sacrifices, in the various declarations of war that occupy him for much of the novel—against the Beast, against the Sea, against Grandfather Anshel—appear, then, to mistake the "real" import of sacrifice as an ethical gesture. Sacrifice is an ethical position when it is for *nothing*—that is, death, matter devoid of meaning—that one is sacrificing oneself.

By the end of the novel, Momik appears to have reached this ethical position: he seems to have grasped the manner in which his repeated "wars" have in fact met a decisive covert need. In the "Absolute Knowing" section of *The Phenomenology*, Hegel exposes this need: self-consciousness does not wish to know the nothingness of the object, which is in fact knowledge of itself. Hegel calls this the "uncultivated consciousness" of religion, and claims that "not until consciousness has given up hope of overcoming that alienation in an external, that is, alien, manner does it turn to itself, because the overcoming of that alienation is the return into self-consciousness; not until then does it turn to its own present world and discover it as its property."²³ The function of Momik's "wars," in other words, is to keep consciousness from taking itself as object, and to see that Absolute Knowledge is nothing but the movement—the restless process of the self superceding the self—in which consciousness takes itself as object. This is why the Subject, the "I," is for Hegel not a substance but rather a relation or an identity, which always indicates a lack of wholeness: "The 'I' is not merely the Self, but the *identity of the Self with itself.*"²⁴ If Momik has before always named his "enemy," and in so doing kept himself from recognizing that the source of his conflicts lies in the deadlock of his self-alienating self-identity, he now rightly sees that act, and the sacrificial economy that undergirds it, as the universal ground beneath the "little nazi" in every one of us: "the disease at the very root of our nature which we proliferate with every move. The Nazis merely outlined it and gave it a name, an army, workers, temples, and sacrificial victims" (296). For Momik, the Nazis only tapped into an already-extant willingness to participate in such sacrificial economies—economies that solve, for the human subject, the impasse of absolute knowing, of an ethics rooted in the sacrifice of oneself for nothing. It is, then, this willingness that must be engaged in the project of historical memory, and Momik engages it in a novel way—not by advancing a simple dismissal of sacrifice, but by exaggerating it to such an extent that its entire economy is unmasked and exposed to nothingness itself.

If the Nazi sacrifice may seem itself already sufficiently exaggerated—and did it not, indeed, result in the most horrible of consequences?—it is, for Momik, never more than the slave's sacrifice for the name of the Master. It is not "absolute" (in the Hegelian sense) because it is a sacrifice *for* something; it freezes the subject at the point where the essentiality of the Master's name is maintained. The Nazi sacrifice, in other words, is one colossal attempt to preserve the illusion that the symbolic is all. All of its activity—its work, its battles, its building of temples, its genocidal acts—points to this end. "The Complete Encyclopedia of Kazik's Life," however, represents a different sort of activity. The real war, Momik realizes, is against nothingness—it is against the experience of the White Room—and the others have been but attempts to occlude this fact. Wasserman's prayer on the final page of the novel, in this context, articulates the larger, formal message of Grossman's novel: "Wasserman raised his eyes to Niegel and said, 'All of us prayed for one thing: that he might end his life knowing nothing of war. Do you understand, Herr Niegel? We asked for so little: for a man to live in this world from birth to death and know nothing of war' " (452). The war to which Wasserman refers resonates beyond the world war he survived, and to the paranoia that structured it. His prayer, then, appears as a prayer for the sort of artistic form in which he has ultimately landed—a form that has given up its belief in the essence of the alterity of the Other or of that kernel of nonsense to which we are subjected. "The Complete Encyclopedia of Kazik's Life," we might say, as a form that knows nothing of war, is an attempt to arrest the paranoid relations that drove the Holocaust itself, and that are handed down from the survivors to the second and third generations which inherit it: "He was finished in this war. This war was finished in him. There was nobody to fight for. For him it was over. He was dead now. He was ready for life" (297).

How is it that a kind of death readies one for life? This paradox is critical for an understanding of Momik's progression in *See Under: Love*, and an ethics of memory that recognizes the absolute or totalizing gesture at the heart of all memorial efforts—that is, that seeks to make us able to experience our death. This is what Hegel is after when he speaks of an End to knowledge: "Within the range of the finite," Hegel writes, "we can never see or experience that the End has been really secured. The consummation of the infinite End, therefore, consists merely in removing the illusion which makes it seem yet unaccomplished."[25] From this standpoint, the virtue of taking up a position of absolute knowledge is to recognize that we are, in a sense, *already* at the end destined for us. The Beast, *The Messiah*, the "eternal" story of Anshel Wasserman—these form the basis, as I have said, of projects that hold out the specter of an End not yet reached. To be "ready for life," however, is to see the symbolic order's precariousness as its condition of possibility, as bereft of an ultimate Object requiring sacrifices capable of bringing about its consummation. The way that memory can work against such a sacrificial structure—and the repetition of fascist aggression it subtends—would be to show that nothing meaningful occupies this place of the Object. Our memorial acts, in this respect, ought to entail sacrifices that appear to make no sense, that appear to be *for* nothing intelligible.

Is it not for this reason that the Reader's Preface to the "Encyclopedia" speaks of removing any and all tensions likely to create the "extraneous illusion of a purpose, as it were, at the root of all things, toward which all 'life' is supposed to flow" (304). Does not a similar "purposelessness" pertain to our act of reading an encyclopedia in its entirety—a work that is explicitly not a narrative? Purpose appears to be what the experience of reading an encyclopedically arranged story appears to lack: the very headings have been selected in the most arbitrary of ways, and our "reading on" is robbed of the enjoyment of believing that we are progressing toward some end (e.g., the "Reader's Preface" reports the fact of Kazik's death before we even encounter it in the narrative proper). For the nine-year-old boy, an Encyclopedia promised comprehensive knowledge:

Momik loves to hold the big books in his hands, and it makes him feel good all over to run his fingers down the smooth pages that seem to have a protective covering that keeps your fingers away, so you won't get too close, because who are you, what are you compared to the *Encyclopedia*, will all the little letters crowded in long, straight columns and mysterious abbreviations like secret signals for a big, strong, silent army boldly marching out to conquer the world, all-knowing, all-righteous [. . .] he likes to touch the pages and feel deep in his stomach and his heart all the power and the silence, and the seriousness and the scientificness that makes everything so clear and simple. (43–44)

Then, it required shrewd and methodical detection strategies—that is, purposeful activity. Now, it is that form which, in arbitrarily organizing the imagined life of a victim of the Holocaust, suggests the stupidity of all our ordering efforts, the impossibility of achieving complete relations within language with history or with those we love. The Encyclopedia reveals its order while at the same time revealing the complete contingency of all order.

The activity that results in the "Encyclopedia" is the product of an ethical realization that the acts in which one must engage are the ones that appear to be without purpose. The most radical act of bearing witness is for Grossman the act that makes no sense. Ayala, then, testifies to the truth of Momik's enterprise in her very condemnation of it:

This whole encyclopedia business is utterly worthless. It doesn't explain anything. Look at it: you know what it reminds me of? A mass grave. That's what it reminds me of. A grave with limbs sticking out in every direction. All disjointed. But not only that, Shlomik. It's also a documentation of your crimes against humanity. And now that you've gotten this far, I hope you see that you've failed, that your whole encyclopedia is not enough to fully encompass a single day or even a single moment of human life. (450)

Momik's crime is the crime of his form—an Encyclopedia that explains nothing. Ayala tells him that she does not expect a "happy ending" from him—"I know your limitations," she says—but what she does expect are stories that affirm the symbolic order that sustains their meaning. Momik can thus reverse his disaster and earn her forgiveness if he writes her a "new story. A good story. A beautiful story"—a story "with MERCY [q.v.], with LOVE [q.v.]! Not *See Under: Love!*" (450). In Ayala's view, crimes can be committed in novels, but novels ought not commit crimes. (It might reasonably be said that the sort of novel Ayala hopes for is one closer to *Doctor Faustus*, which depicts a kind of tragedy without ever being given over entirely to it at the level of form.) The artist, for her, must write with mercy and love in order to transcend the gap between structural and historical trauma. On the level of form, at least, art is to remain in charge of content, no matter how terrible: it is not, in other words, to take on the shape of a mass grave—what Adorno, in his critique of "music's facade of self-sufficiency," refers to as "the heteronomy of scars."[26]

Ayala's analogy is apt, for Grossman seems to have found the only way to treat a "local" facet of the Holocaust without being accused of trying to mitigate its enormity. The attempt to know an individual's life and death under the Nazis absolutely, gives shape to a form that corresponds to that enormity. Taking his positing abilities to their extreme, Grossman's goal is finally to open the subject up to that feeling that is outside all positing. Aaron Marcus is here perhaps our guide, the apothecary who declares "open war on the limitations of human feeling" (441). Wasserman tells us that Marcus "longed to clear a way for himself into unknown territories, the abracadabra realms we feel inside, which nobody dares to touch" (440). And Marcus is not one who shies away from the most ultimate of sacrifices. To know certain feelings, Marcus often undergoes the very dissolution of his identity. It is not so much Marcus's desire to develop a new language of feeling—his "Sentimo" is an attempt to give a name to various shades of feelings, because people are trained to feel only what they can name—as much as it is risk that exemplies the truth of his enterprise. Marcus is one who has "saddened himself to death"— and the important consequence of this effort is not his new language, but his recognition that within language, the most important dimensions of feeling are missing. Perhaps this is why in the very moment of Kazik's death, everyone—except Marcus—experiences a kind of mystical moment of justice, of divine justice:

> Approaching death had roused the same feeling in most of them: it was the right thing. And all of life is a free ticket, but in the end we are returned against our will to the domain of some invisible force, grave and inevitable, which collects its rightful debt, without MERCY [q.v.] or solace. To all of them, suddenly life, their own lives, seemed wrong and dreary and senseless [see under: LIFE, THE MEANING OF], and even those who weren't religious felt a sudden awe of God, while unfamiliar thoughts of sins committed and punishments deserved ran through their minds. (429)

Only Marcus derives a different lesson from the death of the "old boy" (Kazik)—a lesson for the perpetrators and those who carry on their paranoia: "Only Aaron Marcus thought sadly that perhaps death was as arbitrary and inexplicable as life itself" (429). This is our lesson as well: the trauma of the Holocaust is not confined to it, but pertains to the implicit trauma—the inexplicability of our lives and of our deaths—that it makes, and made, explicit. As the Event that attempted to eliminate this inexplicability, the nature and permanence of this trauma is perhaps its greatest, and most difficult, legacy.

Conclusion

In his remarkable chapter in *The Drowned and the Saved*, entitled "The Gray Zone," Primo Levi writes,

> I am not an expert on the unconscious and the mind's depths, but I do know that few people are experts in this sphere and that these few are the most cautious. I do not know, and it does not interest me much to know, whether in my depths there lurks a murderer, but I do know that I was a guiltless victim and I was not a murderer. I know that the murderers existed, not only in Germany, and still exist, retired or on active duty, and that to confuse them with their victims is a moral disease or an aesthetic affectation or a sinister sign of complicity; above all, it is a precious service rendered (intentionally or not) to the negators of truth.[1]

"The Gray Zone" is, of course, Levi's famous and sympathetic meditation on those prisoners who collaborated in one way or another with the authorities of the Lager. Levi refers to such prisoners as comprising "the hybrid class of the prisoner-functionary," and regards their existence as the camp's "most disquieting feature" (42). In his conceptualization of a zone of indistinction where perpetrators and victims converge, Levi contends that such prisoners call into question our need and ability to make hasty moral judgments. When thinking about the guilt of such individuals, Levi claims that "certainly, the greatest responsibility lies with the system, the very structure of the totalitarian state" (44). It is, for him, above all else, "political coercion [that] gives birth to that ill-defined sphere of ambiguity and compromise" (67). And because the particular experience of this coercion is not at all communicable, because we cannot fathom completely the effects of coercion and degradation that led a given prisoner toward compromise, complicity, or both our powers of judgment are paralyzed. What frustrates moral judgment, in short, is ←
a problem having to do with knowledge and with the impossibility of ←

→imagining oneself in the place of another: as Levi puts it, "Nobody can know for how long and under what trials his soul can resist before yielding or breaking" (60).

As the longer passage I have cited above makes clear, however, the ambiguity Levi accords to the behavior of the gray zone's inhabitants must not come at the expense of the collapse of all historically specific distinctions. This is the threshold that Levi's remarks clarify for us, and in insisting on it, Levi functions as one of the standard-bearers for the view held today by many of the leading theorists of Holocaust memory. This is a view espousing caution vis-à-vis the preoccupation with what we cannot know—a preoccupation said to lead ultimately to questions, and sometimes conclusions, that do not respect the historical particularity of the Holocaust. Evoking Levi explicitly, Lawrence Langer, for example, has argued that any memorial effort that aims to adjust one's focus from the behavior of the perpetrators to our own behavior plays a certain "game of evasion."[2] From this standpoint, a kind of ethical trajectory defines Levi's move from ignorance to disinterest in the context of what he refers to as "the unconscious and the mind's depths": what Levi claims he does not know is, at the same time, something it does not interest him much to know. We need only encounter the *but I do know* to perceive the →ethical stakes of the matter: as Levi implicitly suggests, interest in whether →or not we are all capable of murder risks confusing our clear sense of just →who the Nazis were, directing our attention toward broad psychological questions and away from simple and unimpeachable, historical knowledge: "I was a guiltless victim and I was not a murderer."

In this book, I have tried to show how the choice implied by this threshold is ultimately a false one. Rather than conceive the effort to establish particular historical truths and the universal question of our own propensity to murder as two separate projects, I have argued that a post-Holocaust ethics of witnessing committed to avoiding repetition ought properly to see them as inextricably linked. In a sense, much of my effort in the preceding pages has been to establish the centrality of the question Levi leaves aside—"whether in my depths there lurks a murderer"—and to do so in such a way that does not render "precious service" to the "negators of truth." Certainly, it is an indisputable fact that Levi was a guiltless victim and not a murderer. But, as Levi himself would perhaps be the first one to admit, this very knowledge takes us no closer to rendering a meaning unto the particularity of the Event we have come to designate as the Holocaust. Pursuing Hegel's theses on the advent of language and subjectivity—as well as all of the light psychoanalysis sheds on the pathologies coordinated with that advent—my claim has been simply that the traumatic absence or elusiveness of the *real* particularity of history is constitutive when it comes to the consolidation of a linguistic or epistemological order. This is what leads Hegel to claim that the history we can think and speak about is always universal. As Hegel's ← critique of empiricism in the "Sense-Certainty" section of the *Phenomenology* makes clear, even when we are seemingly in the presence of the most particular, historically specific knowledge—for instance, Levi's claim, "I was not a murderer"—we are, at the same time, in fact speaking and thinking from the standpoint of the universal. When grasped at this level, our bearing witness to history leads to a structural encounter with trauma← with significant ethical consequences for the way we conceive of ourselves ← as knowing subjects. Here is, for me, the link between epistemology and← ethics. Indeed, my claim has been that every time we situate our particu- ← lar historical knowledge on its universal basis, we are, at the same time, ← *explicitly grappling with the fundamentally ethical question of our own propen-* ← *sity to murder*.

Much of this argument has rested on a hypothesis regarding the nature and appeal of fascism itself. I am referring here to the very way fascist ideology converts a constitutive problem into a historical one in order to conceptualize (or fantasize) a society rid of antagonism, and as a consequence of this, to achieve a subjectivity characterized by plenitude and autonomy. As I argued in chapter 1, the ultimate shortcomings of today's categorical imperative to historicize lie in this direction: if everything is grist for the historicist mill, the space cleared by logic for a *shared* trauma prior and antithetical to historical trauma is lost. If this hypothesis is correct, then it seems eminently clear to me that part of what it means to bear witness to the past will involve a recognition of the structural imbalance that is constitutive of the social world and our identities within it. This structural imbalance entails a logical locus of nonknowledge that conditions and preserves the consistency of our human world. Ethical consciousness is nothing but the recognition that for us, nonknowledge is part of our knowledge. This is, I think, what David Grossman has in mind when he refers to the "disease at the root of our nature" on which Nazism merely capitalized. Indeed, Grossman sees that the deeper ground of fascism (the ground of what he astutely and cleverly refers to as "the little nazi in you") lies in treating a structural imbalance as a historical matter, as a matter of meaningful knowledge that then becomes the basis of just and necessary violence. In *See Under: Love*, this view is tantamount to finding an enemy to fight, and it ultimately functions as a kind of prescription for war.

The urgent task for Holocaust Studies today, it seems to me, is to theorize a way out of this war. To repeat my remarks regarding Levi's threshold: in this book, I have sought to show that the choice is not between knowledge (liberalism) and its impossibility (deconstruction). Liberal political theory may discover the desire informing the act of Jewish rescue, and derive by way of such knowledge a mobilizing, ethicopolitical maxim for our post–Cold War moment. In response, deconstruction can insist on the discursivity of such knowledge, and thereby destabilize the capacity of such a maxim to arrest the play of signification. The problem is that neither of these significant bodies of knowledge takes us far enough in the direction in which we need to go. Neither enables us to think knowledge and the impossibility of knowledge together, *the former on the basis of the latter.* There are of course risks to conceiving knowledge this way. Indeed, the charge that such a proposal merely licenses our playing fast and loose with history has—most recently in the context of the Wilkomirski affair but well before *Fragments* as well—been made again and again. My own sense is that the *greater risk* lies in failing to avow the traumatic basis of even our most urgent and decisive historical truths. The consequences of this failure are significant. While liberalism develops an ethics aimed at warding off a repetition of the violence of Nazism, the figure of the "enemy"—in the form of those who refuse to fantasize in a politically liberal way—continues to haunt that ethics as a matter of practical politics, despite renewed claims involving a naturally genetic basis for cooperation in groups and for rule-following.[3] For deconstruction, such a haunting itself constitutes the ethical, since, as an entirely discursive entity, the "enemy" is a spectral apparition that always and forever eludes our actual apprehension. My own argument has been that a further step is needed, and it has centered on the contradiction within deconstruction itself and the way its very theses are at odds with its claims regarding the impossibility of definitive knowledge. If our task is to unmask the "enemy" for the phantasm that it is, and if this means challenging the cognitive/linguistic operation whereby this "enemy" is produced and installed in the place of the traumatic particular, then why not actually *bring about* an encounter with such particulars? Why not make explicit the nonknowledge our very knowledge bears deep within it all of the time? This could be the implicit lesson transmitted by the words and images associated with past historical traumas which arrest our capacity to think and speak: such words and images could (and should) function to mark off the structural place of the traumatic particular as *already occupied,* or as *in need of no more occupants.* It is perhaps not an exaggeration to say that the political and ethical possibilities of this century stand or fall on this statement.

How best to bring about such an encounter? As I have said, I have tried to theorize a memorial act that does not arrive at a quantity of self-evident knowledge capable of wresting the signifying chain away from the uncertainties that plague it (as has the liberal focus on rescue exemplified by a film like *Schindler's List*). And I have tried to avoid that path that postpones and prohibits the subject's genuine encounter with historical knowledge (as has the deconstructionist call for proliferation and dissemination and equivocation). Instead, I have suggested that this traumatic encounter is produced most lucidly by an exaggerated, totalizing act of knowing. This is the act that, in the very communication/transmission of historical truth, avoids both liberalism's discovery of a meaningful maxim and deconstruction's infinite conversation in order to make explicit the "stupidity" of the universal order of consciousness and language. Such an act reveals not just how the construction of meaning is always tied to something nonhistorical that cannot be made to mean: it is also part of a mode of witnessing aimed at getting us to encounter the raw material of nonmeaning itself. This encounter is, in one way or another, at the heart of the memory texts I have investigated in this book—of the heroic spirit of a figure like Oskar Schindler in *Schindler's List*, of the mass murder at Babi Yar in *The White Hotel*, of the pure expressions of suffering in Leverkühn's *Apocalypse* and *Lamentation* in *Doctor Faustus*, and finally, of the life and death of a child in the "Encyclopedia" of *See Under: Love*. These works negotiate this encounter to different ends. What makes their outcomes so significant, for me, has again to do with the ever present lure of fascism, the license for aggression it offers, and the way both the lure and the license have coordinates in the ways we think about historical knowledge and our relation as subjects to it. *Schindler's List*, I have argued, is emblematic of a series of various literary and sociopsychological attempts to *know* the spirit informing the ethical acts of those who saved Jews during the Holocaust, and as such, is part of liberalism's post–Cold War confrontation and obsession with a time that radically calls into question the efficacy of its maxims. As a novel full of formal variations and multiple viewpoints, *The White Hotel* exemplifies the deconstructionist critique of positivist historiography, but in its hysterical dissatisfaction with any stable truth, it holds out as a *possibility for knowledge* a scenario that is no less redemptive for being equivocal (in which the massacred at Babi Yar enjoy blissful, pre-Oedipal reunions in the hereafter's version of a displaced persons camp). In the "rigid" style of the composer whose life and death is the novel's subject, *Doctor Faustus* begins to gesture—even as it ultimately maintains a kind of ironic distance—toward an artistic form that would repudiate the meaning or triumph believed to lie in form itself. The significance of Leverkühn's arbitrary form lies in the light it sheds on the link between shared trauma and democracy, on how the very imposition of form responsible for the ordering of our lives is linked inextricably with a particular something that eludes all of our sense-making organs (sight, hearing, etc.). In *See Under: Love*, this very imposition of order is evident in the very form of the novel, whose last section "narrates" a singular story of the Holocaust in the most totalizing, arbitrary form imaginable—an Encyclopedia—and thereby frees the memorial investment in history from the paranoia animating its repetition.

I have spoken in this conclusion about shared trauma and about the
ethics of taking up, in the act of witnessing, a universal position in order
to realize something structural about the nature of our being-in-the-
world. I would like to conclude by referring to a few instances that exemplify universality working in precisely this direction. I will begin by
turning back to Primo Levi himself and to his memoir *The Periodic Table*,
and to the striking suggestion made therein that chemistry might stand
as an "antidote to fascism."[4] Initially, *The Periodic Table*'s advocacy of
chemistry on ethicopolitical grounds is presented simply in the course of
Levi's own attempt to write faithfully of his history as an adolescent
growing up in fascist Italy. Beginning with the recounting of his growing
love for chemistry as a sixteen-year-old boy, Levi, at virtually every turn,
positions science as countering Fascism's (and more generally, philosophy's)
understanding of matter. Chemistry, Levi recalls, "represented an indefinite
cloud of future potentialities which enveloped my life to come in black
volutes torn by fiery flashes, like those which had hidden Mount Sinai.
Like Moses, from that cloud I expected my law, the principle of order in
me, around me, and in the world" (23). Positioned as antithetical to the
abstractions of philosophical discourse—Levi remembers being enervated
and nauseated by lectures having to do with the problem of being and
knowing—chemistry's appeal lies in its concern to understand the smallest and seemingly most insignificant particulars of matter. These are the
everyday mysteries that await revelation and humane understanding—the
mica glint in granite, the old wood of benches, the downward flight of a
fly in early summer—and they are, for Levi, mysteries that fall outside the
purview of philosophy (and the wars to which it is linked). In subsequent
anecdotes, the ethicopolitical dimensions of chemistry are made even
more striking. Recounting his first experiment with zinc in a university
laboratory (at the very moment when the magazine *The Defense of the Race*
had just begun publication), Levi discovers in the behavior of the elements an endorsement of the necessity of impurity and articulates it in
terms that are explicitly antifascist. And in the Periodic Table itself, Levi
finds "the bridge, the missing link, between the world of words and the
world of things," and this makes chemical discourse and discovery something "clear and distinct and verifiable at every step, and not a tissue of
lies and emptiness, like the radio and newspapers" (41–42).

At the level of the book's content, however, the counterfascist force
Levi finds in chemistry only appears explicitly in the initial sections of
The Periodic Table. For this reason, it is difficult not to historicize Levi's
claims on behalf of chemistry, to see something naive or youthful about
them. Indeed, many of them seem entirely a product of his insulation
from the threat of Nazism and his distance from the place that will later
come to define him as a writer—Auschwitz. The very existence of chemi-

cal laboratories in the death camps would seem already to be enough to complicate any claim regarding the irreducibility of chemical science and fascist political power. As Levi himself later reports, his own turn to political resistance following the Nazi occupation of Italy suggests the ultimate fecklessness of what he sees as the "solemn poetry" of chemical processes. We see Levi confessing, for example, that even just prior to the actual occupation, there was something "superficial, passive, and cynical" about participating in the production of such poetry in the midst of an escalating War (128). Perhaps just as troubling, however, is Levi's conceptualization of science as the "shortcut" or "lock-pick" to push open the doors of unimpeachable truth. This conceptualization, at one point, informs Levi's change of allegiance, in his fourth year at the university, from chemistry to physics:

> After having been force fed in *liceo* the truths revealed by Fascist Doctrine, all revealed, unproven truths either bored me stiff or aroused my suspicion. Did chemistry theorems exist? No: therefore you had to go further, not be satisfied with the *quia*, go back to the origins, to mathematics and physics. The origins of chemistry were ignoble, or at least equivocal: the dens of the alchemists, their abominable hodgepodge of ideas and language, their confessed interest in gold, their Levantine swindles typical of charlatans or magicians; instead, at the origin of physics lay the strenuous clarity of the West—Archimides and Euclid. (52–53)

Resting on truths that cannot be proven, chemistry here earns the same sort of suspicion Levi directs at Fascist Doctrine, and this leads to his decision to "become a physicist... [though] perhaps without a degree, since Hitler and Mussolini forbade it" (53).

Though physics is here opposed to fascism, there is perhaps something a bit disconcerting about Levi's fealty to the "strenuous clarity of the West," since that very clarity may have a lot in common with the political power Levi sees it opposing. In our age of deconstruction, we might indeed be tempted to claim here that whatever championing of chemistry on ethicopolitical grounds that Levi has in mind ought to be motivated by precisely its "ignoble" origins and all that such a conception of origins implies. But if the remedial powers of chemistry vis-à-vis fascism seem to lie in the direction of equivocation, what then are we to make of the book's title and form—that is, its explicit valorization of the Periodic Table and its structuring of Levi's own life experiences according to various chemical elements whose properties appear to lend an order and meaning to those experiences (each of the book's twenty-two chapters is named for a chemical element)? What, in other words, are we to make of the *systematic imposition* of a universalizing frame on top of the particulars of Levi's own experiences—a move we do not find in the two renowned memoirs that precede *The Periodic Table* (e.g., *Survival in Auschwitz, The Reawakening*)? What are we to conclude about a memoir that takes its direction ultimately from chemistry and not chronology?

My own sense here is that Levi has grasped the need to expose the very intelligibility of a human being's particular, chronological experience as the product of a systematic, universalizing structure. In *The Periodic Table*, what allows for a chronology to emerge is simply the stupid, arbitrary properties of chemical elements arranged in a table that lays claim to comprehensiveness. Here, the Periodic Table functions as a kind of metaphor for the entirety of language itself: the bridge between the world of words and the world of things, it furnishes Levi with master-signifiers that give an order and a shape to the mass of his experiences. Just as language gives us mastery over experience, the Periodic Table organizes and superintends the emergence of a series of signifiers (e.g., the names of the Table's approximately 113 elements) that allow for nature itself to acquire a measure of consistency. As universal structures, the ethicopolitical thrust both of language and the Periodic Table lies in the fact that the *structures themselves* are not meaningful. This is thus what constitutes their counterfascist potential: the "truths" whose emergence they facilitate are inseparable from the arbitrariness or groundlessness of the structure that facilitates their emergence. What Levi seems to have recognized is that we are often not at all cognizant of this fact in conventional literary and everyday uses of language. This oversight applies to those who would find an inherent affirmation merely in the existence of Levi's memoirs alone, as if Levi's survival and subsequent career as an accomplished memoirist must in itself be said to be meaningful. In other books, Levi tries at the level of argument to disabuse readers of this notion.[5] But in the very form of *The Periodic Table*, this effort finds its most striking expression. As Levi himself makes clear in book's final chapter, an attempt to account for the birth of the most universal of all the elements (carbon), "only the fiction of a story" enables us to distinguish an atom of carbon. That is to say, it is only after its insertion into a structure that we can begin to gain a hold on its emergence, since its emergence, as Levi puts it, cannot be considered a "happening" in the historical sense. Here, we see the culmination of *The Periodic Table*'s Hegelian project: once we have begun to speak of carbon, its real particularity has already vanished. But precisely because "the trade of clothing facts in words is bound by its very nature to fail," the most arbitrary story of carbon's emergence is, for Levi, "nevertheless true" (232). Indeed, because every story of carbon is a universal one, *only the most arbitrary* of stories are true, and *only the most truthful* of truths are arbitrary. "I could tell innumerable other stories," Levi claims, "and they would all be true: all literally true" (232). Ultimately, it is *this* embrace of the universal in all of its arbitrariness that establishes the equivocal nature of truth. In *The Periodic Table*, equivocation comes not in a refusal of the literal but in its embrace. Here, a truth is not equivocal in the sense that it cannot be established, or that it is indeterminate and thus always provisional and subject to historical revision, but rather in the sense that the entire order of language is brought to the precipice of its basis in trauma. The ethical import of Levi's reliance on chemistry is thus: exaggerated, universalizing gestures, far from repeating a kind of fascist gesture, *produce the most literal, which is to say equivocal, of truths.*

To clarify the ethical dimension of this move with two brief final examples, let us return to the idea at the heart of the commission of mass murder—the so-called truth of the Other that marks out the Other as a legitimate object of violence, that necessitates the Other's quarantine, elimination, or both. How might we go about universalizing this "truth," and would such a move in fact work in the service of equivocation? I have in mind here not just the ideology of anti-Semitism and the way in which for it, the word *Jew* signified a particular and unalterable "truth" about the human beings to whom that word was attached, but also the ideology of today's Islamic fundamentalism—what Christopher Hitchens has dubbed "theocratic fascism"—and the way in which the word *American* is believed to name the essence of all who live within its territorial borders or represent its interests abroad. But if the words *Jew* or *American* do not name something particular, if such words are already a universal designation, would not *the* counterfascist ethicopolitical gesture consist of an arbitrary act—rhetorical or otherwise—that would expose the universality of the designation? If we are all Hegelian subjects, then not one of us can be said to be the bearer of a particular truth. Would this not mean that against the fascist partisans of particularity, the most ethical subjects are ← those who would stand up and declare, "I, too, am a Jew"? Is this not the← significance of the most remarkable speech act to emerge in the wake of the September 11 catastrophe—the September 12 headline in *Le Monde* declaring that "We are all Americans now"? Can we not imagine an opposition to fascist ideology and violence by means of such universalizing gestures? And if extended far enough, might this not lead us toward a democracy rooted in a shared structural trauma? Such, finally, is the ⌐ [ ] ⌐ claim of this book. Indeed, my own view is that such gestures might solidify a community besieged not by an embodied exemplar of alterity, the bearer of an already designated particular truth, but rather radically open to the traumatic encounter with a particularity that is not properly speaking historical (and thus incapable of redress).

At the time of this writing, thirteen months removed from the *Le Monde* headline referred to above, one can lament—and of course protest—

America's own seeming unwillingness to advance the cause of universality, to see its own particularity as universal in the Hegelian sense. Indeed, today's revaluation of unilateralism and the doctrine of preemption seem to be aimed at the *securing* of America's insuperable particularity. And the results are hardly surprising: is it any wonder that those around the globe are no longer these days feeling very *American*? To gain a glimpse of how universality might be sustained *without* disintegrating into the struggle to preserve particularity, we might consider a more local example—the response of the neighborhood in Newton Township, Pennsylvania, in December 1996, to the fact that a house displaying a Hanukkah menorah in its window was vandalized. By the next evening, all eighteen homes on the same street and adjoining cul-de-sac displayed lit menorahs in their window. The following evening, homes on nearby streets were doing the same, and even more individuals, according to *The New York Times*, would have participated had not local stores run out of menorahs.[6] Eclipsing the historicist-inflected imperative to respect the specificity of different cultural/religious traditions, the families in this neighborhood acted instead to expose the universality of the particular. Their strategy is akin to Levi's: to render the equivocal nature of the Other's "truth" in an arbitrary act of "becoming Jews"—an act whose very arbitrariness only enhances its claim to literal truth. Here, we see universality that does not aim to secure an inviolable sense of community (as this township had sought to do through bicycle decorating contests for children on Memorial Day, monthly teas for mothers with small children at home, annual parties, etc.), but rather a community opened up to a more unsymbolizable exemplar of otherness—in this case, the possibility of attack. In *The New York Times* article concerning the events in Newton Township, the rationale behind this mass action is clearly articulated in terms of the group's desire to make the risk of attack universal. What the events in Newton Township exemplify is a kind of universalization *in the direction of vulnerability*. The decision to become Jews and to put menorahs in their windows, which might be seen as appropriate or as a failure to maintain critical distance, was driven by the desire to make *more* targets available for whoever had attacked the first home. Here, in a nutshell, lies the political import of a post-Holocaust ethics of witnessing grounded in the embrace of universality. Let us imagine once again a Europe at the point of Nazism's rise and recognize that many in our present historical moment remain seduced by the notion of the (particular) Other's truth. What might have been averted if "ordinary Germans" had become Jews, if there had been *too many Jews*? What violence might be averted today if universalization becomes the cornerstone of ethics? Regarding each and every Other's particular "truth" as universal—as all of ours as well—makes *more and more* targets available. And with more and more targets the possibility of *no more* targets.

Notes

Introduction

1. Michael Geyer, "The Politics of Memory in Contemporary Germany," in *Radical Evil*, ed. Joan Copjec (New York: Verso, 1996), 194–195.

2. Geyer, "The Politics of Memory in Contemporary Germany," 170.

3. Peter Novick, *The Holocaust in American Life* (Boston: Houghton Mifflin, 1999), 257.

4. Novick likens those who still invoke the Holocaust in this way to those secular Jews who annually pledge to carry out next year's Passover observance in Jerusalem. This is, for Novick, "not an expectation, not even an aspiration; rather, a ritualized reminder of expectations and aspirations now tacitly abandoned" (Ibid., 257).

5. Even Novick, who is far from sanguine about the possibility of deriving useful lessons from history in general, concedes that the past must be encountered for what it might portend for the present and future: "I'm skeptical about the so-called lessons of history [. . .] If there *are* lessons to be extracted from encountering the past, that encounter has to be with the past in all its messiness; they're not likely to come from an encounter with the past that's been shaped and shaded so that inspiring lessons emerge" (Ibid., 261).

6. Giorgio Agamben, *Remnants of Auschwitz: The Witness and the Archive*, trans. Daniel Heller-Roazen (New York: Zone Books, 1999), 13–14.

7. From Klemperer's March 18, 1945 entry: "For certain, nothingness—en tant que individual consciousness, and that is the true nothingness—is altogether probable, and anything else highly improbable. But have we not continually experienced, since 1914 and even more since 1933 and with ever greater frequency in recent weeks, the most utterly improbable, the most monstrously fantastic? Has not what was formerly completely unimaginable to us become commonplace and a matter of course? If I have lived through the persecutions in Dresden, if I have lived

through February 13 and these weeks as a refugee—why should I not just as well live (or rather: die) to find the two of us somewhere, Eva and I, with angel wings or in some other droll form? It's not only the word 'impossible' that has gone out of circulation, 'unimaginable' also has no validity anymore" (Victor Klemperer, *I Will Bear Witness: A Diary of the Nazi Years, 1942–1945*, trans. Martin Chalmers [New York: Random House, 1999], 433–434.)

8. "If the Lagers had lasted longer a new, harsh language would have been born; and only this language could express what it means to toil the whole day in the wind, with the temperature below freezing, wearing only a shirt, underpants, a cloth jacket and trousers, and in one's body nothing but weakness, hunger and knowledge of the end drawing near" (Primo Levi, *Survival in Auschwitz: The Nazi Assault on Humanity*, trans. Stuart Woolf [New York: Collier, 1993], 123).

9. Ida Fink, "Description of a Morning," in *Traces: Stories*, trans. Philip Boehm and Francine Prose (New York: Henry Holt, 1997), 81–96. In Fink's playlet, Artur believes that words—and the prewar experiences they evoke—are his and Klara's "only protection." He tries, for instance, to remember the names in alphabethical order of the fifth-grade pupils he used to teach, but gets stuck at *S* and the memory of a "little freckled boy" who used to come and visit them. Klara remembers the boy's name—Süss—and interrupts Artur's recital of the rest of the names with the observation, "I saw them take Süss away." Later, this dynamic is repeated when Artur seeks help in recalling "a poem about a sunset." Klara says, "A poem about a sunset? The sun was setting when they killed our parents."

10. Jonathan Boyarin, *Storm from Paradise: The Politics of Jewish Memory* (Minneapolis: University of Minnesota Press, 1992), xiii.

11. Ibid., 105.

12. Theodor Adorno, *Negative Dialectics*, trans. E. B. Ashton (New York: Continuum, 1966), 365.

13. Dominick LaCapra, *Representing the Holocaust: History, Theory, Trauma* (Ithaca, NY: Cornell University Press, 1994), 64.

14. Ibid., 10.

15. The crux of LaCapra's aim in trying to arrest poststructuralism's extreme dwelling on the unknowable involves a commitment to "social practices and institutions generating normative limits that are not conflated with normalization—limits that are affirmed as legitimate yet subject to disruption, challenge, change, and even radical disorientation." These limits, LaCapra argues, are "crucial in ethico-political education and reasoning." (Dominick LaCapra, *Writing History, Writing Trauma* [Baltimore: Johns Hopkins University Press, 2001], 75).

16. Ibid., 90.

17. See, in this respect, Ernesto Laclau's and Chantal Mouffe's move from Derridean claims regarding the impossibility of fixing ultimate meanings to a "second dimension" in which "the impossibility of an ultimate fixity of meaning implies that there have to be partial fixations" (*Hegemony and Socialist Strategy: Towards a Radical Democratic Politics* [New York: Verso, 1985), 111–112].

18. See, for instance: *Specters of Marx: The State of the Debt, the Work of Mourning, and the New International,* trans. Peggy Kamuf (New York: Routledge, 1994); *The Politics of Friendship,* trans. George Collins (New York: Verso, 1997); *Adieu to Emmanuel Levinas,* trans. Pascale-Anne Brault and Michael Naas (Stanford: Stanford University Press, 1999). Derrida's turn to the political is usually dated to *Specters of Marx* and the notion that deconstruction is "radicalized Marxism" (92). In *Specters,* Derrida hails the formation of a "New International"—"the friendship of an alliance without institution" that he sees working in a "new, concrete, and real way" (85–86). This view is advanced in subsequent works such as *The Politics of Friendship* and *Adieu to Emmanuel Levinas.* In *Politics,* Derrida submits philosophy's canonical, "homo-fraternal and phallogocentric" discourses on friendship to a kind of political critique so that we might begin to think and to implement a democracy uprooted from so many "figures of friendship (philosophical and religious) which prescribe fraternity" (306). For Derrida, the deployment of the word "brother" is always implicitly a political act. In *Adieu,* Derrida links Levinasian notions of hospitality to the political violence and distress produced by Nation-States—especially (but certainly not limited to) Israel. Derrida credits Levinas especially` for the notion of "a Torah before Sinai"—a notion that unseals the law from the event of its message and thus problematizes legitimizing invocations of election.

19. According to Habermas, the "supposition of an achievable consensus" informs the communicative practices of everyday life. For Habermas, we can engage in critical discussions of interpretations of situations *only under the presupposition of intersubjectively identical ascriptions of meaning.* This point is at the heart of his repeated critiques of Derridean deconstruction. See, for instance, Jürgen Habermas, "Excursus on Leveling the Genre Distinction between Philosophy and Literature," *The Philosophical Discourse of Modernity: Twelve Lectures,* trans. Frederick G. Lawrence (Cambridge, MA: MIT Press, 1987), 185–210.

20. Dominick LaCapra, *History and Memory After Auschwitz* (Ithaca, NY: Cornell University Press, 1998), 182.

21. LaCapra, *Writing History, Writing Trauma,* 78.

22. Michael Marrus, "Reflections on the Historiography of the Holocaust," *Journal of Modern History* 66 (March 1994): 93.

23. Inga Clendinnen, *Reading the Holocaust* (New York: Cambridge University Press, 1999), 17.

24. A fundamental statement of this method can be found in the text of Claude Lanzmann's *Shoah: The Complete Text of the Acclaimed Holocaust Film* (New York: Da Capo Press, 1995), 59. The manner of Lanzmann's questioning in his film, of course, takes it cue from Hilberg's method.

25. Binjamin Wilkomirski, *Fragments: Memories of a Wartime Childhood*, trans. Carol Brown Janeway (New York: Schocken, 1996), 4.

26. Ibid., 147.

27. For a definitively thorough overview of the controversy surrounding Wikomirski's memoir—including the determination that the events depicted in Wilkomirski's book "are incompatible with his own biographical reality [. . . .] The story he wrote in *Fragments* and has told elsewhere took place solely within the world of his thoughts and emotions" (268)—see Stefan Maechler, *The Wilkomirski Affair: A Study in Biographical Truth*, trans. John E. Woods (New York: Schocken, 2001). Two shorter, and equally compelling, overviews are Philip Gourevitch, "The Memory Thief," *The New Yorker* (June 14, 1999): 48–68, and Elena Lappin, "The Man with Two Heads," *Granta* 66 (1999): 7–65. For a compelling account of the book's significance in spite of its impugned historical credentials, see Michael Bernard-Donals, "Beyond the Question of Authenticity: Witness and Testimony in the *Fragments* Controversy," *PMLA* 116.5 (October 2001): 1302–1315.

28. See, in this respect, the recent collection of essays that goes by this name: *The Americanization of the Holocaust*, ed. Hilene Flanzbaum (Baltimore: Johns Hopkins University Press, 1999).

29. The link between unchecked transferential relations to the past and simplified historical explanations informs a number of the dismissals of Daniel Goldhagen's controversial *Hitler's Willing Executioners*. For a polemical critique of Goldhagen along these lines, see Hans-Ulrich Wehler, "Like a Thorn in the Flesh," in *Unwilling Germans?: The Goldhagen Debate*, ed. Robert R. Shandley (Minneapolis: University of Minnesota Press, 1998). Wehler suggests that the legitimacy of Goldhagen's thesis is in part undermined by the fact that the author is "the progeny of a victim" (i.e., the son of a Holocaust survivor), and he wonders aloud if other historical atrocities are likewise to be handed over solely to historians who share a national or ethnic link to the victims.

30. This is a question raised explicitly by Clendinnen, for whom the way scholars continue to construe the Holocaust as "morally and intellectually baffling" leads to a "sickening of imagination and curiosity and the draining of the will which afflicts so many of us when we try to look squarely at the persons and processes implicated in the Holocaust." This leads to a dangerous perplexity with grave moral consequences: "In the face of a catastrophe on this scale so deliberately inflicted, perplexity is an

indulgence we cannot afford" (*Reading the Holocaust*, 4–5). See, in this respect, as well Yehuda Bauer's critique of the trend toward a kind of mystification of the Holocaust, including his trenchant claim that "[t]o say that the Holocaust is inexplicable, in the last resort, is to justify it" (Yehuda Bauer, *Rethinking the Holocaust* [New Haven: Yale University Press, 2001], 38.) Sharing this concern—if for more urgent, present political reasons—is Norman Finkelstein, who discerns an ideological utility beneath the insistence on the unthinkability and uniqueness and irrationality of the Holocaust. For Finkelstein, this characterization of the Holocaust is a belated construction designed to secure an unconditional defense of Israel and of Jewish interests. Thus Finkelstein's claim that "the challenge today is to restore the Nazi holocaust as a rational subject of inquiry. Only then can we really learn from it. The abnormality of the Nazi holocaust springs not from the event itself but from the exploitative industry that has grown up around it" (Norman Finkelstein, *The Holocaust Industry: Reflections on the Exploitation of Jewish Suffering* [New York: Verso, 2000], 150.)

31. Omer Bartov, *Murder in Our Midst: The Holocaust, Industrial Killing, and Representation* (New York: Oxford University Press, 1996), 110.

32. Ibid., 132.

33. Saul Friedlander, *Probing the Limits of Representation: Nazism and the "Final Solution"* (Cambridge: Harvard University Press, 1992), 2.

34. The three sections of Friedlander's book engage three related spheres in which these complications have become significant: first, the seeming license for historical relativism that is the offshoot of Hayden White's rejection of "objective historical methodology" as a way to settle truth-claims made by competing historical accounts; second, the problem of using the Holocaust as a sort of capital to affirm Western rationality and ideas about Enlightenment; third, the problem of "postmodern multiplicities" in contemporary aesthetic representations, and whether or not they "convey a complex and multiple message [or] cover a blatantly ideological message" (*Probing the Limits* 10).

35. Slavoj Žižek, *The Sublime Object of Ideology* (New York: Verso, 1989), 6.

36. Slavoj Žižek, *The Indivisible Remainder: An Essay on Schelling and Related Matters* (New York: Verso, 1996), 217.

37. Sigmund Freud, "Negation," in *The Standard Edition of the Complete Psychological Works of Sigmund Freud*, trans. James Strachey, vol. 19 (London: Hogarth Press and the Institute of Psycho-analysis, 1953–74), 235–236.

38. Friedrich Nietzsche, *The Will to Power*, trans. Walter Kaufmann and R. J. Hollingdale, ed. Walter Kaufmann. (New York: Vintage, 1967), 433.

Chapter 1

1. Karl R. Popper, *The Open Society and Its Enemies, Volume 2, The High Tide of Prophecy: Hegel, Marx and the Aftermath*, 5th ed. (Princeton: Princeton University Press, 1971). Popper remains the most vituperative critic of Hegel and the most explicit proponent of a direct causal link between Hegel and totalitarianism. Hegel is, for Popper, the "dictator of philosophy" (35), an apologist for State domination, the purveyor of a "despicable perversion of everything that is decent; a perversion not only of reason, freedom, equality, and the other ideas of the open society, but also of a sincere belief in God, and even of a sincere patriotism" (49). According to Popper, all of the modern totalitarians "have been brought up in the close atmosphere of Hegelianism" (31). Popper's literary equivalent is undoubtedly the narrator of Imre Kertész's *Kaddish For A Child Not Born* who refers to Hegel (not a little sardonically) as "all Führers' and Chancellors' philosopher and chief wine steward" (Imre Kertész, *Kaddish For A Child Not Born*, trans. Christopher C. Wilson and Katharina M. Wilson [Evanston: Northwestern University Press, 1997], 63). Today, the charge of fascism has been by and large replaced by the charge of imperialism. See, for instance, Michael Hardt's and Antonio Negri's recent claim that "it is impossible . . . not to link both Hegel's philosophical recuperation of the Other within Absolute Spirit and his universal history leading from lesser peoples to its summit in Europe together with the very real violence of European conquest and colonialism. In short, Hegel's history is not only a powerful attack on the revolutionary plane of immanence but also a negation of non-European desire" (Michael Hardt and Antonio Negri, *Empire* [Cambridge: Harvard University Press, 2000], 82).

2. Alexander Kojève, *Introduction to the Reading of Hegel: Lectures on the Phenomenology of Spirit*, ed. Allan Bloom, trans. James H. Nichols, Jr. (Ithaca, NY: Cornell University Press, 1980), 194.

3. G. W. F. Hegel, *The Philosophy of History*, trans. J. Sibree (New York: Dover, 1956), 33.

4. This question appears perhaps most consistently in the work of Daniel and Jonathan Boyarin. Citing Paul's famous lines—"There is neither Jew nor Greek; there is neither slave nor freeman; there is no male and female. For you are all one in Christ Jesus"—Daniel Boyarin notes the way in which a universal spirit and its drive for sameness erases various differences: "In the process of baptism in the spirit the marks of ethnos, gender, and class are all erased in the ascension to a univocity and universality of human essence which is beyond and outside the body" (Daniel Boyarin, *A Radical Jew: Paul and the Politics of Identity* [Berkeley: University of California Press, 1994], 24). Calling consistent attention to the dangers of idealization, spiritualization, and totalization—three gestures initiated by Paul

and consummated by Hegel—the Boyarins point out the "fateful conse-
quences" such gestures have had for Jews in the Christian West. See Daniel
Boyarin and Jonathan Boyarin, "Diaspora: Generation and the Ground of
Jewish Identity," *Critical Inquiry* 19 (1993): 693–725.

5. Discussing the place of Judaism in Hegel's progressive narrative
of Spirit coming-to-itself, Emil Fackenheim asks, "What of the 'Lord' of
Judaism and His otherness?" (Emil Fackenheim, *To Mend the World: Foundations of Post-Holocaust Jewish Thought* [New York: Schocken, 1982], 111).
And Jonathan Boyarin, in pointing out the failure of "the ethical narrative
of universal history, observes apropos of Hegel, "contemporary Jews never
fit into his scheme of providential world history" (Jonathan Boyarin, *Storm
from Paradise: The Politics of Jewish Memory* [Minneapolis: University of
Minnesota Press, 1992], 94). For the most recent discussion of the fate of
Judaism within Hegel's dialectical system—"the dialectic itself expresses a
fundamental *in*justice toward Judaism, because it sublates it into Christianity while dismissing its post-Jesus history as meaningless. In this respect, Hegel's dialectic does to Judaism what the medieval church (*ecclesia*)
has done to the synagogue (*synagoga*)—see Yirmiyahu Yovel, *Dark Riddle:
Hegel, Nietzsche, and the Jews* (University Park, PA: Penn State University
Press, 1998), 99.

6. From the standpoint of Jewish philosophy, Emil Fackenheim is
arguably most emphatic on this point, insisting that in our approach of the
Holocaust, "Hegel instructs only by way of contrast. His ultimate Whole
of wholes is one of divine wonder. The Holocaust, on its part, is a whole
of horror. A transcending comprehension of it is impossible, for it would
rest on the prior dissolution of a horror that is indissoluble" (Emil
Fackenheim, *To Mend the World: Foundations of Post-Holocaust Jewish Thought*
[New York: Schocken, 1982], 27). For Fackenheim, the Holocaust—given
its unique, unprecedented horror—simply cannot fall prey to Hegelian
ideas concerning Overcoming. "There can be no thought of a return to
Hegelianism," he claims, since to overcome the Holocaust is somehow to
miss the truth of its horrific dimension. From the standpoint of Holocaust
literature and art, this point is given similar emphasis in the work of Lawrence
Langer, who likewise continually calls attention to the fact that artistic
representation and language are doomed forever to fail to overcome, comprehend, or otherwise transcend in the service of some progressive idea the
catastrophe of Auschwitz. For evidence of this, see his *Holocaust Testimonies:
The Ruins of Memory* (New Haven: Yale University Press, 1991), *Admitting
the Holocaust: Collected Essays* (New York: Oxford University Press, 1995),
and *Pre-empting the Holocaust* (New Haven: Yale University Press, 1998).

7. Emmanuel Levinas, *A Difficult Freedom: Essays on Judaism*, trans.
Seán Hand (Baltimore: Johns Hopkins University Press, 1990), 199. Subsequent references to this edition will be cited parenthetically within the text.

8. Despite important philosophical differences among and between them, this dismissal unites the canonical figures of French postwar philosophy. Levinas and Derrida, for example, may not aim at the complete demolition of metaphysics in the way that Deleuze and Foucault do in their claims for immanence, but all share nonetheless an ethicopolitical hostility to Hegel because of what the latter is said to do to alterity. I have in mind here Derrida's critique of *Aufhebung* in his "From Restricted to General Economy: A Hegelianism without Reserve," in *Writing and Difference*, trans. Alan Bass (Chicago: University of Chicago Press, 1978); Deleuze's critique of dialectic in his *Nietzsche and Philosophy*, trans. Hugh Tomlinson (New York: Columbia University Press, 1983); Foucault's vision of an end to history marked by man's "absolute dispersion," in *The Order of Things: An Archaeology of the Human Sciences* (New York: Vintage, 1994); and finally, Lyotard's critique of totalizing metanarratives in *The Postmodern Condition: A Report on Knowledge*, trans. Geoff Bennington and Brian Massumi (Minneapolis: University of Minnesota Press, 1979).

9. The source text for this summary and subsequent explication is as follows: "The thesis of the primacy of history constitutes an option for the comprehension of being in which interiority is sacrificed. The present work proposes another option. The real must not only be determined in its historical objectivity, but also from interior intentions, from the *secrecy* that interrupts the continuity of historical time. Only on the basis of this secrecy is the pluralism of society possible" (Emmanuel Levinas, *Totality and Infinity: An Essay on Exteriority*. trans. Alphonso Lingis [Pittsburgh: Duquesne University Press, 1961], 57–58).

10. Ibid., 52.

11. The best account of Levinasian ethics in the context of Holocaust memory is James Hatley's *Suffering Witness: The Quandry of Responsibility after the Irreparable* (Albany: SUNY Press, 2000). Despite an uncritical rehearsing of Levinas's construal of Hegel—including the claim that a Hegelian address of the Shoah would necessarily be a redemptive one indifferent to the victims of history—Hatley does unearth the extent to which a nonhistorical moment of witnessing always returns to destabilize or interrupt historical testimony.

12. Levinas, *Totality and Infinity*, 174.

13. Levinas never tires of repeating this important point—that the relationship with alterity instituted by language does not form a totality with it: "The absolute exteriority of the exterior being is not purely and simply lost as a result of its manifestation; it 'absolves' itself from the relation in which it presents itself" (*Totality and Infinity* 50). This is because something about the Other's speech is completely unprecedented and incomprehensible: "The claim to know and to reach the other is realized with the relationship with the Other that is cast in the relation with language,

where the essential is the interpellation, the vocative. The other is maintained and confirmed in his heterogeneity as soon as one calls on him, be it only to say to him that one cannot speak to him, to classify him as sick, to announce to him his death sentence; at the same time as grasped, wounded, outraged, he is 'respected.' The invoked is not what I comprehend: *he is not under a category*. He is the one to whom I speak—he has only a reference to himself; he has no quiddity" (*Totality and Infinity* 69).

14. G. W. F. Hegel, *Science of Logic*, trans. A. V. Miller (New Jersey: Humanities Press, 1969), 146.

15. Levinas, *Totality and Infinity*, 73.

16. As Hegel puts it in the greater *Logic*, "Every beginning must be made *with the absolute*, just as all advance is merely the exposition of it, in so far as it *in-itself* is the Notion" (Ibid., 829).

17. This view is the prevailing one today in Hegel studies: the Hegel who has something to teach us about politics is the one who talks concretely about historical subjects and political theory. Hegel's "logical" works may get us to recognize trauma for what it is, but their political relevance is minimal because insofar as they remain at the level of speculation, the working through they afford is "merely thought" (and thus "obsessional"). This is why many in Hegel studies today argue that Hegel must be saved from himself. Claiming that "speculative logic is dead, but Hegel's thought is not," Allen Wood, for example, urges an understanding of Hegel that would see him as a very practical philosopher. For Wood, Hegel's project is one of "rational ethics," and even though "to read Hegel in this way is, admittedly, to read him in some measure against his own self-understanding; it is nevertheless the only way in which most of us, if we are honest with ourselves, can read him seriously at all" (Allen W. Wood, *Hegel's Ethical Thought* [New York: Cambridge UP, 1990], 8).

18. For clear expressions of praise, see Theodor Adorno, *Hegel: Three Studies*, trans. Shierry Weber Nicholsen (Cambridge, MA: The MIT Press, 1993). There, one finds statements like the following: "The wealth of experience on which thought feeds in Hegel is incomparable; it is put into the ideas themselves, never appearing as mere 'material,' to say nothing of example or evidence external to the ideas. Through what is experienced, the abstract idea is transformed back into something living, just as mere material is transformed through the path thought travels: one could show this in every sentence of the *Phenomenology of Spirit*" (50).

19. Theodor Adorno, *Negative Dialectics*, trans. E. B. Ashton (New York: Continuum, 1966), 320. Subsequent quotations from Adorno are to this edition will be cited parenthetically within the text.

20. It should perhaps be pointed out here that Freud did in fact try to historicize the emergence of this Law/Spirit: the name for that attempt was *Totem and Taboo*.

21. The echo here is to Foucault, whose critique of psychoanalysis rests precisely on its manner of continuing a process begun by Christianity of "disciplining" the body, thus subjecting pleasure to a totalizing discourse of desire and its juridical/confessional restraints. Foucault's lament is that these restraints take sexual conduct away from "pleasure and the aesthetics of its use" and toward a realm of "desire and its purifying hermeneutics" (Michel Foucault, *The Use of Pleasure: The History of Sexuality, Volume 2*, trans. Robert Hurley [New York: Vintage, 1990], 254). Foucault's critique of psychoanalysis has many affinities with Deleuze and Guattari's, which likewise objects to the universalizing tendencies of Freud's epistemology for the harm such tendencies pose to difference and multiplicity. In a paradigmatic articulation of their critique, they claim that "Freud is the Luther and Adam Smith of psychiatry. He mobilizes all the resources of myth, of tragedy, of dreams, in order to re-enslave desire, this time from within: an intimate theatre" (Gilles Deleuze and Félix Guattari, *Anti-Oedipus: Capitalism and Schizophrenia*, trans. Robert Hurley, Mark Seem, and Helen R. Lane [Minneapolis: University of Minnesota Press, 1983], 271).

22. "Hence the greatest and perhaps only benefit of all philosophy of pure reason may be only negative. For such philosophy does not—as an organon—serve to expand [cognition], but—as a discipline—serves to determine the boundary [of cognition]; and instead of discovering truth, it has only the silent merit of preventing errors" (Immanuel Kant, *Critique of Pure Reason*, trans. Werner S. Pluhar [Indianapolis: Hackett Publishing Co., 1996], 728).

23. This is what leads Kant to claim that the *critique* of pure reason is the "true tribunal" for all those controversies of reason rooted in the direct apprehension of objects. Because critique does not deal directly with objects, but with the way we know them, it alone can afford us a measure of tranquillity: "Without such critique reason is, as it were, in the state of nature, and cannot validate or secure its assertions and claims except through *war*. Critique, on the other hand, which obtains all its decisions from the basic rules governing its own appointment—rules whose authority no one can doubt—provides us with the tranquillity of a situation of law, a situation in which we are to carry on our controversy solely through *litigation*" (Ibid., 696).

24. Ibid., 535.

25. Ibid., 541.

26. I owe this insight to Alenka Zupančič's reading of Kant, specifically her claim that "the subject is not divided between the pathological and the pure. The alternative to pathological subjectivity is not pure or immaculate ethical subjectivity but freedom or autonomy" (Alenka Zupančič, *Ethics of the Real: Kant, Lacan* [New York: Verso, 2000], 21–22).

27. Jacques Lacan, *The Four Fundamental Concepts of Psycho-analysis*, trans. Alan Sheridan (New York: Norton, 1981), 250–251.

28. As Hegel sees it, Spirit *is* its own ground, which means quite simply that Spirit's existence, its coming-to-have-agency, its consolidation of itself with itself, comes about by way of some radical, purely performative choice made *from within* for reasons we cannot begin to fathom. Knowledge of Spirit, for Hegel, involves *bearing witness* to this choice—that is, realizing the extent to which we reenact it all the time. Despite all of our attempts to envisage an *external* ground for this choice, this mediation, Hegel always insists that such envisaging constitutes a false move. This is perhaps most clear in Hegel's argument concerning the way one *chooses* God. Hegel claims that the choice of God can never be rooted in external, mediating factors—that is, in factors the Understanding can represent: "My faith may come to me through instruction, miracles, by force of authority, and so on. Thus these things can be the ground of faith as subjective faith. But in this verification the formulation of the content as the 'ground' of my faith is just what is wrong. If it is a matter of faith, this externality, this separation of the ground from myself, must fall away. I appropriate in faith that which is the ground of faith so that it ceases to be something other for me. Authentic faith can be defined as the witness of my spirit, the witness of spirit concerning the spirit, which implies that there is no place in it for any other external content" (G. W. F. Hegel, *Lectures on the Philosophy of Religion, Volume I: Introduction and the Concept of Religion*, ed. Peter C. Hogsdon. trans. R. F. Brown, P. C. Hogdson, and J. M. Stewart [Berkeley: University of California Press, 1984], 337).

29. One way to conceptualize this difference: It is not the necessity *beneath* contingency that lies at the crux of Hegelian phenomenology, but rather the necessity *of* contingency.

30. Harold Kaplan, *Conscience and Memory: Meditations on a Museum of the Holocaust* (Chicago: University of Chicago Press, 1994), 12.

31. Juliet Flower MacCannell, "Fascism and the Voice of Conscience," in *Radical Evil*, ed. Joan Copjec (New York: Verso, 1996), 49.

32. For Rawls's introduction of this concept, see *A Theory of Justice* (Cambridge: Harvard University Press, 1971), 3–22.

33. John Rawls, *Justice as Fairness: A Restatement*. Ed. Erin Kelley (Cambridge, MA.: Harvard University Press, 2001), 87.

34. John Rawls, *Political Liberalism* (New York: Columbia University Press, 1993), 24.

35. Rawls, *A Theory of Justice*, 506.

36. For an elaboration of this point—"The original position is not merely a device to arrive at a contract on justice. It is a creation of morality and human nature, the counterpart of Eden, and Rawls presents himself as the creator of our moral character and nature" (34)—see Roberto

Alejandro, *The Limits of Rawlsian Justice* (Baltimore: Johns Hopkins University Press, 1998), 20–42.

37. Thus Rawls's claim for our occupying an original position characterized by a kind of "reflective equilibrium" in which, for a moment, "everything is in order" but which is not necessarily stable.

38. David Johnston, *The Idea of a Liberal Theory: A Critique and Reconstruction* (Princeton: Princeton University Press, 1994), 113.

39. I take this phrase from Stephen Mulhall's and Adam Swift's account of the communitarian critique of Rawls—especially that of Michael Sandel's—in their *Liberals and Communitarians*, 2nd ed. (Cambridge, MA.: Blackwell, 1996), 40–69.

40. Rawls, *Political Liberalism*, 27.

41. Richard Rorty, *Objectivity, Relativism, and Truth: Philosophical Papers Volume 1* (New York: Cambridge University Press, 1991), 14.

42. The reference here is to Habermas, who likewise conceives of social struggle and social change as an affair of social reality itself—of a "life-world" whose basis is intersubjectivity.

43. Richard Wolin, "Preface to the MIT Edition: Note on a Missing Text," *The Heidegger Controversy: A Critical Reader*, ed. Richard Wolin (Cambridge: The MIT Press, 1993), xvi.

44. See Saul Friedlander's claim that Nazi leaders and some of the rank and file felt they were "accomplishing something truly, historically, metahistorically, exceptional" (Martin Broszat and Saul Friedlander, "A Controversy about the Historicization of National Socialism," Yad Vashem Studies 19 [1988]: 28).

45. For this reason, Richard Wolin laments Heidegger's dismissal of Kantian critical philosophy (i.e., the capacity for thinking to reflect in earnest about its own foundations). We have already seen the extent to which liberalism depends on this self-critical gesture.

46. Kaplan, *Conscience and Memory*, 99.

47. The fundamental desire of political liberalism, according to Rawls—and this is the ground for its ethos of tolerance—is neither to invoke, criticize, or reject any comprehensive doctrines. In Rawls's view, political liberalism "leaves philosophy as it is," abstaining from "assertions about the domain of comprehensive views except as necessary when these views are unreasonable and reject all variations of the basic essentials of a democratic regime" (*Political Liberalism*, 375). Once again, however, this view cannot help but betray a kind of exasperation vis-à-vis those who refuse to be tolerant. Rawls is thus forced to indicate the kernel of "intolerance" *internal to political liberalism* that is its authoritarian underside and that enables the foreclosure and consolidation of its ethos of tolerance. As he puts it, political liberalism must occasionally make assertions regarding certain "unreasonable views" that reject the rules of the democratic universe of meaning.

48. Ibid., lxii.

49. Jacques Lacan, *Seminar III: The Psychoses, 1955–1956*, trans. Russell Grigg (New York: Norton, 1993), 266–267.

50. Slavoj Žižek, *Tarrying with the Negative* (Durham: Duke University Press, 1993), 149. Elsewhere, Žižek makes the obvious claim that follows from his assertion here: that the Jew was Hitler's *point de capiton*. This purely formal gesture, then, promises a way of reversing the absence/loss of enjoyment. As Žižek puts it, "The simply evocation of the 'Jewish plot' *explains everything*: all of a sudden 'things become clear,' perplexity is replaced by a firm sense of orientation, all the diversity of earthly miseries is conceived as the manifestation of the 'Jewish plot' " (Slavoj Žižek, *For they know not what they do* [New York: Verso, 1991], 10).

51. Kaplan, *Conscience and Memory*, 169.

52. Ibid., 177.

53. Ibid., 173.

54. For a similar retroactive, etiological account of anti-Semitism, which likewise posits a intelligible cause for the murder of the Jews—"It is not, I believe, as deicide, as 'God killer,' that the Jew has been loathed and feared in the Christian civilization of the West (although that hideous attribution does play its part). It is as *inventor* of God; it is as spokesman for and remembrancer of an almighty, all-seeing, all-demanding Deity. It is because Judaism has kept man awake"—see George Steiner, "The Long Life of Metaphor: An Approach to the 'Shoah,' " in *Writing and the Holocaust*, ed. Berel Lang (New York: Holmes and Maier, 1988), 164.

55. Kaplan, *Conscience and Memory*, 179.

56. Renata Salecl, *The Spoils of Freedom* (New York: Routledge, 1994), 127.

57. Ibid., 119.

58. Ernesto Laclau and Chantal Mouffe, *Hegemony and Socialist Strategy: Towards a Radical Democratic Politics* (New York: Verso, 1985), 190.

59. Jacques Derrida, *Positions*, trans. Alan Bass (Chicago: University of Chicago Press, 1981), 85–86.

60. Jacques Derrida, *Resistances of Psychoanalysis*, trans. Peggy Kamuf, Pascale-Anne Brault, and Michael Naas (Stanford: Stanford University Press, 1998), 4.

61. Ibid., 33–34.

62. Jacques Derrida, *Aporias*, trans. Thomas Dutoit (Stanford: Stanford University Press, 1993), 12.

63. LaCapra, *Representing the Holocaust: History, Theory, Trauma*, 6.

64. Ibid., 54

65. Ibid., 64.

66. Ibid., 10.

67. Ibid., 47. For a view that joins with LaCapra in acknowledging the role of transference in historical inquiry and in seeking to check its possible abuses, see Inga Clendinnen's suggestion that certain "standards of evidence and inference" function as a way to distinguish and keep apart the "witness" and the "analyst" (Inga Clendinnen, *Reading the Holocaust* [New York: Cambridge University Press, 1999], 9–10).

68. Dominick LaCapra, *History and Memory after Auschwitz* (Ithaca, NY: Cornell University Press, 1998), 47–48.

69. Ibid., 40.

70. LaCapra, *Writing History, Writing Trauma*, 103–104.

71. LaCapra, *History and Memory after Auschwitz*, 40.

72. Ibid., 41.

73. LaCapra, *Writing History, Writing Trauma*, ix

74. Hegel, *Science of Logic*, 129.

75. For Santner's advocacy of the need, as creatures of language, to consider mourning "in structural ways" (as part of a counterfascist ethics), see *Stranded Objects: Mourning, Memory, and Film in Postwar Germany* (Ithaca, NY: Cornell University Press, 1990).

76. Caruth's investigation of this itinerary occurs in her reading of Freud's (and then Lacan's) reading of the famous dream of the child burning. The sequence Caruth sets up from *knowing* to *awakening* strikes me as an unavoidable one in any genuine encounter with the past, and moreover, one that does not automatically rule out *any* knowledge. For Caruth's position, see "Freud, Lacan, and the Ethics of Memory," in *Unclaimed Experience: Trauma, Narrative, and History* (Baltimore: Johns Hopkins University Press, 1996), 91–112.

77. Ruth Leys, *Trauma: A Genealogy* (Chicago: University of Chicago Press, 2000), 275.

78. Leys's book begins by juxtaposing the violent, traumatic fates of young Ugandan girls abducted by a guerrilla army and Paula Jones's claim to have been traumatized by the sexual harrassment of President Clinton. The purpose of this juxtaposition is central to Leys's larger critique of viewing trauma structurally: when trauma is diluted and generalized in this way, victimhood becomes "unlocatable in any particular person or place, thereby permitting it to migrate or spread contagiously to others" (Ibid., 296). For an essay that shares Leys's concern for genealogy, suggesting that the concept of trauma itself needs to be "traumatized" in order to ward off its use as moral capital, see John Mowitt, "Trauma Envy," *Cultural Critique* 46 (Fall 2000): 272–297.

79. See Michael Bernard-Donals astute consideration of this question in "Beyond the Question of Authenticity: Witness and Testimony in the *Fragments* Controversy," *PMLA* 116.5 (October 2001): 1302–1315.

Bernard-Donals and Richard Glejzer's *Between Witness and Testimony: The Holocaust and the Limits of Representation* (Albany: SUNY Press, 2001) appeared too late for me to include in this discussion.

80. James Berger, *After the End: Representations of the Post-Apocalypse* (Minneapolis: University of Minnesota Press, 1999), 31. Berger is especially critical of Derrida, whose wavering about the matter of historical reference and belated mentions of the Holocaust constitute "traumatized responses to the still overwhelming impact of the Holocaust" (120). See, esp. chapter 4, entitled "The Absent Referent: Derrida and the Holocaust."

81. At the time of this writing—in the months following the events of September 11, 2001—this same dynamic can be discerned in the view that America was in full possession of itself prior to the World Trade Center bombings, and in the view (espoused most notably by New York mayor Rudy Guliani) that the scope of the killing of innocent civilians was an unprecedented act in human history.

82. Joan Copjec, *Read My Desire: Lacan against the Historicists* (Cambridge: The MIT Press, 1994), 56.

83. G. W. F. Hegel, *The Phenomenology of Spirit*, trans. A. V. Miller (New York: Oxford University Press, 1977), 10. Subsequent references to this edition will be cited parenthetically within the text.

84. G. W. F. Hegel, *Logic*, trans. William Wallace (New York: Oxford University Press, 1975), 69.

85. Wilkomerski, *Fragments: Memories of a Wartime Childhood*, 4.

86. Adorno's critique of the universal would thus appear to be misplaced, for the very meaning of his critique rests upon a universal ground. In other words, his categorical insistence that thought measure itself by what eludes it—because that insistence is fundamentally a thought—is no less the product of an absolute position.

87. Hegel, *Logic*, 37.

88. Ibid., 32.

89. Robert Pippin, *Hegel's Idealism: The Satisfactions of Self-Consciousness* (New York: Cambridge University Press, 1989), 85–86.

90. This is, for Judith Butler, the key feature of the Hegelian subject—that is, its "rhetorical agency." According to Butler, the Hegelian subject entails an agency whose *enactments* that subject is capable of "reading rhetorically," thus leading to the recovery of "ever greater dimensions of its own identity" (Judith Butler, *Subjects of Desire: Hegelian Reflections in Twentieth-Century France* [New York: Columbia University Press, 1987], 31). This view informs Butler's repeated critique of the traumatic Real— that is, the truth of an unsymbolizable *particularity as such*. In books such as *Bodies that Matter* and *The Psychic Life of Power*, Butler argues that the real is always "figured," that there is no way to posit something prior to self-reflexivity. Thus for Butler, the traumatic real has no credible ontological

claim: whatever is absent from a given sociosymbolic order is, for her, always historical (and futural), depending on projects of cultural translation. For a more recent expression of this position, see Judith Butler, "Restaging the Universal: Hegemony and the Limits of Formalism," in *Contingency, Hegemony, Universality: Contemporary Dialogues of the Left* (New York: Verso, 2000), 11–43.

91. Hegel, *Phenomenology of Spirit*, 66.

92. Jacques Lacan, *The Seminar of Jacques Lacan, Book II: The Ego in Freud's Theory and in the Technique of Psychoanalysis, 1954–1955*, trans. Sylvia Tomaselli (New York: Norton, 1991), 29.

93. There are, in other words, two totalizing operations, and these are often confused—one seeks to secure a ground for the Law and the sociosymbolic order, and one seeks a traumatic encounter with that particular "kernel of the real" that lies on the other side of the Law. The confusion/conflation of these two operations is perhaps most apparent in Adorno's and Horkheimer's insistence that totality and anti-Semitism are always linked. On this point, see Theodor Adorno and Max Horkheimer, *Dialectic of Enlightenment*, trans. John Cumming (New York: Continuum, 1947). My claim here is that the totality to which they refer is *not* Hegel's, and that the totalizing Adorno and Horkheimer see in the Enlightenment project is an operation designed to realize society objectively as a transparent, coherent whole. (Incidentally, this is Rawls' project in *A Theory of Justice*.) As conceived by the purveyors and heirs of Enlightenment, this totality is still symbolic, and this is precisely what points up the un-Hegelian dimension of the society or subject they hope thereby to produce. For Hegel, the symbolic order (i.e., the order of thought and language) depends on some minimal difference, some negativity, and incorporating, adjudicating, or otherwise domesticating this negativity would do nothing to cement social relations; on the contrary, it would bring about their complete collapse. Negativity (i.e., some minimal disparity between subject and substance), in other words, is not just that which eludes the order of thought, it is that order's last support.

94. Gilian Rose, *Hegel Contra Sociology* (Atlantic Highlands, NJ: Athlone, 1981), 183. For Rose, the distinction between Hegel's radical "method" and his conservative "system" is itself a conservative one: "Hegel's thought has *no* social import if the absolute is banished or suppressed, if the absolute cannot be thought" (42).

95. This necessitates, of course, giving up certain anti-Semitic *reasons* for aggression against Jews (e.g., their ill-earned wealth, the killing of Christ, etc.) as well as more honorific explanations. I have in mind here Kaplan's liberal-democratic notion that Jews deserve somehow to be regarded as exemplars of democratic rights or Steiner's notion that the Jews' "invention" of God thus triggered the enmity of Christianity in the

West. I owe this point to Slavoj Žižek, who insists that anti-Semitism is fundamentally a manner of coping with some more primary ontological experience of discomfort. As Žižek puts it, "The (anti-Semitic figure of the) 'Jew' is not the positive cause of social imbalance and antagonisms: social antagonism comes first, and the 'Jew' merely gives body to this obstacle . . . One falls into the ideological trap precisely by succumbing to the illusion that anti-Semitism really *is* about Jews" (Slavoj Žižek, *The Plague of Fantasies* [New York: Verso, 1997], 76–77).

96. Hegel, *Logic*, 274.

97. This phrase is Lacan's, and it points up the homology between the "analytic" discourses of Hegelian phenomenology and psychoanalysis. Lacan credits the latter for "its approach to stupidity," its willingness to get close to stupidity: "Surely it comes closer, since in other discourses stupidity is what one flees" (Jacques Lacan, *The Seminar of Jacques Lacan, Book XX: Encore 1972–1973*, trans. Bruce Fink [New York: Norton, 1998], 13).

Chapter 2

1. See, in this respect, Francis Fukuyama's *The End of History and the Last Man* (New York: The Free Press, 1992).

2. Eva Fogelman, *Conscience and Courage: Rescuers of Jews During the Holocaust* (New York: Anchor, 1994), xix. Fogelman's project to "give altruism back its good name" has been institutionalized in the Jewish Foundation for Christian Rescuers that is now a part of the Anti-Defamation League.

3. Hillel Levine, *In Search of Sugihara: The Elusive Japanese Diplomat Who Risked His Life to Rescue 10,000 Jews from the Holocaust* (New York: The Free Press, 1998), 16.

4. The literature documenting this failure is extensive. See David Wyman's *The Abandonment of the Jews* (New York: Pantheon, 1984), as well as his edited volume *The World Reacts to the Holocaust* (Baltimore: Johns Hopkins University Press, 1996). The persistent obsession with the failure of the Allies to bomb Auschwitz—in which Deborah Lipstadt astutely discerns a form of synechdocical thought—is perhaps also germane here. Lipstadt sees this discussion as a kind of "shorthand for an intricate and complicated web of failures by the British and Americans from 1933 on" (Deborah Lipstadt, "The Failure to Rescue and Contemporary American Jewish Historiography of the Holocaust: Judging from a Distance," in *The Bombing of Auschwitz: Should the Allies Have Attempted It?*, eds. Michael J. Neufeld and Michael Berenbaum (New York: St. Martin's Press, 2000), 227–236.

5. Sigmund Freud, "Notes upon a Case of Obsessional Neurosis" (1909), in *The Standard Edition of the Complete Psychological Works of Sigmund*

Freud, trans. James Strachey, vol. 10 (London: Hogarth Press and the Institute of Psycho-analysis, 1953–74), 246.

6. Claude Lanzmann, "Why Spielberg Has Distorted the Truth," *Manchester Guardian Weekly*, April 3, 1994: 14. The terms of Lanzmann's own critique are taken explicitly from his own film, *Shoah*. As Lanzmann puts it, "The Jewish survivors in *Shoah* are survivors of a special kind; they are not just any old survivors. They were at the end of the extermination process and saw the death of their people with their own eyes. *Shoah* is a film about death, not at all about survival."

7. Lanzmann's entire memorial project depends on a delinking of history and chronology, so as to encounter the "time" of trauma. See, for instance, his critique of chronology in "From the Holocaust to the 'Holocaust.'" *Telos* 42 [Winter 1979–80]: 142).

8. Lanzmann, "Why Spielberg Has Distorted the Truth," 14.

9. Norman Geras, *The Contract of Mutual Indifference: Political Philosophy after the Holocaust* (New York: Verso, 1998), 57.

10. See in this respect, Levine's claim that "There is so much more that we must know about the making of mass murderers; anecdotes of rescue provide fraudulent endings to large-scale processes of destructiveness. Six million killed versus a few thousand saved—in that light, a preoccupation with rescuers becomes unearned and unwarranted comfort. But as we know more about the Holocaust and understand less—to paraphrase Saul Friedländer's apt statement—the story of Sugihara and the making of a mass rescuer should be part of what baffles us" (8). At times, Levine genuinely allows Sugihara's act to baffle us. But at other times, he links Sugihara's act to a mobilizing maxim—for example, the biblical claim in Leviticus, "Do not stand on your neighbor's blood."

11. For books that do reach different hypotheses about the reasons that moved rescuers to act, see Fogelman's *Conscience and Courage*, Samuel P. and Pearl M. Oliner's *The Altruistic Personality* (New York: The Free Press, 1988), and Nechama Tec's *When Light Pierced the Darkness* (New York: Oxford University Press, 1986). For a book that ends up reflecting on the inability to quilt these disparate reasons together, see the epilogue to Eric Silver's *The Book of the Just: The Unsung Heroes Who Rescued Jews from Hitler* (New York: Grove Press, 1992). Silver's book highlights the way the attempt to find an ultimate quilting point ends up providing a sociology or ethnography of moral conduct. Thus Silver can contend that we can never find the "sufficient and necessary condition for moral courage." But he does not see the absence of such a condition as *the* feature of an act of moral courage itself.

12. Quoted in Mark Miller, "The Real Schindler," *Newsweek* (December 20, 1993), 118.

13. Keneally, 14. Keneally warns against reading the novel he is about to tell under easy character headings. "It is a risky enterprise to have to write of virtue" (14).

14. This is, in my view, the question that deserves to be posed apropos the "heroic" act at the core of Roberto Benigni's *Life Is Beautiful*. Certainly on one level, the film depicts a father's desperate attempt to save his son by providing an understandable—if comic—framework for the boy to make sense of his surroundings. The father's desire is apparently so self-evident we do not even bother to interrogate it. But what if beneath this heroic act we can also detect the most selfish of acts—that is, the father's desire to save himself and his own status as the locus of authority? There is indeed a key scene in which the boy clearly already knows what's really behind the game his father has devised. His claim to know what is really going on is then met by his father with an even more tenacious application of the game. Thus, while the entire sentimental thrust of the rescue motif lies in our identification with the little boy, the film contains within it an opposite narrative concerning the father's rescue and its failure.

15. See Ron Rosenbaum, *Explaining Hitler: The Search for the Origins of His Evil* (New York: Random House, 1998). The final paragraph of Ron Hansen's recent novel, *Hitler's Niece* (New York: HarperCollins, 1999), positions Hitler's murder of Geli Rebaul as a potentially decisive point in a telos leading to mass murder.

16. G. W. F. Hegel, *Phenomenology of Spirit*, trans. A. V. Miller (New York: Oxford University Press, 1977), 394.

17. Hegel, *Phenomenology*, 194.

18. Ibid.

19. Richard Rorty, *Contingency, Irony, Solidarity* (New York: Cambridge University Press, 1989), 189. Subsequent references to this edition will be cited parenthetically within the text.

20. Part of Rorty's effort is to rid us of *explanations* for inaction such as "inhumanity," "hardness of heart," or "lack of sense of human solidarity." This at least has the advantage of clearing a space for anti-Semitism as a specific mobilizing factor for indifference. Rorty hints at as much when he claims that "there are, presumably, detailed historicosociological explanations" for why one particular description of the Other that did not mobilize action (e.g., "She is a Jewess") often outweighed a competing description of the Other that might have mobilized action (e.g., "She is, like me, a mother of small children" [Ibid., 191].

21. Norman Geras, *Solidarity in the Conversation of Humankind: The Ungroundable Liberalism of Richard Rorty* (New York: Verso, 1995), 66.

22. Norman Geras, "Progress without Foundations" in *The Contract of Mutual Indifference*, 137.

23. See his critique of Ernst Mandel's doctrinaire Marxist "explanation" of the Holocaust in "Marxists Before the Holocaust," in *The Contract of Mutual Indifference*, 139–170. For Geras, Mandel's invocation of the "destructive tendencies present in bourgeois society" to explain the Holocaust seriously diminishes its significance. We might point out here that omission and minimization has given way, among certain Marxists in France, to outright revision and denial. For an account of this phenomenon, see Alain Finkielkraut, *The Future of a Negation: Reflections on the Question of Genocide*, trans. Mary Byrd Kelly (Lincoln: University of Nebraska Press, 1998). Finkielkraut's book deals with the uniqueness of the revisionists in France—the fact that they emerge from the Left. From such a perspective, the Holocaust is a myth aimed at sapping anticapitalist radicality.

24. This is the crux of Geras's socialist critique of liberalism—his sense that "liberal culture underwrites moral indifference" by failing to see indifference to the calamities and sufferings of others as a form of moral depravity (*Contract*, 58–59). As Geras puts it, "On its own, self-interest, even if this is the interest of a group, offers an improbable route towards a state of things in which sympathetic care and support for others will have come to occupy a much more prominent place. Furthermore, self- or group interest and the interest in a juster, more compassionate world are the less likely to coincide the further away are the supposed agents of change from the achievement of that world. And they *are* a long way from it, whoever they may be thought to be" (75).

25. Geras, *The Contract of Mutual Indifference*, 90.

26. Geras's argument here bears affinities to Mordecai Paldiel's. The director for the Righteous at Yad Vashem, Paldiel has located, in several books, the significance of rescuers' deeds in the good side of human nature. In a paradigmatic statement, Paldiel writes, "The Righteous show us that the individual does have an intrinsic wisdom of what constitutes good and evil behavior, and the individual's decision to act does make a difference; that even when one is living under totalitarian conditions, social pressure can be overcome. By identifying with the Righteous, we lay claim to the goodness in us, which is as inherently human, as the other less pleasant manifestations in our behavior" (Mordecai Paldiel, *Sheltering the Jews: Stories of Holocaust Rescuers* [Minneapolis: Fortress Press, 1996], 202). As I have suggested, the ethical dimension of the act is incompatible with any foreordained notion as to its "goodness" or positive outcome. Indeed, the most amazing aspect of the rescuers' conduct, it seems to me, is that the "difference" it would make was far from certain—and yet the decision to act was still undertaken.

27. For another instance of the way understanding appears to mandate a remaining at the level of language and conscious reality, see Gay

Block and Malka Drucker, *Rescuers: Portraits of Moral Courage in the Holocaust* (New York: Holmes & Meier), 1992. Block and Drucker aim to convey the "major issues of Holocaust rescue not by means of objective analysis but through personal narratives, lived experiences as remembered and recounted by the rescuers. Told in the rescuers' words, the stories reveal the interaction of social and psychological factors that led these people to intervene on behalf of Jews" (7).

28. For an interesting reading that, though traveling a somewhat different path, lands on a point similar to my own, see David Brenner, "Working through the Holocaust Blockbuster: *Schindler's List* and *Hitler's Willing Executioners*, Globally and Locally," *Germanic Review* 75.4 (Fall 2000): 296–316. Focusing on the political contexts and subtexts of *Schindler's List*, Brenner discerns a "globalizing American discourse" beneath the film's seeming commitment to particularity (or literalism). This discourse is aimed in part at defending the liberal capitalist American film industry.

29. Quoted in David Gritten, "Grim. Black and White . . . Spielberg?" *Los Angeles Times* (May 9, 1993): 9.

30. Bryan Cheyette, "The Uncertain Certainty of *Schindler's List*," *Spielberg's Holocaust: Critical Perspectives on* Schindler's List, ed. Yosefa Loshitsky (Bloomington: Indiana University Press, 1997), 235. Cheyette's otherwise finely argued analysis of the Manicheanism of Spielberg's film is for me only problematic in its suggestion that Spielberg's Manicheanism works on a tabula rasa: "To be sure, Schindler begins as a tabula rasa on which both the potential for good and for evil can be inscribed. He is, in other words, initially suspended between Stern's unequivocal virtue and Goeth's complete viciousness" (235). In my view, a Manichean aesthetic operates not so much *on* a blank state but rather as a *defense against* some terrifying, pathological presence—for example, Schindler's desire from the first frame of the film.

31. Perhaps the ultimate instance of this link is Spielberg's January 1996 donation of a part of the profits of *Schindler's List*—$1.6 million— to Brandeis University for the purposes of, according to press releases, "giv[ing] young men and women an opportunity to explore and define their Jewish identity" (Bernard Weinraub, "Spielberg Recording Holocaust Testimony," *New York Times* [November 10, 1994]: C22).

32. For the link between *Schindler's List* and the history of Spielberg's relation to Judaism, see David Ansen, "Spielberg's Obsession," *Newsweek* (December 20, 1993): 113–116, and Bernard Weinraub, "Steven Spielberg Faces the Holocaust," *New York Times* (December 12, 1993), section 2: 1, 28. Ansen makes, but does not explore, the connection in this context between *Schindler's List* and the "alien" presence in *E.T.*

33. Quoted in John H. Richardson, "Steven's Choice," *Premier* (January 1994): 93.

34. Ibid., 92.

35. As Bryan Cheyette points out, in his close comparison of Keneally's novel and Spielberg's film, "Spielberg leaves out many more concrete instances of dehumanization of the *Schindlerjuden* recounted by Keneally" (Bryan Cheyette, "The Uncertain Certainty of *Schindler's List*, 234–235).

36. *Schindler's List*, Universal Pictures Production Information (Universal City, n.d.), 6.

37. David Ansen, "Spielberg's Obsession," *Newsweek* (December 20, 1993): 114.

38. *Schindler's List*, Universal Pictures Production Information (Universal City, n.d.), 8–9.

39. Keneally, *Schindler's List*, 133.

40. As more than a few of *Schindler's List*'s detractors have pointed out, this position beyond struggle and mystery is part and parcel of an exercise of mastery highly consonant with an apologetic approach to historical memory. The response to the film in Germany provides evidence of this. On the cultural page of one of Germany's most important conservative newspapers, Gertrude Koch writes, *Schindler's List* was praised for showing how "all this bullshit the intellectuals tell about aesthetics after the Holocaust is just not true, because one can narrate it. What Spielberg has shown the world is there is nothing that can't be narrated. And, therefore, it tells us that aesthetics in general has to come back to these kinds of conventional forms." In short, one can get *beyond* desire—the desire of the perpetrators, the desire of the dead, the desire of the survivors, and so on. (Quoted in J. Hoberman et al. "*Schindler's List*: Myth, Movie, and Memory," *Village Voice* 39.13 [March 29, 1994]: 29–30).

41. The line is an ideological joke of sorts: how can the Russian army—the military arm of Stalin—liberate anyone?

42. This is especially evident at Jerusalem's Yad Vashem, where, as James Young writes, the contemplation of remembrance is carried out "within an ever-vigilant context: exile, memory, and redemption. The 'end of the Holocaust' comes only with the survivors' return to and redemption in Eretz Israel" (James Young, *Writing and Rewriting the Holocaust* [Bloomington: Indiana University Press, 1988], 187). For a further investigation of the nationalist/Zionist connection to this positive emphasis, see James Young, *The Texture of Memory* (New Haven: Yale University Press, 1993), 268–281. According to Young, "After being twinned with heroism for so many years, the Shoah itself no longer signifies defeat in many of the young soldier's eyes, but actually emerges as an era of heroism, of triumph over past passivity" (275).

Chapter 3

1. Elisabeth Bronfen, *Hysteria and Its Discontents* (Princeton: Princeton University Press, 1998), xii.

2. Saul Friedlander, *Probing the Limits of Representation: Nazism and the "Final Solution"* (Cambridge: Harvard University Press), 2.

3. D. M. Thomas, *The White Hotel* (New York: Pocket, 1981), 289. All subsequent citations are to this edition and will be referred to parenthetically in the text.

4. Sigmund Freud, *Introductory Lectures on Psycho-Analysis* (1916–1917), in *The Standard Edition of the Complete Psychological Works of Sigmund Freud*, trans. James Strachey, vol. 16 (London: Hogarth Press and the Institute of Psycho-analysis, 1953–74), 404.

5. Sigmund Freud, *Civilization and Its Discontents* (1930), in *The Standard Edition of the Complete Psychological Works of Sigmund Freud*, trans. James Strachey, vol. 21 (London: Hogarth Press and the Institute of Psycho-analysis, 1953–74), 76.

6. Sigmund Freud, *New Introductory Lectures on Psycho-Analysis* (1933), in *The Standard Edition of the Complete Psychological Works of Sigmund Freud*, trans. James Strachey, vol. 22 (London: Hogarth Press and the Institute of Psycho-analysis, 1953–74), 93–94.

7. In another novel inhabited by Freud (and his family), Thomas's belief in the prophetic dimension of the symptom gets an expression perhaps even more startling than *The White Hotel*'s linking of Lisa Erdman's hysteria and Babi Yar. In *Eating Pavlova* (London: Bloomsbury, 1994), Freud himself dreams, before the fact, the death of Jews in gas chambers, the dropping of the atomic bomb on Hiroshima, the Eichmann trial in Israel, Vietnam, and San Francisco bath houses.

8. C. G. Jung, *Modern Man in Search of a Soul*, trans. W. S. Dell and Cary F. Baynes (New York: Harcourt Brace, 1933), 67.

9. Ibid., 122.

10. The first World War and its traumatized veterans were examples, for Freud, of this "failure." Thus, in *Beyond the Pleasure Principle*, his well-known call "to abandon the belief that there is an instinct towards perfection [i.e., pleasure] at work in human beings, which has brought them to their present high level of intellectual achievement and ethical sublimation and which may be expected to watch over their development into supermen. I have no faith, however, in the existence of any such internal instinct and I cannot see how this benevolent illusion is to be preserved" (Sigmund Freud, *Beyond the Pleasure Principle* [1920], in *The Standard Edition of the Complete Psychological Works of Sigmund Freud*, trans. James Strachey, vol. 18 (London: Hogarth Press and the Institute of Psycho-analysis, 1953–74), 23.

11. Freud, *Beyond the Pleasure Principle*, 42.

12. D. M. Thomas, *Memories and Hallucinations* (New York: Viking, 1988), 40.

13. Ibid., 46.

14. Immanuel Kant, *The Critique of Pure Reason*, trans. Werner S. Pluhar (Indianapolis: Hackett Publishing Company, 1996), 343.

15. Ibid.

16. Jacques Lacan, *The Seminar of Jacques Lacan, Book XX: Encore, 1972–1973*, trans. Bruce Fink (New York: Norton, 1998), 76.

17. Rowland Wymer, "Freud, Jung and the 'Myth' of Psychoanalysis in *The White Hotel*," *Mosaic* 22 (1989): 67.

18. For these displacements, see Sander L. Gilman, "The Jewish Psyche: Freud, Dora, and the Idea of the Hysteric." *The Jew's Body* (New York: Routledge, 1991), 60–103.

19. Gilman, *The Jew's Body*, 77.

20. Laura Tanner, "Sweet Pain and Charred Bodies: Figuring Violence in *The White Hotel*," *Boundary* 2, 18 (1991): 134.

21. Cowart, David. "Being and Seeming: *The White Hotel*," *Novel* 19 (1986): 221.

22. Mary F. Robertson, "Hystery, Herstory, History: 'Imagining the Real' in Thomas' *The White Hotel*," *Contemporary Literature* 25 (1984): 462–463.

23. Wymer, "Freud, Jung and the 'Myth' of Psychoanalysis in *The White Hotel*," 67.

24. Indeed, we appear here to be in the presence of poststructuralism's underside: more attention to narrative/authorial situatedness—more seeming giving up of control—works in fact to solidify the position and control, if covert, of the author.

25. For a discussion of the novel's "triumphant" postmodernism, see Linda Hutcheon, "Subject In/Of/To History and His Story," *Diacritics* 16 (1986): 78–91 and Ellen Y. Siegelman, "*The White Hotel*: Visions and Revisions of the Psyche," *Literature and Psychology* 33 (1987): 1, 69–76. And also: Marsha Kinder, "The Spirit of the White Hotel," *Humanities in Society* 4 (1981): 2–3, 143–170.

26. For a reading that insists on the link between Freud's presence—literal and textual—and the novel's refusal of closure, see Robert E. Lougy, "The Wolf-Man, Freud, and D. M. Thomas: Intertextuality, Interpretation, and Narration in *The White Hotel*, *Modern Language Studies* 21 (1991): 3, 91–106.

27. This is why virtually every single survivor account is marked by lack and a sense of insignificance. In *The Drowned and the Saved*, Primo Levi makes just this point, and it is one that seriously challenges the kind of universal significance Thomas wants to derive from survivor accounts:

"We, the survivors, are not the true witnesses [. . .] we are those who by their prevarications or abilities or good luck did not touch bottom. Those who did so, those who saw the Gorgon, have not returned to tell about it or have returned mute, but they are [. . .] the complete witnesses, the ones whose deposition would have general significance" (Primo Levi, *The Drowned and the Saved*, trans. Raymond Rosenthal [New York: Vintage, 1990], 83–84).

28. Jung, *Modern Man*, 163.

29. "My novel wasn't about the holocaust, but about the journey of the soul, which I believe is endless" (Thomas, *Memories and Hallucinations*, 49).

30. Adolf Hitler, *Mein Kampf*, trans. Ralph Manheim (Boston: Houghton Mifflin, 1943), 339.

31. Thomas's claim, in his memoir, that the "poet writes from his feminine unconscious" is a clear echo of Jung, who says that "the creative process has a feminine quality, and the creative work arises from unconscious depths—we might say, from the realm of the mothers" (Jung, *Modern Man in Search of a Soul*,170).

32. Roberston, "Hystery, Herstory, History," 465.

33. "The feminine body is peculiarly psychosomatic; that is, there is often close connection between the mental and the organic" (Simone de Beauvoir, *The Second Sex*, trans. H. M. Parshley [New York: Vintage, 1989], 391).

34. Juliet Mitchell, "Introduction I," *Feminine Sexuality: Jacques Lacan and the ecole freudienne* (New York: Norton, 1983), 20.

35. For this encounter as the basis of a feminist practice, see Joan Copjec, "Sex and the Euthanasia of Reason," *Read My Desire: Lacan Against the Historicists* (Cambridge: The MIT Press, 1994), 201–236.

36. Frances Bartkowski and Catherine Stearns, "The Lost Icon in *The White Hotel*," *Journal of the History of Sexuality* 1 (1990): 283–295. Bartkowski's and Stearns's argument exemplifies a feminist attempt to challenge the characterization of pre-Oedipal, mother-child dyads as antisocial. Referring explicitly to Kristeva, Luce Irigaray, and Cynthia Willett (and to her own work), Kelly Oliver, for example, speaks of "the need to refigure maternity and mother-child relationships as social relationships that don't require the violent intervention of paternal authority to socialize the child. This work is itself an attempt to make the social space in which maternal affects can be symbolized in order to demythologize the natural antisocial image of maternity upheld by patriarchy" (Kelly Oliver, *Witnessing: Beyond Recognition* [Minneapolis: University of Minnesota Press, 2001], 80–81.)

37. Jacqueline Rose, "Introduction II," *Feminine Sexuality: Jacques Lacan and the ecole freudienne* (New York: Norton, 1983), 38.

38. Altruism is far from posing a challenge to the subject's fantasy of omnipotence. As Lacan puts it: "My egoism is quite content with a certain altruism, altruism of the kind that is situated on the level of the useful" (Jacques Lacan, *The Seminar of Jacques Lacan, Book VIII: The Ethics of Psychoanalysis, 1959–1960*, trans. Dennis Porter [New York: Norton, 1993], 187).

39. Bronfen, *The Knotted Subject*, xi–xii.

40. Juliet Mitchell, "Psychoanalysis and Hysteria," Unpublished paper, 2.

41. Mitchell, "Psychoanalysis and Hysteria," 14. Bronfen's interest in arguing for the navel as the anatomical sign for the source of traumatic knowledge is apt here, since the navel is the fundamentally unreadable, unravelable cluster of evidence of a once-enjoyed plenitude and power.

42. Thomas, *Memories and Hallucinations*, 39–40.

43. Mitchell, "Psychoanalysis and Hysteria," 17.

44. Thomas: "I tried to mix realistic, down-to-earth images, of sand and dust and refugee huts, with lyrical passages: *I am the rose of Sharon* . . . Above all I tried to convey that it was a place where people still suffered" (Thomas, *Memories and Hallucinations*, 49).

45. For an essay justly critical of Thomas's use of erotic language to explore the notion of death in the Holocaust, see Rebecca Scherr, "The Uses of Memory and the Abuses of Fiction: Sexuality in Holocaust Fiction and Memoir," *Other Voices: The (e)Journal of Cultural Criticism* 2.1 (February 2000): <http://www.othervoices.org>.

46. For this notion—"hysteria is the subject's way of resisting the prevailing, historically specified form of interpellation or symbolic identification. Hysteria means failed interpellation"—see Slavoj Žižek, *For they know not what they do* (New York: Verso, 1991), 99–103, 142–146.

47. Jean-Paul Sartre, *The Emotions: Outline of a Theory*, trans. Bernard Frechtman (New York: Philosophical Library, 1949), 32.

48. Thomas, *Memories and Hallucinations*, 49.

Chapter 4

1. John Fetzer has noted that for early readers of the novel (and more recently), the very fact of Mann's exile contravenes the novel's historiographical warrant (let alone accuracy). For the particulars speaking to this point, see John Fetzer, *Changing Perspectives of Thomas Mann's Doctor Faustus, 1947–1992* (Columbia, SC: Camden House, 1996), 2, 67–68.

2. Erich Heller, *The Ironic German: A Study of Thomas Mann*. (Boston: Little, Brown, and Company, 1958), 25. For Heller, the achievement of *Doctor Faustus* lies in the fact that Mann is *neither* "a mere Serenus

Zeitblom, humanistic country-cousin to the metropolitan desperadoes of art" *nor* an Adrian Leverkühn, forswearer of all tradition in the name of an aesthetic freedom that can easily deteriorate into an alliance with evil.

3. Thomas Mann, *Doctor Faustus*, trans. H. T. Lowe-Porter (New York: Vintage, 1992), 482–483. All subsequent references are to this edition of the novel and will be cited parenthetically in the text.

4. Egon Schwarz, "Jewish Characters in *Doctor Faustus*," *Thomas Mann's Doctor Faustus: A Novel at the Margins of Modernism*, eds. Herbert Lehnert and Peter C. Pfeiffer (Columbia, SC: Camden House, 1991), 118.

5. Adolf Hitler, "Nation and Race," *Mein Kampf*, trans. Ralph Mannheim (Boston: Houghton Mifflin, 1971), 310, 314.

6. See my discussion in chapter 1 of the quilting point, and the way the Jew functions as a transcendental locus of causality imagined as a site of plenitude. On this reading, anti-Semitism is not purely a matter of inclusions and exclusions, but rather the way exclusions can, themselves, preserve the Other as enjoying full self-possession, as nonsplit. This is one of the problems with Zeitblom's scenario in which the German nation becomes like a Jewish ghetto.

7. The primary historical line on German soil runs from Johann Spies's chapbook *Historia Von D. Johan Fausten* (1587)—in which Faust is denied redemption—to Goethe's *Faust II* (1832)—in which Faust achieves grace and redemption. For an overview, see Klaus L. Berghahn, "Georg Johann Heinrich Faust: The Myth and Its History," in *Our Faust?: Roots and Ramifications of a Modern German Myth*, eds. Reinhold Grimm and Jost Hermand (Madison: University of Wisconsin Press, 1987), 3–21.

8. As Mann put it, "It *is* true and self-evident: how could such a radical book not extend into the religious sphere. And yet it has been called 'godless.' That shows you the caliber of those who professionally write on 'belles lettres' " (qtd. in Gunilla Bergsten, *Thomas Mann's Doctor Fautus: The Sources and Structure of the Novel*, trans. Krishna Winston [Chicago: University of Chicago Press 1969], 213.)

9. Etienne Balibar, "The Nation Form: History and Ideology." *Race, Nation, Class: Ambiguous Identities*. eds. Etienne Balibar and Immanuel Wallerstein (New York: Verso, 1991), 94.

10. Slavoj Žižek, *Enjoy Your Symptom! Jacques Lacan in Hollywood and Out* (New York: Routledge, 1992), 41.

11. This is, admittedly, a generalization. I take without objection the point raised by a reader of this manuscript that the citizens of Buchenwald did on occasion show spontaneous remorse, particularly in lesser-known (and color) footage of their being led through Buchenwald.

12. This is not an argument against Eisenhower's act—recorded by Zeitblom in the novel—of forcing the citizens of Weimer to walk through

Buchenwald after the Allies had liberated the camp. (Eisenhower wanted those who had lived in proximity to the camp to see with their own eyes the crematoria that had been operating in their midst.) It is to note instead the way that act can so quickly become another exercise of a mode of conduct that necessitated it in the first place.

13. Nietzsche's critique of Christianity—"the courage of a Christian, of a believer in God in general, can never be a courage without witnesses—this fact alone degrades it" (*Will to Power*, trans. Walter Kauffman [New York: Vintage, 1967], 443)—is perhaps the clearest expression of the manner in which belonging to a community is not the fruit of particular decisions, but rather their underlying cause. Is this not the consistent feature of Zeitblom's personality—the need to be among a community necessarily selected by History? The pleasure he experiences here by feeling himself part of a (German) collective appears to be analogous to the pleasure he experienced in fighting in World War I: "It is a great pleasure to the superior individual, just once—and where should one find this once, if not here and now?—to lose himself altogether in the general" (301).

14. I have in mind here Žižek's insistence, contra Dominick LaCapra, that "transference is not a kind of 'theater of shadows,' where we settle past traumas *in effigia*, it is repetition in the full meaning of the term, i.e., in it, the past trauma is literally repeated, 'actualized' " (*Enjoy Your Symptom!*, 102). In risking his place within the social order, Leverkühn follows the path from historical to structural trauma that I endorse in chapter 1. For a view critical of Žižek's—that repeating trauma in the full sense of the term is without "constructive ethicopolitical possibilities," appearing only as a "lucidly theorized" option—see Dominick LaCapra, *Representing the Holocaust: History, Theory, Trauma* (Ithaca, NY: Cornell University Press, 1994), 205–224.

15. Mann—intentionally or otherwise—is ambiguous in *The Story of a Novel* when he recalls the task he set for himself in *Doctor Faustus* as to write "to write nothing less than the novel of my era, disguised as the story of an artist's life, a terribly imperiled and sinful artist" (*The Story of a Novel*, trans. Richard and Clara Winston [New York: Knopf, 1961], 38.) In Zeitblom's attempt to know the desire of the Other (i.e., Adrian)—his consistent efforts to invest the latter and his art with a sensible meaning and purpose—Mann has indeed written the novel of his era.

16. Patrick Carnegy, *Faust as Musician: A Study of Thomas Mann's Novel Doctor Faustus* (London: Chatto and Windus, 1973), 29. Gunilla Bergston, *Thomas Mann's Doctor Faustus*, 128. Erich Heller, *The Ironic German*, 24. Donna Reed, *The Novel and the Nazi Past* (New York: Peter Lang, 1984). Herbert Lehnert, "Introduction," *Thomas Mann's Doctor Faustus: A Novel at the Margins of Modernism* (Columbia, SC: Camden

House, 1991), 14, 10. Criticism of Mann's novel is too extensive to do complete justice to here. But, to remain with the sources in English, it is fair to say that the equation of Leverkühn's music with Nazi barbarism has been overwhelmingly prevalent. This view begins with Fritz Kauffman's *Thomas Mann: The World as Will and Representation* (Boston: Beacon, 1957), which finds in the tragic greatness of the trinity Faust-Nietzsche-Leverkühn "the stains of murder and the germs of the travesty known as Nazism" (200). And it extends to the essays in Herbert Lehnert and Peter C. Pfeiffer's *Thomas Mann's 'Doctor Faustus'* [Columbia, SC: Camden House, 1991]), all of which argue, or tacitly assume, Adrian as the figure of evil in the novel. Even those who see Mann intending a kind of ambiguity apropos our judgment of Adrian still implicitly assume Adrian's "damnation." The ambiguity, in this view, pertains solely to the fate of Adrian's music a propos a future German cultural tradition. (See, e.g., Judith Ryan, *The Uncompleted Past* [Detroit: Wayne State University Press, 1983].) One exception to this tradition of approaching Leverkühn as representative of fascism may be found in Marc Weiner, *Undertones of Insurrection: Music, Politics, and the Social Sphere in the Modern German Narrative* (Lincoln: University of Nebraska Press, 1993), 213–245.

17. Heller, *The Ironic German*, 22.

18. See G. W. F. Hegel, *Phenomenology of Spirit*, trans. A. V. Miller (New York: Oxford University Press, 1977), 132.

19. On the refusal of this sacrifice, see Kretschmar's lecture on Beethoven's final piano sonata (Op. 111). There, Kretschmar identifies Beethoven's excessive reflection and inwardness—a sign of his degeneracy in the eyes of critics and friends—and links it precisely with the task of the genuine artist to expose the abyss that the sonata form, for example, stands in for. In the incredible changes that mark the encounter with this abyss—in the long second movement—are the kind of explorations after which there can be no return. Thus, no third movement.

20. For Kant, the mathematical sublime of nature—that is, the stuff of Adrian's investigations—resides not so much in a large numerical concept (a content), but rather in its offering of a "unit" for the measure of the imagination (a form)—that is, a way of approaching these phenomena at all: "The sublime in the aesthetical judging of an immeasurable whole like this lies, not so much in the greatness of number [of units], as in the fact that in our progress we ever arrive at greater units. To this the systematic division of the universe contributes" (*The Critique of Pure Judgment*, trans. J. H. Bernard [New York: MacMillan, 1951], 95.). This is clearly a "progress" Adrian is out to throw into question.

21. Marguerite de Huszar Allen, *The Faust Legend: Popular Formula and Modern Novel* (New York: Peter Lang, 1985), 94.

22. Zeitblom would appear to be retelling yet another the story of "paradise lost": Adrian's (Adam's) downfall is traced in the manner of Milton to Esmeralda (Eve).

23. G. W. F. Hegel, *Logic*, trans. William Wallace (Oxford, 1973), 44.

24. Thus Hegel's claim that the original state (Eden) must be likened to a zoological garden—a garden of savagery. The original state is for Hegel *foundational* but not *actual*. For his fullest critique of those views which hold to the *actuality* of a lost paradise, see G. W. F. Hegel, *Lectures on the Philosophy of Religion, Volume II: Determinate Religion*, eds. Peter C. Hogsdon, trans. R. F. Brown, P. C. Hogsdon, and J. M. Stewart (Berkeley: University of California Press, 1897), 521–530.

25. On ironic distance as a form of ideology, see Slavoj Žižek, *The Sublime Object of Ideology* (New York: Verso, 1989), 11–53.

26. We might here mention Lukács's paradigmatic misreading of *Doctor Faustus*. Leverkühn's realization of the "stupidity" or "silliness" of the social order is for Lukács evidence of a consciousness that needs only to mature. What Lukács would have Adrian and Mann see (he says, in fact, that they do eventually see it) is that there exists another, more "intelligent" order out there—the order of the socialist revolution. Adrian's pact with the devil, for Lukács, points to Marx. Unable to see order in its very constitution as "stupid" or "silly," Lukács here appears in the company of Zeitblom (see "The Tragedy of Modern Art," in *Essays on Thomas Mann*, trans. Stanley Mitchell [London: Merlin, 1964], 47–97.)

27. Hegel, *Phenomenology of Spirit*, 68.

28. Even Arnold Schoenberg might have made this equation. In his famous letter to the editor in the *Saturday Review of Literature*, Schoenberg objected strenuously not only to Mann's use of his "literary property" (i.e., the twelve-tone method of musical composition), but also to the character of the fictional composer into which Mann placed his property. For Schoenberg, Adrian Leverkühn was to be regarded "from beginning to end, as a lunatic" ("Doctor Faustus' Schoenberg?" *Saturday Review of Literature* [Jan., 1949], 22). Noting this deeper source of Schoenberg's disaffection, Michael Mann suggests that Schoenberg made the equation between Adrian and Nazi Germany. What Schoenberg was principally upset with, Mann suggests, was that his invention seemed to be "involved with a sick-minded fictional character or even with German National Socialism" ("The Musical Symbolism in Thomas Mann's *Doctor Faustus*," *Music Review* 17 [1956], 318–331).

29. Fred Chappell, "What Did Adrian Leverkühn Create?" *Postscript* 2 (1985), 12. This view recurs again and again in criticism of the novel. Donna Reed likens Adrian's return to the archaic and primitive as symbolizing the irrationalism, formal introversion, and social aloofness of

expressionism (Donna Reed, *The Novel and the Nazi Past*, 86). Brigitte Prutti, too, reads Adrian's turn to the twelve-tone system as part of an " 'archaic' regression [. . .] into an order of his own making over which he has total control" (Brigitte Prutti, "Women Characters in *Doctor Faustus*," *Thomas Mann's Doctor Faustus: A Novel at the Margins of Modernism*, Eds. Herbert Lehnert and Peter C. Pfeiffer [Columbia, SC: Camden House, 1991], 104). And Manfred Dierks goes as far as to see in this "regression" the narcissist's fantasy of omnipotence (see his "*Doctor Faustus* and Recent Theories of Narcissism: New Perspectives," *Thomas Mann's Doctor Faustus: A Novel at the Margins of Modernism*, eds. Herbert Lehnert and Peter C. Pfeiffer [Columbia, SC: Camden House, 1991], 53).

30. This point repeats those made in my discussion, in chapter 1, of the "Sense Certainty" section of the *Phenomenology*, pages 65–68. Though we speak all the time from the position of the absolute, it is significant whether or not we take this position up absolutely: to do so is to expose the manner in which even the universal Law that structures the order of language lacks stability and substance; not to do so is to maintain the natural, essential universality of that Law—to keep that Law from encountering the real.

31. Walter Davis has rightly claimed that this forms the basis of Mann's insight into the nature of dialectical thought, his recognition, if you will, of Absolute Knowledge as the recognition of what Davis calls " 'the true or ultimate dichotomy': that single comprehensive opposition which generates and sustains the progressively more inclusive oppositions which make up the dialectical process" (*Inwardness and Existence: Subjectivity in/and Hegel, Heidegger, Marx, and Freud* [Madison: University of Wisconsin Press, 1989], 330). Adrian's twelve-tone method of composition would seem to dramatize this "single comprehensive opposition" in its most developed form.

32. Weiner, *Undertones of Insurrection*, 219.

33. Ibid., 232.

34. Ibid., 236.

35. Weiner is less than optimistic about the efficacy of the modernist aesthetic strategies given the extent to which they rely on the reader's capacity to interact with demanding aesthetic structures.

36. The stupidity of attempting to "solve" this estrangement is made unequivocal by none other than Adrian. In the Christian Society Winifried gathering, Adrian responds to the notion that "Youth" is some positive German metaphysical endowment with a short laugh and with this line: "And his [the German's] revolutions . . . are the puppet-shows of world history" (118).

37. Theodor Adorno, *Philosophy of Modern Music*, trans. Anne G. Mitchell and Wesley V. Blomster (New York: Continuum, 1994), 118.

38. Ibid., 67.

39. Ibid., 112.

40. In his book on Schreber's delusions (*My Own Private Germany: Daniel Paul Schreber's Secret History of Modernity* [Princeton, NJ: Princeton University Press, 1996]), Eric Santner speaks of Schreber as exemplifying a new strategy of "sapping the force of social fantasies that might otherwise lend support to the totalitarian temptation" (144). For Santner, Schreber does this, in part, by laying bare the drive dimension of signification, by "beating the repetition machine at its own game" (93). Despite obvious differences between them, we might join Leverkühn with Schreber at least on this count: both reveal that the authority believed to lie in institutions (Law, music, etc.) rests not in an external legitimizing entity, but in the repetition of immanent processes of enunciation.

41. Mann's regression strikes me, in any case, as much more defensible than Spielberg's (and the others focused on Jewish rescue taken up in chapter 2). They move from the present, post–Cold War moment back to the Holocaust to discover something meaningful that (though it failed at the time to have a large enough appeal) can prevent repetition. Mann moves from his present moment to a composer who lived from 1885–1940 (the last ten years, severed almost entirely from reality) in order to land on a trauma whose avowal may have prevented the calamity in the first place.

42. When Adorno read Mann's rendering of *The Lamentation*, he could not abide the redemptive quality the latter had given it. "He had no objections to make on musical matters, but took issue with the end, the last forty lines, in which, after all the darkness, a ray of hope, the possibility of grace, appears. I had been too optimistic, too kindly, too pat, had kindled too much light, had been too lavish with the consolation" (Mann, *The Story of a Novel*, 158). Mann's modifications, one suspects—given the "high G" given to Adrian's last work—did not exactly address Adorno's critique.

43. Hans Rudolf Vaget, "Mann, Joyce, and the Question of Modernism," *Thomas Mann's Doctor Faustus: A Novel at the Margins of Modernism*, eds. Herbert Lehnert and Peter C. Pfeiffer [Columbia, SC: Camden House, 1991], 184. The significance of the *Lamentation*'s final note forms the basis of one of the novel's enduring interpretive controversies. Vaget is one who has repeatedly sought to contest the view that Mann ultimately complied with the redemption-less views of Adorno. See, in this respect, Hans Rudolf Vaget, "Amazing Grace: Thomas Mann, Adorno, and the Faust Myth," *Our Faust?: Roots and Ramifications of a Modern German Myth*, eds. Reinhold Grimm and Jost Hermond (Madison: University of Wisconsin Press, 1987), 168–189.

Chapter 5

1. David Grossman, *See Under: Love*, trans. Betsy Rosenberg (New York: Simon Schuster, 1989), 3. All subsequent citations from this novel are to this edition and will be indicated parenthetically in the text.

2. See G. W. F. Hegel, *Phenomenology of Spirit*, trans. A. V. Miller (New York: Oxford University Press, 1977), 21.

3. See, in this respect, Grossman's two journalistic accounts: *The Yellow Wind*, trans. Haim Watzman (New York: Farrar, Straus, and Giroux, 1988) and *Sleeping on a Wire: Conversations with Palestinians in Israel*, trans. Haim Watzman (New York: Farrar, Straus, and Giroux, 1993). One of the historicist coordinates of the novel pivots fundamentally around the analogy to Nazism as it has functioned in Israeli political discourse. In short, which side in the political struggle reproduces the violence of Nazism? Grossman's status as critic of Israel has led some to suggest that the construction of the Nazi beast is an allegory for the Zionist construction of the Palestinian/Arab "enemy" against whom one must fight. Even more significantly, the paranoia underwriting this construction comes, in the "Wasserman" section, to bear a more explicit affinity with that universally fascistic disposition Grossman designates with the acronym "LNIY" (the little nazi in you).

4. See Yael S. Feldman, "Whose Story Is It, Anyway?: Ideology and Psychology in the Representation of the Shoah in Israeli Literature, *Probing the Limits of Representation: Nazism and the 'Final Solution,'* ed. Saul Friedlander (Cambridge: Harvard University Press, 1992), 223–239. Gilead Morahg, "Israel's New Literature of the Holocaust: The Case of David Grossman's *See Under: Love*," *Modern Fiction Studies* 45.2 (Summer 1999): 457–479 and Johanna Baum, "A Literary Analysis of Traumatic Neurosis in Israeli Society: David Grossman's *See Under: Love, Other Voices: The (e)Journal of Cultural Criticism* 2.1 (February 2000): <http://www.othervoices.org.>

5. Feldman, "Whose Story Is It, Anyway?," 236.

6. For this connection, see pages 44–46 in chapter 1 of this book. History has no immanent meaning for Momik until it is "given a name." His literal adoption of Bella's accidental mention of a Nazi Beast is what quilts together all of the various and seemingly chaotic behaviors and symptoms he is daily privy to. It is perhaps not a stretch to see the person of Eichmann functioning in a similar way. Lyotard's claim regarding the traumatic import of a "Nazi name" such as Eichmann is pertinent here. For Lyotard's view of the covert benefits met by the Eichmann trial (benefits akin to those Momik stands to gain by materializing a Nazi Beast), see Jean-François Lyotard, *The Differend: Phrases in Dispute*, trans. George Van Den Abbeele (Minnesota: University of Minnesota Press, 1988), 56–57.

7. Grandma Henny has given Momik "a hundred names," and the latter is charged with the task of listening for the names of "a lot of lost Neumans" (37) on the lunchtime radio-show, "Greetings from the New Immigrants and Locating Lost Relations."

8. Despite worries regarding the link between this uncertainty and extreme ideological polarization, Yael Feldman does credit Grossman's novel for "releas[ing] the Shoah from the shackles of the collective and reclaim[ing] it as a subjective experience." See Yael Feldman, "Whose Story Is It, Anyway?," 236.

9. Slavoj Žižek has shown how the very intersubjective function of questions is already of a piece with fascist ideology, since every posed question is tacitly held to have an answer. "Totalitarian power," Žižek claims, "is not a dogmatism which has all the answers; it is, on the contrary, the instance which has all the questions" (Slavoj Žižek, *The Sublime Object of Ideology* [New York: Verso, 1989], 179).

10. The entirety of Wordworth's poetry stages the difficulty of accessing the thing-in-itself and avoiding solipsism at the same time. As Book IV of *The Prelude* puts it, the poet's eye can discover "many beauteous sights—weeds, fishes, flowers,/Grots, pebbles, roots of trees—and fancies more,/Yet often is perplexed, and cannot part/The shadow from the substance, rocks and sky,/Mountains and clouds, from what which is indeed/The region, and the things which there abide/In their true dwelling" (William Wordsworth, *The Prelude, 1799, 1805, 1850*, eds. Jonathan Wordsworth, M. H. Abrams, and Stephen Gill [New York: Norton, 1979], 138). This inability to distinguish between substance and shadow, between vision and revision, is perhaps best captured by the speaker's famous final line in Keats's "Ode to a Nightingale": "Do I wake or sleep?"

11. Indeed, for Hegel, the body always fails to express or reflect something unique at the core of subjectivity, because the instant we accord it a signifying function, we are no longer speaking of its individuality. This is why Hegel claims that every linguistic statement regarding the being of spirit is *really* a claim that spirit is a bone. For this point, see G. W. F. Hegel, *Phenomenology of Spirit*, 207–208.

12. The political salience of this recognition is entertained in Grossman's first novel, *The Smile of the Lamb*, which is aimed, in part, at documenting the vicious circle of hatred and violence produced by Israel's occupation of the West Bank and Gaza. In the novel's penultimate scene, Khilmi (an aged Palestinian Arab and fantastical storyteller) articulates a mode of resistance in which Palestinians would refuse to play their part in a cause for which Israelis would sacrifice themselves.

13. It is thus the case that even after the last Jew's death, the German Nazi would still experience the "loss of the real." More Jews would have to be invented in order to locate the enjoyment the German Nazi

still experiences as lacking, the enjoyment "stolen" from him. This is why the surest way to undo the anti-Semitic construction of the Jew is to insist that the Jew, too, has no real relation to his or her enjoyment—that is, the Real Jew does not exist.

14. Yael Feldman's claim that Grossman, in his first novel (*The Smile of the Lamb*), was "the first Israeli to imagine from within the psychological world of another victim" is pertinent here. So, too, are Grossman's journalistic attempts to document the daily lives (and indignities) of Palestinians in *The Yellow Wind* and *Sleeping on a Wire*.

15. Bruno Schulz, "The Age of Genius," *Sanitorium Under the Sign of the Hourglass*, trans. Celina Wieniewska (New York: Penguin, 1979), 14.

16. Ibid., 14.

17. Derrida makes the (Hegelian) point that will be developed more fully in the discussion of the "Encyclopedia" section below—that is, that because the Law is the result of a purely performative, senseless act, its essential integrity is undermined by its very existence. As Derrida puts it, "There is something decayed or rotten in law, which condemns it or ruins it in advance. Law is condemned, ruined, in ruins, ruinous" (Jacques Derrida, "Force of Law: The 'Mystical Foundation of Authority,'" *Deconstruction and the Possibility of Justice*, ed. Drucilla Cornell et al. [New York: Routledge, 1992], 39).

18. See Giorgio Agamben, *Homo Sacer: Sovereign Power and Bare Life*, trans. Daniel Heller-Roazen (Stanford: Stanford University Press, 1998). Though Agamben is critical of the manner in which sovereign power assumes the mantle of constituting power, he remains squarely in favor of the necessary, generative capacity of constituting power. Indeed, as Agamben sees it, we must not dismiss the notion of an originary violence that founds the differential relation on which language is staked. For Agamben, the future of democratic politics depends on this differential relation, since only the originary violence executed by the signifier *as such* can call a halt to the sacralization of bare life. Thus, though Agamben basically agrees with Foucault's thesis regarding biopower—that sovereign power works today by taking charge of life—he argues not for a taking back of life, but rather for the split that grants particular ways of living their intelligibility. What Agamben calls the "fundamental biopolitical fracture" is, as it is for Hegel, there *from the beginning*. For the development of these ideas as they pertain to politics, see Giorgio Agamben, *Means Without End: Notes on Politics*, trans. Vincenzo Binetti and Cesare Casarino (Minneapolis: University of Minnesota Press, 2000).

19. Schulz, "The Age of Genius," 21.

20. The other version of this question is: What does the baby *want* from me? For Lacan, the formulation of this question is a sign that the subject is becoming true to his/her desire. It is, for Lacan, "the question

of the Other which comes back from the place from which he expects an oracular reply" (Jacques Lacan, "The Subversion of the Subject and the Dialectic of Desire," *Ecrits: A Selection*, trans. Alan Sheridan [New York: Norton, 1978], 312). It is at the level of Lacan's *Che Vuoi?* (i.e., What do you want?) that Grossman demonstrates the real predicament in its properly absolute or formal dimension. The disagreement between Wasserman and Niegel about the fate of the baby is a disagreement concerning content only.

21. G. W. F. Hegel, *Phenomenology of Spirit*, trans. A. V. Miller (New York: Oxford, 1977), 492.

22. To return to the Israeli-Palestinian conflict with which Grossman has involved himself: at the time of this writing (October, 2002), the vicious circle of suicide bombings and Israeli retaliatory aggression has arguably reached its most terrible and crystalline form. The prospect of an act that might reveal the hole in the universe of meaning governing events seems remote. Now more than ever, we need, I believe, to resist the inscription in which the agents and victims in the struggle are seen as sacrifices in a larger cause. When I suggested to a friend that the events were confirming for me the radicality of Christ's injunctions against re-taliation; and that the latest suicide bombing ought to result in the uni-lateral withdrawal of Israeli forces from the West Bank and Gaza, as well as internationally assisted efforts at reparations for lost lands and liveli-hoods; and that any and every subsequent suicide bombing should be met each time with *more and more* infrastructural support (e.g., roads, schools, etc.) for a Palestinian state, my friend assumed I was jesting. When I said I was serious, he quickly said that there was no question but that Israel must retaliate.

23. Hegel, *Phenomenology*, 488.

24. Hegel, *Phenomenology*, 489. Hegel's emphasis.

25. G. W. F. Hegel, *Logic*, trans. William Wallace (New York: Oxford University Press, 1975), 274.

26. Theodor Adorno, *Philosophy of Modern Music*, trans. Anne G. Mitchell and Wesley V. Blomster (New York: Continuum, 1994), 39.

Conclusion

1. Primo Levi, *The Drowned and the Saved*, trans. Raymond Rosenthal (New York: Vintage, 1989), 48–49.

2. Lawrence Langer, *Preempting the Holocaust* (New Haven: Yale University Press, 1998), xiv.

3. See Francis Fukuyama, *The Great Disruption: Human Nature and the Reconstitution of Social Order* (New York: Free Press, 1999).

4. Primo Levi, *The Periodic Table*, trans. Raymond Rosenthal (New York: Schocken, 1984), 42. Subsequent references to this edition will be cited parenthetically.

5. In the context of a discussion of the survivor's shame in *The Drowned and the Saved*, Levi repudiates the providential notion that discerns in his subsequent career as a writer the *reason* for his having survived. There, Levi asserts that there is no "proportion between the privilege [of having survived] and the outcome [i.e., testimony]." This assertion directly precedes his oft-quoted claim that those who survived are not the "true witnesses" (see Levi, *The Drowned and the Saved*, 81–85). The critique of those who would inscribe survival within a larger providential narrative is already telegraphed in Levi's powerful depiction of the "selection" in *Survival in Auschwitz*, and in particular, his attitude toward the aged figure of Kuhn, who thanks God for not having been chosen while the twenty year-old Beppo, destined for the gas chamber the following day, lays in the bunk next to him. Imagining himself the auditor of Kuhn's words of thanks, Levi writes, "If I was God, I would spit at Kuhn's prayer" (*Survival in Auschwitz*, trans. Stuart Woolf [New York: Collier, 1993], 130).

6. See Jennifer Preston, "Menorahs Bloom From Act of Vandalism," *New York Times*, December 13, 1996, A 18.

Index

234 *Index*